CRACKER
PARTIES

CRACKER PARTIES

BY

HORACE MONTGOMERY

LOUISIANA STATE UNIVERSITY PRESS

BATON ROUGE

MANUFACTURED IN THE UNITED STATES OF AMERICA
BY THE VAIL-BALLOU PRESS, INC., BINGHAMTON, N. Y.

To
Gladys Day
Montgomery

PREFACE

PARTY battles in Georgia have rarely been dull affairs. In late ante-bellum times (1845–1861) few states produced a greater number of more purposeful politicians. Some of these men attained national prominence; others, while scarcely known beyond the State's borders, nevertheless made significant contributions to State and regional politics. Working closely with the politicians of this age was a group of zealous editors whose specialty was to write about party leaders and dogma. Many of these editors were fierce antagonists; some were sensationalists; few were graceful. In an age when it was easy to accept "causes," it is not strange that editors, like politicians, were well stocked with devious questions and trite explanations all neatly arranged in a brace of sweeping alternatives.

While the locale in this study is Georgian, the view into the regional and the national arenas is never closed. The fifteen years under observation comprise a sort of golden age in Georgia's history. Of her political figures who achieved national prominence, I have deliberately emphasized Howell Cobb. None of his Georgia contemporaries possess his peculiar diagnostic significance. The central theme of Georgia's political history during this era was the growing power of the Democratic party. The manner of its conversion from Jacksonian dogma to the credo of John C. Calhoun is the essence of this study. The agonies of Howell Cobb are the symptoms of this conversion. Had Cobb lived in Pennsylvania, it is not inconceivable that he would have followed David Wilmot into the Republican party, which had adopted many of the Jacksonian creeds and symbols. He would thus have been spared a brooding anxiety over the "Calhounization" of his party. In Georgia and the South there were many who, like Cobb, frustrated and despairing, sought a verdict by appealing to the sword.

In 400 B. C. Chuang-Tze declared that "with a learned person it is impossible to discuss the problems of life; he is bound by his system." Many Georgians found it increasingly necessary to believe and to claim more for the Southern system than was warranted. What had once been assurance became intransigence. Equally finalistic was the mood of many of the South's critics. They, too, had their "eternal verities." Such a mentality, North and South, precluded a hearing for fresh compromises. It was in this sense that the Civil War was an "irrepressible conflict." This account purports to show how Georgia's party structure reflected the growing mood of finality.

A number of years ago Dr. E. Merton Coulter suggested that I undertake a study of Georgia parties of the late antebellum age. The result of that study, with some revision, is herewith presented. To Dr. Coulter, therefore, I am heavily indebted and hereby express my thanks for many helpful suggestions. Others have assisted in one way or another, especially Professor A. J. McMullen of Markleysburg, Pennsylvania. It is with a special sense of gratitude that I acknowledge his helpfulness. The *Georgia Historical Quarterly* has kindly permitted me to use in slightly altered form the substance of Chapters I and II, which originally appeared in that journal.

HORACE MONTGOMERY

Athens, Georgia
January, 1950

CONTENTS

I.

MOTIF

IT required the impact of the Jacksonian surge to shatter the provincialism which, during the decade and a half after the War of 1812, had clung so stubbornly to Georgia's party system. By the end of the Jacksonian era in 1841 the national Democratic-Whig party pattern had been superimposed, with necessary modifications, upon the old Troup-Clark structure. Thus it was that Georgians came to live in a climate of thought which compelled them frequently to accord strictly local issues the chilliest receptions.[1] Only the bitter personal rivalry so characteristic of Troup-Clark days seems to have survived the advent of this new era in Georgia politics.[2]

Never has Georgia's two-party system stood higher than during the 1840's. So evenly matched in strength were her Whig and Democratic parties then that journalists came to regard their State as inscrutable. Hopkins Holsey, editor of the *Southern Banner* at Athens and impetuous disciple of Andrew Jackson, editorialized during the Towns-Hill gubernatorial fight in 1849 that "if there be any state in the union to which the maxim peculiarly applies, that 'no one can tell who is to be Governor until after election,' it is

---

[1] Interesting discussions of this phase of Georgia politics appear in Ulrich B. Phillips, *Life of Robert Toombs* (New York, 1913), 26 ff., and E. Merton Coulter, *Georgia: A Short History* (Chapel Hill, 1947), 238–48. See also, Ulrich B. Phillips, "The Southern Whigs," *Essays in American History* (New York, 1910), and *Georgia and State Rights* (Washington, 1902). For an excellent treatment of the national party picture, see Wilfred E. Binkley, *American Political Parties: Their Natural History* (New York, 1944), 120–260.

[2] Athens *Southern Whig*, November 1, 1849, for a North Carolina editor's impressions of Georgia politics.

our own state." [3] Georgia voters frequently selected four Whigs and four Democrats to represent them in the popular branch of the national legislature. In the Congressional elections of 1846 the Democrats cast a total of 30,300 votes, while the Whigs were not far behind with 29,526 votes.[4] In 1847 George W. Towns, the Democratic candidate for Governor, defeated his Whig opponent, Duncan Clinch, but Whiggery succeeded in winning control of both houses of the State's lawmaking body.[5]

During the forties Georgia's political leadership reposed in capable hands. The Whig party was ably directed by John M. Berrien, George Crawford, Charles J. Jenkins, Alexander H. Stephens, and Robert Toombs. Democracy boasted such leaders as G. W. Towns, Howell Cobb, Henry L. Benning, Charles J. McDonald, John H. Lumpkin, Herschel V. Johnson, John E. Ward, and Henry R. Jackson. An alert set of party journalists spun pretty fictions in defense of conventional articles of faith. At Athens the Democratic *Southern Banner* and the *Southern Whig* defended party dogmas. Partisan interests at the State capital in Milledgeville were zealously guarded by the *Southern Recorder* and the *Federal Union*, Whig and Democratic organs respectively. Chatham County Whigs were served able editorials by the Savannah *Republican*, while Democrats were carefully instructed by the rival *Georgian*. In Macon the Democratic *Georgia Telegraph* and the rival *Journal and Messenger* looked after Bibb County affairs. Muscogee County Democrats boasted two journals, the *Times* and the *Sentinel*, both of Columbus, while Whigs of that county were trained in their party's ideology by the *Enquirer*, also of Columbus. In Richmond County the influential *Chronicle and Sentinel* and the *Constitutionalist*, both of Augusta,

   3 Athens *Southern Banner*, August 30, 1849.
   4 Quoted in Milledgeville *Federal Union*, November 3, 1846.
   5 Quoted *ibid.*, October 12, 1847.

dispensed Whig and Democratic doctrines respectively.[6]

It was the Jacksonian era that produced a fusion within each party of Northern and Southern interest groups. True to their Jacksonian traditions, Cobb and his Georgia followers kept up a fatherly interest in the "wool hat boys" of Cherokee (North Georgia) and the pine barrens as well as the small planters of the downstate region. Their natural partners in the Northern states were the factory workers. After the middle forties when both parties were struggling for planter support, Georgia's Democratic leaders insisted on the wisdom of an *entente cordiale* between planters and Northern workers.[7] Such a union would make the Democratic party a truly liberal party, contended Hopkins Holsey. The endemic conservatism of planters, he continued, would hold in abeyance radical labor tendencies, while labor ideology would in turn preclude a conservative party outlook.[8] To discourage the planters from joining the Democratic party the Whig press focused its editorial spotlight on the "Red Republicanism" and the Locofocoism in the Democratic household.[9] The Democracy, insisted the Brahmins of Whiggery, was giving aid and comfort to subversive social doctrines. "True Patriots" were urged to don the raiment of Whiggery and go forth in defense of the "American Way." [10]

[6] According to surveys conducted by the Milledgeville papers there were in Georgia during the forties approximately forty-five journals. Adiel Sherwood, *A Gazeteer of Georgia* (Atlanta, 1860), 167–68, lists forty-four newspapers for 1859.

[7] Howell Cobb and Others, "To Our Constituents," quoted in *Federal Union*, March 20, 1849; Howell Cobb to Jackson Day Committee, January 1, 1852, in Cobb MSS.; Howell Cobb to Thomas Morris, March 21, 1853, in Robert P. Brooks (ed.), "Howell Cobb Papers," in *Georgia Historical Quarterly*, VI (1922), 43.

[8] Athens *Southern Banner*, May 27, 1852.

[9] Athens *Southern Whig*, June 22, 1848; Augusta *Chronicle and Sentinel*, July 25, 1849; Binkley, *American Political Parties*, 142–43.

[10] Athens *Southern Whig*, June 22, 1848.

While Georgia's Democracy was flirting with the Northern proletariat, rival Whig leaders, on the other hand, were playing up the advantages of continuing the old alliance between Southern planters and the robust industrial group of the North. Hence it was natural for Whig spokesmen of the forties frequently to chant the ritual of Henry Clay's American System.[11] Editors frequently appealed to Georgians to divert some of their talents and substance to the establishment of an industrial economy.[12] The campaign to industrialize Georgia was especially energetic in such centers as Athens, Augusta, and Savannah, cities in which the Whig party was particularly strong. The *Republican* of Savannah boasted during the debate over the adoption of the Walker tariff that "it is the Whig party of Georgia, that has shown itself publicly, openly, as a matter of political faith, the true friend of the manufacturing industry, and therefore, of all education and comfort and happiness to the people at large, which always in our happy country go hand and hand with that industry." [13] It was by these combinations between Northern- and Southern-interest groups that Georgia's party system was drawn into the vortex of a balance-of-power discipline. As long as this was the prevailing motif, parties would be national, rather than sectional, in character. Within this party design it was next to impossible for anti-Union threats to develop.

From the standpoint of practical planter politics, balance-of-power strategy possessed at least the merit of keeping the North divided, thereby immunizing the South to the dangers suggested by the rapid growth of Northern population. By the same token it kept the South divided and for this reason a respectable number of Georgians of both parties viewed it with suspicion. Astute Southern-rights propo-

[11] Macon *Journal and Messenger* quoted in Athens *Southern Whig*, October 8, 1846; Athens *Southern Whig*, February 18, September 2, 1847.
[12] Augusta *Chronicle and Sentinel*, March 22, 1849.
[13] Quoted in Milledgeville *Federal Union*, June 22, 1847.

nents detected the economic revolution then in progress in America and realized that it was subtly rending the nation's constitutional fabric. John Forsyth, Jr., of the Columbus *Times,* frequently delivered sledge-hammer blows against the constitutional repercussions of this economic drift. At no time was his logic more compelling than in 1851 when with characteristic nostalgia he instructed the Southern-rights committee of Charleston, South Carolina, as follows: "I would to God, we had fewer miles of railway, fewer millions invested in manufactures and stocks, fewer proofs of enterprise and thrift and money-making; and *more* of the spirit and chivalry of Georgia of olden time, which on more than one occasion, has interposed her sovereignty to check the usurpation of the Federal Government." [14] Here was a plea for the Union of the Fathers of 1787, a Union which had been formed by a society of small traders, merchants, planters, and farmers, a Union which Forsyth was complaining in 1851 no longer existed because the search for profits was producing more railroads and factories and less of that brand of "chivalry" which had made Georgia famous as the defender of the old Union.[15]

No Southern leader viewed with greater alarm the "entangling alliances" of balance-of-power politics than John C. Calhoun. This celebrated Carolinian advocated a fundamentally different party design. To him Southern rights required an all-Southern party.[16] Such a plan, he asserted in his far-famed "Southern Address" of 1849, was the most

[14] John Forsyth, Jr., to Carolina Southern Rights Committee quoted in Athens *Southern Banner,* September 25, 1851. The complete story of Georgia's dramatic struggle with the Federal government is told in Phillips, *Georgia and State Rights.*

[15] John Forsyth, Jr., to Carolina Southern Rights Committee quoted in Athens *Southern Banner,* September 25, 1851; Avery O. Craven, *The Coming of the Civil War* (New York, 1942), 253–54.

[16] Milledgeville *Federal Union,* January 3, February 6, 13, 1849, for reflections on the "Southern Address" by a Southern-rights editor; Robert P. Brooks, "Howell Cobb and the Crisis of 1850," in *Mississippi Valley Historical Review,* IV (1917), 281–82.

promising method of assuring the South control of its domestic affairs and of arresting the Northern threat to white
supremacy.[17] Calhoun had a reputable following among
Georgians. Some were party leaders and others were journalists. In addition to Forsyth such prominent Democrats
as former Governor C. J. McDonald, H. V. Johnson, H. L.
Benning, David C. Campbell of the *Federal Union,* and
Samuel J. Ray of the *Georgia Telegraph* were all disciples
of Calhoun's geographic notion of party discipline.

Among Whig leaders the tendency to disagree over the
relative merits of the respective party disciplines became
evident soon after the gubernatorial contest of 1847. As a
rule the followers of J. M. Berrien gravitated in the direction of the Calhoun notion. Hence this contingent of
Whiggery come to feel that it had more in common with
Southern-rights Democrats than with the Union Whigs.
Therefore Berrien refused to be pressed into the Cobb-
Democratic Union-Whig fusion movement which got under
way in the late forties. Instead, this influential Whig leader
sought comradeship with the anti-Cobb, or Southern-rights,
Democrats.[18] A. H. Stephens and Robert Toombs, on the
other hand, believed that planter interests would benefit
most by the preservation of the natural character of the
party design. Consequently they gave generously of their
time and talents to further the balance-of-power scheme.[19]
Once it became evident that balance-of-power politics could
be preserved only by scuttling the old parties, Stephens and
Toombs set out to fuse their followers with the Cobb
Democrats in the hope of capturing that balance of social

[17] "Southern Address" quoted in Milledgeville *Federal Union,* January
3, 1849; Ulrich B. Phillips, *The Course of the South to Secession* (New York,
1939), 145.

[18] H. V. Johnson to J. M. Berrien, October 13, 1854, MS. in Governor's
Letter Book, 1847–1861, in Georgia Department of Archives and History,
Atlanta; *Congressional Globe,* 30 Cong., 1 Sess., XVIII, 1042 ff., for the vote
on the Oregon bill; Milledgeville *Federal Union,* August 29, 1848.

[19] Phillips, *Life of Toombs,* 33.

forces which appeared to be eluding the old parties. Necessarily there began to emerge late in the forties the substructure of a new party arrangement.[20]

The high command of Georgia's Whig party stubbornly assailed the Mexican War, which broke out in 1846, the second year of President James K. Polk's administration. Whigs admonished the President for having "unconstitutionally begun" an uncalled-for war. It was freely asserted that needless domestic strife would be precipitated by a reopening of the slavery controversy. Yet almost from the start of the war the Southern Whig delegation in Congress showed a disposition to co-operate with the main contingent of the Democratic party, which was, of course, supporting President Polk. The war had scarcely begun when David Wilmot, a Pennsylvania Democrat, touched off a national explosion by presenting Congress his celebrated Proviso. The "Provisoists," as the supporters of Wilmot came to be labeled, were determined to prevent the extension of slavery into such territory as might be acquired from Mexico as a result of the war. The entire Southern delegation in the House of Representatives, excepting two Kentucky Whigs, voted against this measure during the first session of the Twenty-ninth Congress.[21]

The Wilmot Proviso severely jarred Georgia's party structure. The Savannah *Republican* sized up the situation perfectly when early in 1847 it concluded an editorial on the Proviso with these words: "We mention these things mainly to show the tendency of the country towards the formation of geographical parties." [22] Some months later

[20] John W. Burke to Howell Cobb, March 22, 1849, in Ulrich B. Phillips (ed.), *The Correspondence of Robert Toombs, Alexander H. Stephens, and Howell Cobb,* in American Historical Association, *Annual Report,* 1911, II (Washington, 1913), 158.

[21] *Cong. Globe,* 29 Cong., 1 Sess., XV, 1217; Arthur M. Schlesinger, Jr., *The Age of Jackson* (Boston, 1946), 451; Bernard De Voto, *The Year of Decision: 1846* (Boston, 1943), 297–300.

[22] Quoted in Athens *Southern Whig,* February 15, 1847.

the legislature's Committee on the State of the Republic had the following to report with respect to the Wilmot Proviso: "Georgia has but one mind—is as one man—all parties are ready and willing to plant themselves upon the same *platform,* and join *heart* and *hand.* . . ."²³ That the conventional party system was on trial after 1846 is evident from the multiplicity of nonpartisan gatherings which assembled to protest against "Provisoism." One such meeting in Richmond County boasted that "we know no party feeling . . . on this question [Wilmot Proviso]. . . ."²⁴ Despite the virulence of this wave of popular indignation the old parties refused to melt away. Georgians were still Whigs and Democrats, and they remained so until 1850. Editorial sentiment warrants the inference that the gubernatorial contests of 1847 and 1849 stimulated enough conventional partisan enthusiasm to enable the old party structure to resist the violent impact of Provisoism.²⁵

While Whigs the country over had freely lectured President Polk for his "needless war" against Mexico, they did not hesitate to appropriate the military fame of the war's leading hero, General Zachary Taylor of Louisiana.²⁶ Realizing their idol was without benefit of having killed a Mexican, Clay Whigs were soon eclipsed by a "Taylor boom." ²⁷ Thus it was that General Taylor, the Louisiana planter, came to be selected in June of 1848 as the Whig

---

²³ Quoted *ibid.,* December 9, 1847.

²⁴ Quoted in Milledgeville *Federal Union,* March 20, 1849.

²⁵ *Ibid.,* September 4, 1849; Augusta *Chronicle and Sentinel,* April 25, 1849; Macon *Journal and Messenger,* February 28, 1849; Columbus *Enquirer* quoted in Augusta *Chronicle and Sentinel,* September 5, 1849; Athens *Southern Whig,* May 31, 1849; Savannah *Republican* quoted in Milledgeville *Federal Union,* June 26, 1849.

²⁶ On January 21, 1847, the *Southern Whig* claimed to have inaugurated the Taylor boom in Georgia. This journal was, of course, opposed to the war.

²⁷ Robert Toombs quoted Henry Clay as having declared in a speech at New Orleans, "I wish I could kill a Mexican." Speech of Toombs quoted in Milledgeville *Federal Union,* April 18, 1848.

candidate for the presidency. In the contest which followed, the General, who was presented as the "Hero of Buena Vista," defeated Lewis Cass, his Democratic opponent, whom the Whigs painstakingly advertised as the "Hero of Hull's Surrender." [28]

Like Provisoism, the Taylor-Cass contest revealed the precarious state of Georgia's party structure. The very manner in which Taylor was presented to the South constituted a real threat to the existing party design. The General was offered to Georgia electors as a true son of the South. Much was made of the fact that he was a large slaveholder. Whig editors kept up a steady plea for him as the "safe" candidate. Taylor was hardly the Whig nominee, but rather the Southern champion. Stephens and Toombs, both experienced campaigners, reported six weeks in advance of the election that this "no-party-appeal" was producing favorable results. [29]

Mindful of their successful tactics of eight years earlier when they had elevated General William Henry Harrison to the presidency, Whigs methodically set out to entertain the electorate. They organized "Rough and Ready Clubs" all over the State and freely asserted that these clubs were nineteenth-century editions of the Revolutionary clubs of 1776. [30] Distinctly a party of the "haves," Whiggery was forever plagued with the necessity of wooing the "have nots." [31] This was the recurring motif of the Whig party, both locally and nationally. In 1848 the wool-hat boys of Cherokee and the pine barrens were fed a steady diet of barbecue and eighteenth-century natural-rights political philosophy in

[28] Lewis Cass had served with General William Hull at Detroit in 1812. Hull surrendered Detroit without firing a shot.

[29] A. H. Stephens to John J. Crittenden, September 26, 1848, and Robert Toombs to John J. Crittenden, September 27, 1848, in Phillips (ed.), Correspondence, 127.

[30] Athens Southern Whig, July 6, 1848.

[31] Binkley, American Political Parties, 180.

the hope that on election day they would cast their votes for "Rough and Ready," a sort of Whig edition of Old Hickory.

Representing General Taylor as a second Washington was more than the sober-minded Judge Thomas W. Thomas of Elberton could stand. Writing Cobb in midsummer that the "fool idea constantly harped upon by the Whig press, of having a second Washington in the chair, has turned some weak heads," he recommended that the Whig nominee for President be attacked as a partisan.[32] Taylor, however, was a difficult target. Not only had the Whigs "unwhigged" him with their "no-party-appeal," but it would seem that their spellbinders had succeeded in making him both a Jackson and a Washington as well. One can imagine the exasperation of the *Federal Union* as its editor exploded that "he [Taylor] tells Col. Haskell of Tennessee, he is 'a Whig and *a quarter over.*' Now we seriously ask, can any man, calling himself a Democrat . . . think of voting for Zachary Taylor, a Clay Whig, a Fillmore Whig—'*a Whig and a quarter over*'?" [33]

Georgia's Democratic leaders encountered difficulty in meeting the nonpartisan appeal of the Whigs. Taylor's almost complete lack of a public record made him an elusive target for the tilted lances of a frantic Democracy.[34] However, the General's Northern apologists, anxious to sell the slaveholder north of Mason and Dixon's line, exposed the Taylor candidacy to a flank attack in the South. Georgia Democrats lost no time in bringing it within range of their most deadly fire. Almost a year in advance of his nomination Taylor had declared in a letter to the Cincinnati *Signal* that "the personal opinion of the individual

[32] Thomas W. Thomas to Howell Cobb, July 7, 1848, in Phillips (ed.), *Correspondence,* 115.

[33] Milledgeville *Federal Union,* October 24, 1848.

[34] For an excellent treatment of the presidential election of 1848 see Brainerd Dyer, *Zachary Taylor* (Baton Rouge, 1946), 265–301.

who may happen to occupy the Executive chair ought not
to control the action of Congress upon questions of domestic
policy." [35] Northern Whigs, notably Andrew Stewart of
Pennsylvania, frequently cited the letter in the *Signal* during the canvass of 1848 to appease the "Conscience Whigs."
If elected, explained Stewart, Taylor would not interfere
with those acts of Congress which were designed to extend
the free-soil "principles of the Ordinance of 1787." [36] Stewart's plan for selling Taylor to Northern voters could have
but one interpretation among Georgia Democrats, namely,
that if elected, the General would subscribe to good Whig
doctrine and therefore not invoke the veto power to prevent antislavery legislation. Democrats were careful to warn
that the South needed a strong executive, one who would
use the veto freely when Southern institutions were under
attack in the Congress. Democracy, notably the Southern-
rights wing, was thus beginning to attach a special importance to the presidency. [37]

As already observed, Clay Whigs were displeased at
Taylor's nomination. The high command of Georgia's
Democracy naturally hoped to annex these dissident Whigs.
When shortly after Taylor's nomination the *Federal Union*
lamented that "the few successful battles which Gen. Taylor
has won, have eclipsed the glory of his [Clay's] long civil
career . . . ," the editor was simply grappling with the
politician's perpetual problem of devising means to attract
the opposition's dissonant elements. [38] While Stephens and
Toombs were laboring well in the Taylor vineyard, Berrien

[35] *Signal* letter quoted in Milledgeville *Federal Union,* July 13, 1847.

[36] Stewart's opinion in Richmond *Enquirer* is quoted in Milledgeville
Federal Union, July 18, 1848.

[37] Milledgeville *Federal Union,* June 20, 1848; *Cong. Globe,* 30 Cong.,
1 Sess., Appendix, 963, for comments of Congressman Alfred Iverson, Georgia
Democrat, on the *Signal* letter. See also Wilfred E. Binkley, *The Powers of
the President* (New York, 1937), 107–108, for an analysis of Zachary Taylor's
conception of the presidency.

[38] Milledgeville *Federal Union,* June 13, 1848.

was recognized as the leader of Georgia's Clay Whigs. Smarting under the sting of his favorite's repudiation and disappointed at the failure of his party's convention to define its position in respect to slavery in the territories, Berrien recommended the mild nonintervention plank of the Democratic national platform.[39] His choice was widely advertised by the Democrats. Aside from purely political considerations it would appear to have been dictated by a preference for the written word of the Democratic platform over the rather ambiguous position selected by the Whigs, a weakness which Whiggery attempted to conceal by its manner of presenting General Taylor to the electorate.

Throughout the campaign of 1848 Berrien behaved in a manner that must have been disconcerting to the Taylorites. When he supported the Senate's move to incorporate the Missouri Compromise line in the Oregon bill in the place of the Wilmot Proviso, he was theoretically sustaining the right of Congress to decide the question of slavery in the territories.[40] To be sure, by voting to replace the Wilmot Proviso with the Missouri Compromise line, he was acting to substitute a mild form of intervention for the severe Proviso.[41] Actually the controversy over the Oregon bill would seem to have been quixotic. Few could seriously have believed that slavery could ever exist in faraway Oregon. Yet it must be remembered that 1848 was a presidential election year; and Congressmen, anxious to provide copy for certain interest groups among their constituents, sounded off freely. Apparently hopeful of arresting this flow of dialectics, Stephens had the Senate's version of the Oregon bill tabled when it reached the House.[42] Led by

[39] *Ibid.*, August 1, 1848.

[40] Georgia's other Senator, H. V. Johnson, a Democrat, was in agreement with Berrien on the Oregon bill.

[41] Milledgeville *Federal Union*, August 29, 1848; *Cong. Globe*, 30 Cong., 1 Sess., XVIII, 1043 ff.

[42] Milledgeville *Federal Union*, August 29, 1848.

the *Federal Union,* the Democratic press lost no time in pouncing on Stephens. His action in tabling the Oregon bill was represented as tantamount to approval of the hated Proviso. Wailing bitterly, the *Federal Union* editorialized that by such actions as Stephens' ". . . the enemies of the South abroad will learn, that . . . under the influence of party drill and for the purpose of promoting the ambitious views of *a few* party leaders, a viper is cherished in her bosom. . . ." [43]

If Stephens could be repudiated in the October Congressional election, then, hopefully reflected the Democrats, perhaps Georgia would decide against Taylor in the November presidential voting. Thus the Democrats of Stephens' Congressional district paid a warm tribute to Berrien when they met in Milledgeville to nominate a candidate to oppose the incumbent. Joseph Day, the nominee, was characterized as "one who would have voted with Berrien and the South on the Oregon Bill." [44] The correspondence of both Stephens and Toombs would indicate that Democracy's efforts to detach Berrien were causing Taylor men considerable anxiety. In late September, Stephens complained that the "whole campaign . . . has rested entirely on the shoulders of Mr. Toombs. . . . The real Clay men here as elsewhere I believe are doing nothing for Taylor, while many of them are openly in opposition; but I think we shall triumph notwithstanding." [45] On the following day Toombs noted that the "Clay men in the State will do nothing; some of them would be glad to lose . . . with the hope of breaking down Stephens and myself. . . . They will lessen my vote in my district some two or three hundred unless I can get them from the Democrats. I think I shall do it. Had not Mr. Clay put himself up there would

[43] *Ibid.* [44] *Ibid.,* September 12, 1848.
[45] A. H. Stephens to John J. Crittenden, September 26, 1848, in Phillips (ed.), *Correspondence,* 127.

not have been even a contest in Georgia, the friends of Clay being the only men here who ever dared to attack Taylor." [46]

A few days after Georgia voters registered a preference for General Taylor, one of Howell Cobb's Cherokee (North Georgia) friends wrote the Athens Democrat that he could not even console him with "an explanation, other than the indisputable truth that very many Democrats have voted for Taylor." [47] A comparison of October's Congressional election returns with November's presidential voting will suffice to show how severely the Taylor avalanche smashed party lines. In October, Cobb, the Democratic nominee for Congress, carried the sixth district by a majority of 1,477 votes. Taylor lost this traditional Democratic stronghold a month later by slightly over two hundred votes. In the fourth district, where Democracy's Hugh Haralson had won in October, Taylor carried off the honors in November. In the second district, Cass lost to Taylor in November after the Democratic candidate for Congress, Marshall Wellborn, had emerged the winner a month earlier. Both Wellborn and Haralson were recognized Southern-rights champions. [48] Planters predominated in both the second and fourth districts. [49] The fact that Taylor carried both districts only a month after they had registered Southern-rights

[46] Robert Toombs to John J. Crittenden, September 27, 1848, *ibid.* Toombs was to regret his enthusiastic support of Taylor. Long after the Civil War he was quoted in an interview with a reporter of the Philadelphia *Times* as having reflected that of all the Presidents he had known (he boasted to have been on at least speaking terms with all the Presidents who served before the Civil War, except the first three), Taylor was the most ignorant. "It was amazing," he told the reporter, "how little he knew." This interview was quoted in the Pittsburgh *Daily Post*, July 9, 1879.

[47] James F. Cooper to Howell Cobb, November 11, 1848, in Phillips (ed.), *Correspondence,* 137.

[48] Official returns quoted in Athens *Southern Whig,* November 30, 1848.

[49] See series of maps in Phillips, *Georgia and State Rights,* Appendix; E. Merton Coulter, *College Life in the Old South* (New York, 1928), 223.

preferences lends weight to the belief expressed by the *Federal Union* that many Democrats supported the General because he was a slaveholder.[50] The presiding officer of Georgia's electoral college paid a warm tribute to the high command of the State's Whig party when he announced in December that "I think it may be said with truth, that this is not the triumph of party—Whigs and Democrats everywhere . . . have voted for General Taylor." [51]

The Democratic caucus which assembled in Washington just before the opening of Congress in December, 1849, reflected the nervous feeling which at that time prevailed throughout the nation. Democracy's leaders were in a bad humor. This was particularly the case with Southern-rights Democrats who were inclined to view as a victory for abolitionists General Taylor's election to the presidency.[52] It was generally predicted that Cobb, the Athens Democrat, would be nominated by his party's caucus for the speakership, if he could get the support of the Southern Democrats of the Calhoun stripe.[53] Northern Democrats were as a rule friendly to Cobb. While his record in Congress and his refusal to sign Calhoun's "Southern Address" had weakened him with Southern-rights leaders, his public career had, on the other hand, made him a favorite with those Northern Democrats who, like himself, were determined to preserve the national character of their party.[54]

Early in December, after a vain fight against Cobb in the party's nominating caucus, the Southern-rights faction suddenly joined the Georgia Democrat in preparation for the speakership fight against Robert C. Winthrop of Massa-

[50] Milledgeville *Federal Union*, November 28, 1848.

[51] Quoted *ibid.*, December 26, 1848.

[52] *Ibid.*, October 24, 1849.

[53] Athens *Southern Whig*, November 8, 1849; James Buchanan to Howell Cobb, June 12, 1849, in Phillips (ed.), *Correspondence*, 162; John L. Robinson (Indiana Democrat) to *id.*, August 24, 1849, *ibid.*, 174.

[54] Athens *Southern Whig*, November 8, 1849.

chusetts, the Whig nominee.[55] Northern Democrats were
now in a quandary. They had loyally stood by Cobb before
and during the bitter caucus fight. The picture had changed,
however, and many of those Northern Democrats who had
sustained Cobb in the intraparty feud were beginning to
betray a reluctance to support him in the race against
Winthrop. Many of them felt that a too evident show of
interest in Cobb's success would at this stage be interpreted
by some of their constituents as the product of a complete
surrender to the Southern "fire-eaters." [56] Northern Democrats thus confirmed the belief, already widespread among
extreme Southern-rights men in Georgia, that the South
could expect very little from the national Democratic
party.[57] The campaign among them for Southern unity now
became more determined than ever.[58] Three days before
Christmas, Cobb was chosen Speaker by an angry House
of Representatives. He was now more closely wedded to
the national Democratic party than at any previous time
in his career. His late triumph was a vindication of balance-
of-power methodology. As Speaker he intended to protect
it. Committee appointments were therefore judiciously
divided between Northern and Southern Congressmen for
the purpose of arresting the drift toward sectional parties
which had been given a giant shove by Provisoism and General Zachary Taylor's election to the presidency of the
United States. Thus did Howell Cobb hope to preserve the
motif of the national Democratic party.

[55] Howell Cobb to his wife, December 4, 1849, Phillips (ed.), *Correspondence,* 176–77.

[56] *Id.* to *id.,* December 20, 1849, *ibid.,* 184; Milledgeville *Federal Union,*
December 14, 1849; Savannah *Georgian,* January 29, 1851.

[57] Phillips, *The Course of the South to Secession,* 135–36.

[58] Milledgeville *Federal Union,* December 14, 1849; Savannah *Georgian,*
January 29, 1851.

II

CRISIS

NO sooner had the excitement over the Speaker's election subsided than the House of Representatives found itself caught in the tough web of the slavery struggle. California had forced the issue by applying late in 1849 for admission into the Union. For months Congress debated a series of proposals which, under the skillful leadership of Henry Clay, was cut and polished so as finally to emerge in the form of the celebrated Omnibus bill, more commonly called the Compromise of 1850. The main features of Clay's plan were as follows: the admission of California as a free state; the assumption by the Federal government of the debt of Texas contracted before annexation and the surrender of her claims to a large part of eastern New Mexico; a more effective fugitive-slave law; the creation of the territories of New Mexico and Utah without restrictions as to slavery; and the prohibition of the slave trade in the District of Columbia.[1]

Georgia's determined blasts against the Wilmot Proviso formed a fitting prelude to the venomous effusions which were hurled at Clay's proposals during the winter of 1849–1850. Shortly before the opening of Congress in December, Governor Towns, with a fresh mandate from the people, outlined a plan of action.[2] He recommended a State convention to consider measures for self-protection in case an effort were made by the forthcoming Congress to apply the

---

[1] Daniel Mallory, *The Life and Speeches of Hon. Henry Clay* (New York, 1853), II, 610–34, contains many speeches, mostly by Clay, on this subject.

[2] Governor Towns was re-elected in 1849, defeating Edward Y. Hill, the Whig nominee.

Proviso treatment to slavery in any part of the Mexican cession.[3] This was, of course, precisely the formula Clay was shortly to prescribe.

The legislature which assembled in November, 1849, for its regular biennial session gave more than passing attention to affairs at the nation's capital. The State's lawmakers were no doubt moved by the Governor's admonitions. However, it seems they hoped to avert the crisis he warned of in his message. It was in this spirit that a series of declarations known as the Wiggins Resolutions was introduced in the lower house soon after the session opened in November. These resolutions plainly instructed Georgia's Congressional delegation to resist whatever efforts were made in the national legislature to admit California as a free state.[4] Thus it was clear in advance of the opening of Congress how Georgia would regard the free admission of California.

Caught in the swirling vortex of popular indignation at the threatened adoption by Congress of Provisoism, party lines in Georgia were torn to shreds. Whigs and Democrats all over the State suspended partisan zeal during January and February, 1850, assembled in county meetings and aimed blistering protests at a menacing leadership in the nation's capital.[5] Aware of this state of popular feeling back home, Senator Berrien broke with Clay at this time, declaring the great Kentuckian was trying to trick the South into accepting the Proviso.[6] The *Southern Whig*, father of the Taylor boom in Georgia, began to reflect the growing coolness between the Taylor administration and the Southern contingent of Whiggery.[7] John B. Lamar, Cobb's brother-

[3] Governor's message quoted in Milledgeville *Federal Union*, November 6, 1849.

[4] *Georgia House Journal, 1849–1850 Session* (Milledgeville, 1850), 136, 309. Hereafter cited *House Journal* with appropriate date.

[5] Milledgeville *Federal Union*, January 8, 1850; Athens *Southern Whig*, January 17, 1850.

[6] Milledgeville *Federal Union*, February 5, 1850.

[7] Athens *Southern Whig*, February 11, 21, 1850.

in-law in Macon, wrote the Speaker early in February that disunion was inevitable. Howell Cobb, defender of the Union, was hardly comforted by his kinsman's gloomy prediction that ere long the Athens Democrat could lay claim to the distinction of having served as the last Speaker of the United States Congress.[8]

Shortly after the legislature returned from its Christmas recess, Lucius J. Gartrell, a Wilkes County Whig, acted on Governor Towns's recommendation by presenting a convention bill. This measure was to empower the Governor to summon a State convention in case California was admitted as a free state. The House adopted it late in January by a vote of 106 to 12, only Whigs dissenting.[9] In the Senate the convention idea was strongly defended by Joseph E. Brown, a Cherokee Democrat who was later to become famous as Georgia's "War Governor." The Gartrell bill came to a vote in the upper chamber early in February. It was passed by a vote of 35 to 3.[10] Thus by the end of the first week in February Georgia had made preparations to meet the impending crisis. In so doing she had manifested an impressive unanimity of purpose. Calhoun's plea for Southern unity, it appeared, had at last triumphed in the Empire State of the South.

Southern-rights Democrats hailed the adoption of the convention bill as a vindication of Governor Towns, whose notions of party discipline bore a striking resemblance to those of Calhoun.[11] Whig leaders, on the other hand, particularly those with balance-of-power leanings, were disturbed by the sudden show of confidence in the Democratic administration at Milledgeville. Thus it was that an attempt to revive partisan feeling was undertaken in the

[8] Quoted in Phillips (ed.), *Correspondence*, 183.

[9] *House Journal, 1849–1850*, 350, 383, 520; Milledgeville *Federal Union*, January 29, 1850.

[10] *Georgia Senate Journal, 1849–1850 Session* (Milledgeville, 1850), 509.

[11] Milledgeville *Federal Union*, January 29, 1850.

House by A. H. Stephens' half-brother, Linton, of Talia-
ferro County. During the House discussion of the Report of
the Committee on the State of the Republic, Linton Stephens ascribed the prevailing threat against Southern rights
to the policies of the Democratic administration of James
K. Polk. The Mexican War, explained Stephens and his colleagues, lay at the root of the South's ills. Whigs had warned
against that war, they continued, and had accurately predicted what had since come to pass.[12]

Georgia's lawmakers had performed well at fanning the
flames of Southern fire during the months of January and
February of 1850. In fact, at times the legislature actually
degenerated into little more than a propaganda machine for
the extreme Southern-rights leaders. Consequently, after
adjournment in February, passions cooled quickly and
Georgians settled down to do some sober thinking on the
issues raised by Clay's proposals. Extreme Southern rightists, however, did not intend to lose by default their brilliant conquests of legislative days. Hence their journals kept
up a steady assault on the Clay program during the late
winter and early spring months.[13] A wise legislature, declared an able battery of Southern-rights journalists, had
authorized a State convention. Thus Georgia was enabled,
went the argument, to protect herself against the Clay
heresies, which were, of course, steadily moving nearer
adoption.

Meanwhile preparations were under way to try the case
against the Compromise in the high court of public opinion.
As early as the spring of 1849 Mississippi extremists, acting
on Calhoun's plea for Southern unity, had prepared the
stage for a cotton-states convention which was to meet in

[12] Speeches quoted *ibid.*

[13] With the exception of the *Southern Banner,* Cobb's Athens journal, the
Democratic press lined up solidly against the Compromise of 1850. Two
Whig papers, the Athens *Southern Whig* and the Augusta *Republic,* joined
the attack against the Compromise.

Nashville, Tennessee, sometime during the summer of 1850. The promoters of this convention planned to have the delegates publish an address to the nation. This address was to set forth the causes of Southern grievances and warn of the consequences that would follow failure to redress them.[14] Calhoun's correspondence with the Mississippi extremists indicates that he desired at this time to force a showdown on the question of Southern rights. The Nashville convention was to serve precisely this purpose.[15]

According to the plan adopted by the legislature, each of Georgia's eight Congressional districts was to select by popular vote two delegates to attend the Nashville Convention.[16] With the adjournment of the legislature in February, Southern-rights forces began a concerted drive for full representation at this convention. They were a sanguine lot as they approached what amounted to their first real test of strength. Two preliminary rounds, namely, the State convention-bill fight and the struggle to provide means for selecting representatives to the Nashville gathering, had been won by comfortable margins. The popular excitement of legislative days, which had been largely responsible for these successes, quickly gave way, however, to a puzzling indifference. By the middle of March this widespread lack of interest in the Nashville convention had created perceptible alarm in Southern-rights circles.[17] Sensing this popular indifference and anxiously awaiting an opportunity to strike at the Towns administration, the Whig press suddenly sprang to life. The Southern-rights proclivities of the

[14] John C. Calhoun to Collin S. Tarpley, July 9, 1849, quoted in Philip May Hamer, *The Secession Movement in South Carolina, 1847–1852* (Allentown, Pa., 1918), 39; Howard C. Perkins, "A Neglected Phase of the Movement for Southern Unity, 1847–1852," in *Journal of Southern History*, XII (1946), 162.

[15] John C. Calhoun to Collin S. Tarpley, July 9, 1849, quoted in Hamer, *The Secession in South Carolina*, 39.

[16] *Acts of the State of Georgia, 1849–1850* (Milledgeville, 1850), 418–19.

[17] Milledgeville *Federal Union*, March 19, 1850.

Democratic party were roundly denounced, the influential *Chronicle and Sentinel* describing the forthcoming Nashville convention as a "miserable abortion." [18] Thus did the project for cotton-states unity become tangled in the vicissitudes of partisan politics.

Despite grim warnings by Southern-rights journals during the spring of 1850, Georgians were apparently not even mildly alarmed over the alleged threat that was then being prepared in Congress by the designing Henry Clay. This disposition was reflected early in April by the light vote cast in the election of delegates to the Nashville convention. The *Southern Recorder* estimated that less than one twenty-fifth of the State's eligible electors had voted. [19] The *Chronicle and Sentinel* reported that in many counties not even a single vote was cast, while in others the polls were not even opened. Of the 1,200 eligible voters in Richmond County only 127 were interested enough to vote. "The popular voice," declared the *Chronicle and Sentinel,* "has condemned the Convention . . . as premature—unnecessary—mischievous at the present time." [20] Howell Cobb's *Southern Banner,* the lone Democratic organ failing to join the Southern-rights movement, thought that it was "worse than folly to think of holding a sectional convention . . . at a moment when every mail informs us of the probability of a fair and pacific adjustment by Congress." [21]

Despite their miserable showing, Southern-rights leaders could lay claim to a majority of the State's delegates elected to attend the Nashville convention. [22] Whatever solace they might have derived from this fact was short-lived, for three

[18] Quoted *ibid.,* April 2, 1850.

[19] Quoted in Augusta *Chronicle and Sentinel,* May 3, 1850.

[20] *Ibid.,* April 17, 1850.

[21] Quoted in Milledgeville *Federal Union,* May 14, 1850.

[22] An interesting discussion of this phase of the Southern-rights movement appears in Percy Scott Flippin, *Herschel V. Johnson of Georgia, State Rights Unionist* (Richmond, 1931), 32 ff.; Richard H. Shryock, *Georgia and the Union in 1850* (Durham, 1926), 264 ff.

Unionists (opponents of the Nashville convention) announced they would not attend the cotton-states meeting. Judge James S. Scarbrough, delegate-elect in the third district, publicly declared shortly after the April election that the forthcoming convention was part of a movement designed to excite disunion by unconstitutional means. For this reason, he explained, he would not go to Nashville in June.[23] The behavior of Scarbrough is significant because it represents that strategy which the disciples of Howell Cobb, Robert Toombs, and A. H. Stephens (the balance-of-power proponents) were at the moment preparing to invoke in order to put over Clay's Compromise in Georgia. The third district's delegate-elect had simply pinned the badge of disunion on the Southern-rights crowd. This was soon to become the most devastating weapon in the balance-of-power arsenal. Judge John A. Billups and Junius Hillyer, delegates-elect in the fifth and sixth districts respectively, likewise declined to serve because popular opinion in their districts, they asserted, was averse to the convention idea.[24]

"None but knaves," remonstrated D. C. Campbell of the *Federal Union,* "ever conceived that the Nashville Convention was designed for the purpose of disunion." [25] He continued by justifying the winter demonstrations in behalf of Southern rights, professing to have seen a softening of Northern attitude as a result of those demonstrations. However, he lamented, the late failure of the people of Georgia to support the Nashville convention would fan the flames of abolition. The resourceful Campbell blamed the Whigs for the April mishap. As was to be expected, he cajoled,

[23] Quoted in Milledgeville *Federal Union,* May 7, 1850.

[24] Henry G. Lamer to John T. Smith, May 21, 1850, MS. in Telamon Cuyler Collection in University of Georgia Library; Athens *Southern Whig,* May 23, 30, 1850.

[25] Milledgeville *Federal Union,* May 7, 1850; Perkins, "A Neglected Phase of the Movement for Southern Unity, 1847–1852," *loc. cit.,* 161–62.

they had yielded to party considerations when their duty had plainly been to co-operate with patriotic Georgians then engaged in an effort to arrest the "mad career" of the South's enemies. The intrepid John Forsyth, Jr., of the Columbus *Times* took much stronger ground. He reminded those who held the forthcoming convention in Nashville to be unconstitutional that the Congress which drafted the Declaration of Independence had also been unconstitutional. Moreover, he was at a loss to understand how a protest against Clay's "violations of the Constitution" could possibly be considered "unconstitutional." [26]

The political consort of early 1850 was but a memory by May. It had been dissolved during March and April by the invective-drenched exchanges over the Nashville convention. Old party lines, however, failed to reappear. Instead, a new pattern was emerging. This new design conformed with the specifications dictated by the rival notions of party discipline. Putting aside the prejudices of nearly two decades, balance-of-power proponents were preparing to quit the Whig and Democratic parties to build a new party dedicated to acceptance of the Compromise of 1850. Their opponents, likewise recruited from the old parties, hoped that acceptance of the Compromise would at least be contingent upon pledges underwriting Southern rights. Consequently by late spring of 1850 the political architecture erected in Georgia during the Jacksonian era had become a jumbled ruin.[27]

On June 3, while Congress was still debating specific features of Clay's proposals, the long-heralded cotton-states convention assembled in Nashville. Walter T. Colquitt,

[26] Quoted in Athens *Southern Whig*, May 7, 1850.

[27] On June 6 the Athens *Southern Whig*, one of the two Whig papers which refused to support the Compromise, carried an editorial in answer to the Richmond (Virginia) *Republican's* plea for a restoration in the South of the traditional two-national-party system. This journal declared that the passing of the old parties was an omen of better times. Only the demagogue, it asserted, profited by the existence of strong party ties.

Simpson Fouche, Andrew H. Dawson, and H. L. Benning —all conspicuous Southern-rights Democrats from Georgia —played leading roles in its deliberations.[28] The "Address to the Southern People," which accompanied the convention's thirteen resolutions, reviewed Northern aggressions in typical Southern-rights style.[29] On June 12 the delegates adjourned to await the action of Congress. The most sanguine of the all-Southern adherents admitted that this "disunion conclave," as the Nashville gatherings was labeled by its opponents, had not spoken for a united South.[30]

During the summer of 1850 Clay's proposals, daily moving nearer adoption by Congress, became the subject of extravagant claims and counterclaims. Friends of Clay's plan insisted that a majority of Georgians were eagerly awaiting the opportunity to acclaim the finished product.[31] The *Federal Union,* on the other hand, was able to report by mid-August at least two dozen counties in which Southern-rights meetings had gone on record against the "Omnibus surrender" and in favor of the Nashville convention's injunction that the Missouri Compromise line be applied to California.[32]

Anticipating the adoption of the Omnibus surrender, Georgia's Southern-rights leaders assumed that Governor Towns would summon a State convention, as indeed he had been directed to do by the State legislature. They therefore decided to stage a grass-roots demonstration. Accord-

[28] Proceedings of the Nashville convention quoted in Milledgeville *Federal Union,* June 18, 1850.

[29] Quoted *ibid.,* June 25, 1850.

[30] *Ibid.,* June 4, 11, 18, 1850; Shryock, *Georgia and the Union,* 273; Perkins, "A Neglected Phase of the Movement for Southern Unity, 1847–1852," *loc. cit.,* 175. On November 11, 1850, the Nashville convention reassembled for a listless session.

[31] J. B. Lamar to Howell Cobb, July 3, 1850, in Phillips (ed.), *Correspondence,* 191–92; John H. Lumpkin to *id.,* July 21, 1850, *ibid.,* 207–208; Macon *Journal and Messenger* quoted in Augusta *Chronicle and Sentinel,* July 3, 1850.

[32] Milledgeville *Federal Union,* July 10, August 13, 20, 1850.

ingly there assembled in Macon on August 21 an elaborate
Southern-rights conclave. The Whig press was quick to
label this meeting a failure. The *Republican* thought that
fewer than 1,500 were in attendance; the *Southern Recorder*
fixed the number at 2,000; and the *Chronicle and Sentinel*
boldly asserted that the Southern-rights movement had now
received "a signal rebuke from the people of Georgia." [33]
These journals were naturally interested in discrediting
the Macon gathering, chiefly because its flavor was pre-
dominantly Democratic. Unquestionably this object moti-
vated the charge that none but "disunionists" had been in
attendance at Macon. The *Federal Union* admitted that a
few intemperate speeches had been made. It strongly denied, however, that these outbursts had committed the
Southern-rights movement to secession. [34] The report of the
Macon convention's proceedings suggests the tone of an
ultimatum. This was particularly true in respect to the
California bill. This feature of Omnibus surrender and the
plan to reduce the size of Texas were emphatically condemned by the Macon delegates. They took violent exception to the Proviso formula and insisted that Clay was applying it to California; they expressed a preference for the
Missouri Compromise line as a means of treating slavery
in California; and all references to the Nashville convention were sympathetic. [35]

The Macon meeting of August speeded up that realign-
ment of Georgia parties which had been in the making since
early 1850. It was at Macon that the Democratic party as
it had been known in Georgia for a decade and a half was
disbanded and a new party was born. Committed to the
Calhoun notion of Southern unity, this new party quite

[33] Savannah *Republican*, August 23, 24, 1850; Milledgeville *Southern Recorder*, August 27, 1850; Augusta *Chronicle and Sentinel*, August 28, 1850.
[34] Milledgeville *Federal Union*, September 10, 1850. The speeches in question were made by South Carolina's Rhett and Alabama's Yancey.
[35] Proceedings of the Macon convention quoted *ibid.*, August 27, 1850.

naturally chose the name "Southern Rights." While the Southern Rights party's stand on secession was never very clearly defined, yet a determined minority, which historians have frequently called "fire-eaters," refused to conceal its contempt for the Union. It was the presence of this element in the new party which caused a great many influential Union Democrats to repudiate it. These Union Democrats began to labor in the Cobb-Stephens-Toombs vineyard, where they gave generously of their time and talents to promote the credo of balance-of-power politics, namely, the preservation of the Union. Inspired by D. C. Campbell of the *Federal Union*, moderate Democrats refused to support secession, except the so-called "abstract right" to secede. However, these moderate Democrats kept up their vigorous assaults against "submission" to Clay's "surrender bills," as they had facetiously stamped the Compromise of 1850. Editorial sentiment and the speeches and letters of prominent Georgians of this age warrant the inference that it was these moderates who comprised the bulk of the Southern Rights following. Naturally those Whigs who were opposed to the Compromise joined the Southern Rights party. They were in the minority in this new party and would seem never to have exerted much influence in shaping its destiny.[36]

By mid-September Clay's celebrated Compromise of 1850 had become law. On September 23 Governor Towns issued his long-awaited call for a State convention. It was to gather at Milledgeville on December 10.[37] Delegates were to be elected in each county on November 25. Georgians were thus to decide for their nation the fate of the Compromise. The action of Governor Towns had created for them this unique role. Accordingly the nation's center of political

[36] Shryock, *Georgia and the Union*, 287; Phillips, *The Course of the South to Secession*, 128–49.

[37] Proclamation quoted in Milledgeville *Federal Union*, September 24, 1850.

gravity was suddenly shifted in late September from Washington to the South's Empire State, where A. H. Stephens, Robert Toombs, and Howell Cobb were hurriedly mobilizing an emotional drive dedicated to the great dogma of the Union. The Georgia triumvirate astutely resolved matters by presenting the issue in terms of sweeping alternatives. Georgians would either accept the Compromise and save the Union, or they would by rejecting the Compromise dissolve the Union. Southern Rightists were thus promptly stigmatized with the derisive epithet of disunion. John W. Forney, editor of the Washington *Union,* knew Georgia's three famous "Union savers" of 1850. Years later he was still impressed with the strange contrast of the "feeble health of Stephens, his treble or tenor voice, his light boyish frame, his deadly pale face," to the "stern visage, imperious tones, and fierce swagger of Toombs, and the laughing face and rotund figure of Cobb." [38]

Calling themselves Unionists, the friends of the Compromise of 1850 entered the fall campaign for the selection of convention delegates with such political advantage as accrues to those who promise not to disturb prosperity. In Georgia in 1850 there were 40 cotton mills, employing 60,000 spindles and consuming 45,000 bales of cotton annually.[39] It was at this time too that enterprising Georgians were beginning to reap enormous profits from an elaborate network of railroads and a successful banking business.[40]

[38] John W. Forney, *Anecdotes of Public Men* (New York, 1881), II, 312.

At this time Georgia arranged to have her Congressional delegation take office in December immediately after the October elections. Thus Georgia's newly elected members of Congress waited two instead of thirteen months to take office. This arrangement lasted until the Civil War.

Where reference is made to the Southern Rights party both words will appear in the upper case; where reference is made to Southern rights per se "rights" will appear in the lower case.

[39] Washington (D.C.) *United States Journal* quoted in Milledgeville *Federal Union,* November 12, 1850.

[40] Balthasar H. Meyers, *History of Transportation in the United States before 1860* (Washington, 1917), 438–57.

The Savannah correspondent of the Boston *Courier* would seem to have made a fair appraisal of the relation between political temper and prosperity when in the fall of 1850 he observed that "it is very fortunate for this Union that cotton is thirteen cents a pound, instead of four to five. There is now a state of prosperity they do not care to disturb —but were it otherwise, all the depression in trade and prices would be attributed to the burden of the Union and to the baneful effects of national legislation and northern agitation." [41] It is doubtful whether Southern Rights strategists could have selected a more unfavorable locale in which to try their case than the prosperous Empire State of the South.

During the early weeks of the campaign the Union cause was further aided by the intemperate language of the extreme Southern Rights press. The Savannah *Georgian,* Columbus *Times,* Augusta *Republic,* Macon *Georgia Telegraph,* Augusta *Constitutionalist,* and Columbus *Sentinel* all expressed at one time or another during the fall canvass that type of dialectics which was easily represented as anti-Union.[42] Even the normally moderate *Federal Union* at times veered dangerously close to this verbal precipice.[43] Actually it became a simple matter for Union strategists to pin the label of disunion on the entire Southern Rights crowd.

Southern Rightists hoped to avoid a fight over the Compromise in the carefully prepared Union arena of sweeping alternatives. They countered with their own brand of alternatives. "Resistance or submission" to the Clay Compromise, not "union or disunion" was the real issue, protested

[41] Quoted in Shryock, *Georgia and the Union,* 291; Milledgeville *Federal Union,* December 3, 1850.

[42] Macon *Journal and Messenger* quoted in Augusta *Chronicle and Sentinel,* October 9, 30, 1850; Augusta *Republic* quoted in Milledgeville *Federal Union,* October 8, 1850.

[43] Milledgeville *Federal Union,* October 1, November 5, 1850.

the *Federal Union* during the early weeks of the campaign.[44]
"Submission now," it added six weeks later, "is Abolition
and ultimate Disunion; Resistance now with the Rights of
the South may save the Union." [45] How was the South to
resist? In the first place, effective resistance called for an all-
Southern party "linked together by the ties of a common
kindred and a common interest. . . ." [46] Southern alliances
with Northern Democrats and Whigs had placed the rights
of the South on the auction block of party expediency.[47]
Little by little they had almost all been bartered away.
This "sale" of Southern rights must end and Georgia must
take the lead in bringing it to an end by repudiating
the system of balance-of-power politics.[48] In the second
place, it was urged by representative Southern Rightists
that the forthcoming State convention "examine into and
deliberate, as a remedy, of non-intercourse; of retaliation
by reprisals and by a system of discriminatory taxation."
Should such economic pressure appear impracticable, then
it was recommended that an ordinance be adopted asserting
Georgia's rights in the territories of the United States. The
convention, it was further urged, should "take such course
as in their wisdom shall be most condusive to their [South-
ern states] security." [49] This was bold language. That many
Georgians believed it was the language of secession cannot
be doubted. That many Unionists deliberately classified
all Southern Rightists as secessionists for political effect
would appear a fair assumption. That some Southern
Rightists, perhaps a small minority, wanted secession is
probably an equally valid assumption. That all Georgians

[44] *Ibid.*, October 1, 8, 1850.   [45] *Ibid.*, November 19, 1850.

[46] *Ibid.*, October 1, 1850; H. V. Johnson to Washington County citizens,
November 5, 1850, quoted in Flippin, *Herschel V. Johnson*, 37.

[47] Milledgeville *Federal Union*, November 26, 1850.

[48] Augusta *Constitutionalist* quoted *ibid.*, October 8, 1850.

[49] "The True Platform" as published in Milledgeville *Federal Union*, October 8 through November 5, 1850; *To the Voters of Newton County*, in
possession of Dr. E. Merton Coulter, University of Georgia.

of 1850 were neatly arranged in a pretty brace of sweeping alternatives is not demonstrable.

Southern Rights strategists made a bid for traditionally Democratic Cherokee, where Howell Cobb's "horny handed" constituents were manifesting an inclination to support the Compromise. Late in September between two thousand and three thousand North Georgians trekked to Kingston (Cass County), where, according to prearrangement, they ate barbecue and listened to an abundance of anti-Compromise rhetoric.[50] The latter was ably served by such astute orators as H. L. Benning, Judge W. T. Colquitt, and James M. Smythe, editor of the Augusta *Republic*. In reflecting on this monster demonstration, the *Federal Union* apostrophized that "they [nonslaveholders] know that when the slave population shall be let loose among them, that the lordly owner of hundreds of them, with his pockets well lined by the product of their labor, can and will remove to other regions, but that they must remain, and become the associates and equals if not inferiors of the African race." [51]

As the campaign to elect delegates to the State convention progressed, there was a perceptible tendency for both the Southern Rights party and the friends of the Compromise to move nearer common ground. By pegging themselves on the credo of resistance rather than secession, Southern Rightists executed a swing to the right. On the other hand, the "Submission" party (Unionists) stiffened appreciably.[52] Meanwhile the Compromise was having trouble in the dominion of the abolitionists. On October 14 a great mass meeting in Boston, presided over by Charles Francis Adams, was counseled to look upon the new fugitive-

[50] Athens *Southern Herald,* September 12, 1850; Milledgeville *Federal Union,* October 1, 1850. The *Southern Herald* was the successor to the *Southern Whig.*

[51] Milledgeville *Federal Union,* October 1, 1850.

[52] Shryock, *Georgia and the Union,* 310.

slave law (a part of the recently enacted Compromise) as a dead letter.[53] A short time later a certain Mr. Knight of Macon hurried to Boston to recover some fugitive slaves. After an exciting experience with enraged New England vigilantes, among whom were Charles Sumner and Richard Henry Dana, Jr., the Macon planter returned home without his Negroes. In the name of "virtue" Massachusetts had thus successfully nullified the new fugitive-slave law in less than two months after its adoption. Lashed to the neck of the South by the New England concept of morality, this "yoke of sin" bred frustration and fear, a culture where the yeastier kind of fanaticism fermented rapidly.[54]

According to the *Federal Union*, "Submission" spokesmen were infuriated by the Boston slave hunt. The *Southern Recorder, Journal and Messenger,* and *Republican,* all of whose editors had urged at the start of the campaign that the forthcoming convention meet and "summarily adjourn," now insisted the delegates had important work to do. By early November these journals, asserted the *Federal Union,* were for the convention's adjournment "only after it lays down a fighting line." Except for such extreme Union journals as the *Chronicle and Sentinel,* this fighting line would seem to have made the preservation of the Union contingent upon Northern fidelity to the fugitive-slave law.[55]

Georgians decided on November 25 by the heavy majority of 42,000 to 24,000 that the Compromise of 1850 was to be accepted. According to the tabulations of the *Federal Union,* fewer than twenty of the ninety-three Georgia coun-

53 Proceedings quoted in Milledgeville *Federal Union,* October 29, 1850.

54 Washington (D.C.) *Southern Press,* and Boston *Times,* quoted in Milledgeville *Federal Union,* November 5, 1850; New York *Tribune* quoted *ibid.,* November 12, 1850, for the roles of Charles Sumner and R. H. Dana, Jr., in the Boston slave hunt. For a stimulating treatise of morality and war in a cause and effect relationship, see G. B. Chisholm, "The Reëstablishment of Peacetime Society," in *Psychiatry,* IX (1946), 3–11.

55 Milledgeville *Federal Union,* November 12, 1850.

ties chose Southern Rights delegations to attend the State convention.[56] Unionists were naturally jubilant over the outcome. Southern Rightists ascribed defeat to a conspiracy of circumstances, the most important elements of which were thirteen-cent cotton and wanton misrepresentation of theirs as a secession party.[57]

Two hundred and sixty-four delegates gathered in Milledgeville on December 10 to attend what was to become one of the most important conventions in the State's history.[58] According to the correspondent of the *Journal and Messenger* they were men of age, property, education, and high responsibility. More than half of them owned from thirty to four hundred slaves each.[59] Thomas Spalding sounded the keynote of this celebrated gathering when, on assuming its presidency, he announced that ". . . rather than have the states separated, I should prefer to see myself and mine slumbering under the load of monumental clay." [60]

On December 14, after a top-heavy Union majority had struck innumerable sledge-hammer blows, the convention completed its work by adopting the famous Georgia Platform.[61] This proclamation was the product of the joint labors of the Unionists of both Whig and Democratic parties.[62] Because it decided the fate of the Compromise

[56] Official returns quoted in Savannah *Georgian*, November 29, 1850; Milledgeville *Federal Union*, December 3, 10, 1850.

[57] Milledgeville *Federal Union*, December 3, 1850.

[58] Proceedings quoted *ibid.*, December 17, 1850.

[59] Quoted in Augusta *Chronicle and Sentinel*, December 24, 1850.

[60] Quoted in Milledgeville *Federal Union*, December 17, 1850; E. Merton Coulter, *Thomas Spalding of Sapelo* (University, La., 1940), 265–67.

[61] Proceedings quoted in Milledgeville *Federal Union*, December 17, 1850; *Debates and Proceedings of the Georgia Convention, assembled in Milledgeville, at the Capitol, December 10, 1850* (Milledgeville, 1850).

[62] The origin of the Georgia Platform is carefully recounted by Dr. R. D. Arnold (Savannah Unionist) in a letter to J. W. Forney (editor of the Washington *Union*), December 18, 1850, in Richard H. Shryock (ed.), *Letters of Richard D. Arnold, M.D., 1808–1876* (Durham, 1929), 42.

of 1850, the Georgia Platform was the State's most significant utterance since Governor Troup's bellicose oratory of
1827. It embraced a preamble and five resolutions.[63] The
preamble and the first three resolutions reflected the conciliatory tone expressed by President Spalding at the
convention's opening session. Georgia would accept the
Compromise "as a permanent adjustment of the sectional
controversy," although some of its provisions were not
fully approved. The North was plainly instructed to banish
abolitionists from high places as an evidence of good faith.
The fourth and fifth resolutions laid down the fighting line,
which if violated would automatically render the Compromise a nullity and the Union a memory. The nation was
tersely warned by the fourth plank that Congress must not
interfere with slavery in the District of Columbia, with the
interstate slave trade, with slavery in New Mexico, or with
the enforcement of the new fugitive-slave law. Mindful ot
the late Boston slave hunt, the convention concluded (the
fifth plank) the Georgia Platform with a plain ultimatum
to the effect that preservation of the Union was contingent
upon the faithful execution of the recently adopted fugitive-
slave law.

The Georgia Platform, says Professor Avery O. Craven,
was either a bristling Southern Rights ultimatum or a pious
Submission document, according to a mere shift of em-
phasis.[64] Hence it is not surprising that each group (Southern Rights and Union) heralded the work of the convention as a vindication of its own particular credo.[65] At any
rate a national disaster had been successfully averted and
the nation was inclined to give the credit to Georgia. The

[63] Quoted in Milledgeville *Federal Union*, December 17, 1850.

[64] Avery O. Craven, "Georgia and the South," in *Georgia Historical Quarterly*, XXIII (1939), 219–36.

[65] Typical Southern Rights praise appears in Milledgeville *Federal Union*,
December 17, 1850; typical Union praise appears in Augusta *Chronicle and
Sentinel*, December 15, 1850.

Providence (Rhode Island) *Journal*, New York *Express*, Philadelphia *Pennsylvanian*, and the New York *Tribune* generously complimented Georgia for her patriotic service.[66] The Union had been rescued, a nation was grateful, and, save for a few fire-eaters, each political faction in Georgia insisted that to it had fallen the special privilege of slaying the horrible secession monster.

The convention completed that reshuffling of Georgia parties that had long been under way. It has been observed how the Southern Rights party emerged from the Macon grass-roots convention of August, 1850. While the Union party was perhaps a reality by August, yet prior to the December convention it had lacked a formal organization. This it acquired during the convention period (December 10–14) when the fusion of Unionists from both Whig and Democratic parties was given a sort of formal christening. On December 11 and 12 the correspondent of the Savannah *Republican* wrote from the State capital that two meetings had been held for the purpose of organizing a "National Union Party." [67] The *Southern Recorder* reported that both A. H. Stephens and Robert Toombs had spoken to at least one of these gatherings.[68] Since this project had the support of the *Southern Banner* it may be assumed that Howell Cobb was at least a sympathetic observer, if not an active participant, in the political complots then afoot.[69] The *Southern Recorder* reported a third meeting as having been held on December 13, when the work of organization was

[66] Quoted in Shryock, *Georgia and the Union*, 338; Augusta *Chronicle and Sentinel*, January 1, 1851. See Henry S. Foote, *War of the Rebellion; or, Scylla and Charybdis, consisting of Observations upon the Causes, Course and Consequences of the Late Civil War in the United States* (New York, 1866), 171, for a Mississippi Unionist's appraisal of the Georgia Platform; Phillips, *The Course of the South to Secession*, 139.

[67] Quoted in Augusta *Chronicle and Sentinel*, December 18, 1850.

[68] Quoted *ibid.*, December 24, 1850.

[69] Augusta *Republic* quoted in Milledgeville *Federal Union*, December 31, 1850.

completed. Before this meeting adjourned, a resolution was adopted calling a State gubernatorial convention for June, 1851. Provision was also made for sending delegates to a National Union party convention which was to be held at the nation's capital on Washington's birthday, 1851.[70]

According to the *Republican* correspondent the National Union party of Georgia was to be part of a nationwide movement designed to arrest the tendency toward geographical parties.[71] In other words, the old balance-of-power stratagem so effectively practiced during the forties by both Whig and Democratic parties was to be revived and to serve as a buffer against the Southern Rights plea for an all-Southern party.[72] The sympathetic *Journal and Messenger* declared that the new party would become so powerful in the North that the abolition party there would "fall into obscurity, and agitation would cease." Thus was the wine of violence to be confiscated. Here was a pretty maneuver which would remove the pretext for a Southern Rights party. Such at least was the hope of the Unionists.[73]

By mid-December of 1850 Georgia's Whig and Democratic parties had vanished. Their places had been taken by two new political groups, the Constitutional Union and the Southern Rights parties. These were the so-called Crisis parties. In the Constitutional Union organization were those former Whigs and Democrats who believed the balance-of-power scheme of party discipline offered the most effective means of preserving Southern interests. The Southern Rights party was composed of those former Whigs and Democrats who believed that Calhoun's idea of an all-Southern party offered the best method of protecting the

[70] Quoted in Augusta *Chronicle and Sentinel,* December 24, 1850.

[71] *Ibid.,* December 18, 1850.

[72] This was precisely the impression D. C. Campbell noted in the Milledgeville *Federal Union,* December 17, 1850. This erudite journalist had attended one of the "National Union Party" meetings.

[73] Quoted in Augusta *Chronicle and Sentinel,* December 31, 1850.

Southern way of life. Both parties then had a common objective. Each held, however, that its scheme of party discipline offered the better chance of realizing this objective. It has been observed how the pre-Crisis (before 1850) clash between the proponents of these rival procedures was a constant source of embarrassment to both Whig and Democratic parties. This had been so because at that time lines of cleavage on the important question of methodology inexorably cut across rather than between the party organizations. The Crisis of 1850 reshaped Georgia's party structure in such a way as to permit each school of party discipline to organize itself into a single-interest group. Procedurally Georgians were now organized into vertical instead of horizontal groups.

III

REACTION

ORGANIZED to preclude the "coincidence of a moral principle and a geographical line," the Constitutional Union party was at best a temporary expedient.[1] It quickly became a political monstrosity, nurtured for the most part by a flow of intemperate rhetoric from the fire-eaters of the Southern Rights party.[2] Sensing the weakness of their antagonists, a majority of the Southern Rights strategists hastily climbed aboard the Georgia Platform and with ironic jest broadcast philippics against the labors of the Constitutional Union party.[3] Insisting that they had thwarted the secessionists in 1850, Constitutional Union party leaders hopefully continued their appeal to the great dogma of the Union in a language reminiscent of the best efforts of Jacksonian Democrats and Webster Whigs. In this manner did they hope to start an overwhelming emotional drive which would provide the cohesion necessary for a permanent organization of national proportions.[4]

As already observed, many Southern Rights strategists saw the advantage of accepting the Georgia Platform. However, the fire-eaters presented a problem. Led by the editors

---

1 Phillips, *The Course of the South to Secession*, 144.

2 Athens *Southern Banner*, June 19, 1851; Savannah *Georgian*, May 1, 1851; Milledgeville *Federal Union*, February 18, 1851.

3 Athens *Southern Banner*, June 19, 1851; Savannah *Georgian*, May 26, 1851; Milledgeville *Federal Union*, March 18, April 1, 1851.

4 Athens *Southern Banner*, January 16, 1851; James A. Nisbet to Howell Cobb, February [?], 1851, in Cobb MSS.; Milledgeville *Federal Union*, March 25, 1851.

of the Columbus *Times,* the Augusta *Constitutionalist,* and the Macon *Georgia Telegraph,* they comprised a compact minority.[5] They hated the Compromise and despised the Georgia Platform. Their contempt for the Union savers was withering. They greeted with frozen apathy the suggestion that the Democratic party be revived.[6] Hence whatever efforts were made to revive the Democratic party during the year or so after 1850 were bound to be abortive. If the leaders of the Southern Rights party could appease the fire-eaters and draw the Union Democrats away from the Constitutional Union party, the chances for victory in the gubernatorial fight of 1851 would be improved. With these objectives in mind they prepared their verbal blasts of 1851. Hence the Constitutional Union party was denounced as the "submission" party and the Compromise was characterized as the "surrender bills." [7] As a result, fire-eaters let go with a round of approval, while Union Democrats scampered into the Constitutional Union party tent, where they were frantically reminded of their unholy alliance with Whiggery.[8] Such was the party picture on the eve of the gubernatorial fight of 1851.

Nominating the former Democratic Governor C. J. McDonald on a platform which leaned strongly in the direction of fire-eater notions, the Southern Rights party opened the Governor's race of 1851. Among the resolutions adopted was one asserting the right of secession; another insisting it was the duty of the Federal government to extend its protective arm to all species of property in any section of

[5] Athens *Southern Banner,* June 19, 1851; Savannah *Georgian,* May 1, 1851; Milledgeville *Federal Union,* February 18, 1851.

[6] Savannah *Georgian,* May 1, May 26, 1851; Athens *Southern Banner,* June 19, 1851; Milledgeville *Federal Union,* February 18, March 18, April 1, 1851.

[7] Savannah *Georgian,* April 26, 1851.

[8] Athens *Southern Banner,* February 6, 1851; James A. Nisbet to Howell Cobb, February [?], in Cobb MSS.; Milledgeville *Federal Union,* March 25, 1851.

the Union; and a third constituting a strongly worded appeal to all state-rights sympathizers.[9] Howell Cobb, also formerly a Democrat and currently the Speaker of the United States House of Representatives, was nominated by the Constitutional Unionists. This convention glorified the Georgia Platform, insisting that it was the special creation of the Constitutional Union party, and warned of the calamity that would befall Georgia in the event of a Southern Rights party victory.[10] The fact that both candidates were former Democrats would indicate that the old party structure was still unhinged and that the gubernatorial contest was to follow the pattern set by the fall contest of the preceding year.[11]

Cobb proved an elusive target. One of the most astute politicians of his time, he had a large personal following among the small farmers of Cherokee and the pine barrens. Further, he was the safe candidate and for this reason acceptable to the planter and business interests. Both groups were pleased with the "peace" of 1850, which he had done so much to forge. More than any other Georgian, Cobb symbolized in 1851 the emotions of a people who were anxious for a stoppage of the slavery controversy. Under the impact of Southern Rights blows, however, a new emotional drive was shortly to get under way. In this instance Cobb was by 1852 to fall behind long enough to lose to men of less moderate manners the leadership he enjoyed in 1850 and 1851.[12]

If, as Professor Shryock has asserted, ". . . the extremists, in the process of losing the election of 1851, . . . prepared the way for victory in 1861," then the reaction against

[9] Savannah *Republican,* May 30, 1851; Milledgeville *Federal Union,* June 3, 1851.

[10] Milledgeville *Federal Union,* June 10, 1851.

[11] Savannah *Republican,* May 30, 1851.

[12] Helen Ione Greene, "Politics in Georgia, 1853–54: The Ordeal of Howell Cobb," in *Georgia Historical Quarterly,* XXX (1946), 185–86.

Constitutional Unionism may be said to have begun with the gubernatorial contest of 1851.[13] For the first time in their history Georgians were to be given a thorough indoctrination on secession. Although both candidates were careful to deny secessionist intentions, each defended by deft verbal thrusts the right of secession. Neither Cobb's loyalty to the Union nor his faith in the Federal government can be questioned at this stage of his political career.[14] In fact, an anxiety to demonstrate his feelings would appear to have caused him to utter certain indiscretions in respect to state rights. Within three weeks after the campaign had begun, the Constitutional Union nominee was charged with having urged his party's convention boldly to declare itself in favor of more federalism and less state rights.[15] This federalist ideology was anathema to the Southern Rights crowd. All conceivable sorts of accusations were fired at Cobb, including the charge that he was backing off the Georgia Platform.[16] From this welter of verbal missiles the astute Constitutional Union party's candidate emerged with a fancy rejoinder by which he admitted the abstract right of secession to be inherent in the American political system.[17] Thus within less than a year after the Union saving of 1850, the foremost of the Union savers was saying in effect that without a sanction there was no possible way to save the Union. This was, of course, good natural-rights

[13] Shryock, *Georgia and the Union*, 356; Craven, *Coming of the Civil War*, 302.

[14] Burton J. Hendrick, *Statesmen of the Lost Cause: Jefferson Davis and His Cabinet* (Boston, 1939), 77; Forney, *Anecdotes of Public Men*, 40.

[15] See issues of the Milledgeville *Federal Union* and Athens *Southern Banner* for June and July for elaborate editorials on the "right" of secession; Robert Toombs to Howell Cobb, June 9, 1851, in Cobb MSS.

[16] Savannah *Georgian*, June 26, 1851; Milledgeville *Federal Union*, July 1, 1851; Columbus *Times* quoted in Milledgeville *Federal Union*, July 22, 1851.

[17] Milledgeville *Federal Union*, July 29, 1851; Arthur Cole, *The Whig Party in the South* (Washington, 1913), 204; Brooks, "Howell Cobb and the Crisis of 1850," *loc. cit.*, 292-93.

political doctrine, the very procedure that Southern Rights leaders had consistently been recommending.[18]

Cobb and his coterie of Constitutional Union strategists planned carefully. Insistence upon the abstract right of secession was intended to appease extreme state-rights elements. On the other hand, Unionists elements were reminded that the opposition had attempted to break up the Union a year earlier. McDonald, the Southern Rights nominee, was accused of being foolhardy. It was pointed out that in 1850 he had labored assiduously for the Nashville convention and the Macon Southern-rights meeting.[19] Both efforts were labeled as the diabolic inventions of treacherous Georgia secessionists, who then, as in 1851, were suckling at the breasts of the incendiary South Carolina fire-eaters.[20] Georgia voters were urged to still the voice of these disturbers of the peace. All that was needed, it was explained, was a repetition of the performance of 1850.[21] "By your special verdict," exhorted the *Southern Recorder*, "confirm the justice and wisdom of your former verdict." [22] The special verdict was an 18,000 majority for Cobb, a majority almost identical to that received by the Unionists a year earlier. That it was a confirmation of the preceding year's action was the contention of the Constitu-

[18] Milledgeville *Federal Union*, June 24, August 16, September 16, 23, 1851; Savannah *Georgian*, September 22, 1851.

[19] Savannah *Republican*, June 16, July 1, 9, 19, August 6, 1851; Athens *Southern Banner*, June 5, 19, 1851; Augusta *Chronicle and Sentinel*, June 4, 8, July 16, 1851; Howell Cobb's speech to Savannah Union meeting quoted in Augusta *Chronicle and Sentinel*, May 21, 1851.

[20] Augusta *Constitutionalist* quoted in Milledgeville *Federal Union*, July 22, 1851; Milledgeville *Federal Union*, August 5, 1851; Savannah *Georgian*, July 15, 1851; Columbus *Times* quoted in Savannah *Georgian*, July 18, 1851. The traditional contempt for Georgia across the Savannah caused rival Georgia parties of ante-bellum times to accuse each other of following the South Carolina "line." For a brief account of the genesis and development of South Carolina's contempt for Georgia see Coulter, *Georgia*, 152.

[21] Augusta *Chronicle and Sentinel*, June 18, 1851.

[22] *Ibid.*, September 30, 1851.

tional Union party press.[23] Significantly, however, this second Union saving followed the admission by Cobb, foremost among the Union savers of 1850, that given the proper conspiracy of circumstances the Union could not be saved.[24]

The political shuffle of Crisis days had completely unhinged Georgia's national party structure. From the latter part of 1850, when the Crisis parties were organized, until preparations for the presidential campaign of 1852 unscrambled this party design, the State was without benefit of communion with the national Whig and Democratic parties.[25] At this time Georgians settled their major political differences as Constitutional Unionists and Southern Rightists, not as Whigs and Democrats. Georgia had saved the Union in 1850 at the cost of this political isolation. There were several methods by which this state of affairs might have been altered. Some advocated a new national party design to reflect the emotions of the past two years. They were most numerous in the ranks of the Constitutional Union party. They desired a national organization held together by the great dogma of the Union. However, a restoration of the pre-Crisis party structure presented the most feasible way of bringing the State back into the national party picture. It was a modification of this arrangement that eventuated, and naturally so, because the magnetism of pre-Crisis attachments had been tempered by the experience of the past two years. Georgians did not forget easily the old days when, as Whigs and Democrats, they had done battle. Perhaps one of Howell Cobb's friends, writing during the heat of the Crisis struggle, expressed a

[23] Milledgeville *Southern Recorder,* October 21, 28, 1851.

[24] See page 41; Georgia held its Congressional elections at this time too as a result of an agreement reached in early 1850 to postpone for twelve months these elections. Six of the eight Congressmen elected were Constitutional Unionists. Of these six, four had been Democrats.

[25] Augusta *Chronicle and Sentinel,* October 22, November 12, 1851; Milledgeville *Southern Recorder,* October 28, 1851.

rather common nostalgia when he prophesied that it would not be long before the Democratic party would be reunited.[26]

Precisely when the movement to unscramble the Constitutional Union and Southern Rights parties began is difficult to ascertain. It is conceivable that many Georgians never considered themselves anything but Whigs and Democrats. In Savannah, for example, it was reported that the extreme Southern Rightists of October and November, 1850, called themselves Democrats a month later.[27] In this city, too, the victor in the mayoral race of late 1850 ran as a Democrat, the loser charging he had done so to attract Irish votes.[28] Meeting in Savannah in the early spring of 1851, the Chatham County Southern Rights convention selected delegates to represent the "Democratic" party at the State convention which, as already observed, nominated former Governor McDonald to oppose Howell Cobb.[29] On the eve of this State convention the *Georgian,* formerly one of the foremost Democratic journals of the State, exhorted Chatham County's delegates to hold on to the Democratic label, insisting that the national organization was being purged of its antislavery elements.[30] Reflecting on McDonald's defeat in the gubernatorial race of 1851, the *Georgian* thought the failure of Southern Rights leaders to make the fight against Cobb as Democrats had been fatal.[31]

Two successive victories kept Constitutional Unionists satisfied with their organization. On the other hand, failure to win in 1850 and again in 1851 had convinced Southern

[26] Luther J. Glenn to Howell Cobb, November 28, 1850, in R. P. Brooks (ed.), "Howell Cobb Papers," in *Georgia Historical Quarterly,* V (1921), 44.

[27] R. D. Arnold to J. W. Forney, December 18, 1850, in Shryock (ed.), *Arnold Letters,* 46–47.

[28] *Id.* to *id.,* September 9, 1850, in Shryock (ed.), *Arnold Letters,* 55. Arnold, a Savannah physician, was a Union Democrat. He was beaten for mayor by the "Democratic" candidate.

[29] Savannah *Georgian,* April 5, 1851.   [30] *Ibid.,* April 24, May 19, 1851.
[31] *Ibid.,* October 16, 1851.

Rights leaders that they must change their strategy. Hence, within a few weeks after Cobb's election in October, 1851, the movement to restore communion with the national Democratic party took definite form. Meeting in the State capitol in mid-November, prominent members of the Southern Rights party began the task of drafting a blueprint for the restoration of Democracy in Georgia.[32] To study the problem and to make specific recommendations, a committee was appointed with H. V. Johnson serving as its chairman.[33] According to prearrangement the Johnson committee reported to a second convention meeting in Milledgeville on November 25. In an atmosphere of hope and anxiety the Johnson committee resolved the issue by recommending that delegates be sent to the national Democratic convention which was to meet at Baltimore in June.[34] Prefacing its approval of this recommendation with a resolution describing the Georgia Platform as the "Rubicon beyond which Congress must not pass," the convention adjourned after making preparations for a State gathering to name delegates to the Baltimore meeting of the national Democratic party.[35] Thus within less than five weeks after their defeat in the gubernatorial contest of 1851, H. V. Johnson and his colleagues had performed the last rites over the dead body of the twice-beaten Southern Rights party; and by the same token these former Southern Rightists had begun the revival of Georgia Democracy.

[32] *Ibid.;* Augusta *Constitutionalist* quoted in Milledgeville *Federal Union,* October 21, 1851; Augusta *Chronicle and Sentinel,* November 12, 1851; Milledgeville *Federal Union,* November 18, 1851.

[33] Milledgeville *Federal Union,* November 18, 1851; Athens *Southern Banner,* December 4, 1851. See Flippin, *Herschel V. Johnson,* 43, for an account of Johnson's role in the reorganization of the Democratic party. D. C. Campbell, former editor of the Milledgeville *Federal Union,* James Gardner, editor of the *Constitutionalist and Republic* of Augusta, former Governor C. J. McDonald, and Joseph E. Brown were among the more prominent members of the Johnson committee.

[34] Athens *Southern Banner,* December 4, 1851.

[35] *Ibid.;* Milledgeville *Federal Union,* December 2, 1851.

Astounded by the opposition's boldness, the Constitutional Union press scorched Johnson and his disunionist associates. Accusing the "Coon Killer," as Johnson was called, of having placed his "seceders" aboard the Georgia Platform, an excited Consitutional Union press insisted that he had done so for the purpose of concealing beneath the Platform the fraud of "Southern rights." [36] Were Northern Democrats, Union Democrats of Georgia, and Southern-rights Whigs so naïve, asked Constitutional Unionites, as to yield to such an outrageous proposal as the revival of the Democratic party? [37] "As well might . . . Satan and his rebellious legions endeavor to gain admittance into Heaven by putting on the garb of the angel Gabriel," was the sarcastic reflection of Hopkins Holsey of the *Southern Banner*.[38] Here was another "Armageddon," the third in two years, and Union savers were again enjoined "to battle for the Lord." In 1850 they had come forward with the Georgia Platform. In the gubernatorial contest of 1851 they had elected Howell Cobb. Could they now, in the waning months of 1851, head off the movement to restore the Democratic party by appealing again to the dogma of the Union?

It will be recalled how Johnson and his colleagues had, by the end of November, prepared the way for a revived Democracy's participation in the presidential contest of 1852. Johnson's performance had thrown the Constitutional Unionists on the defensive for the first time in two

[36] During the early forties Johnson had won considerable fame as a stump speaker. He toured the State denouncing the youthful Whig party, which, in its anxiety to win popular support, had adopted many homely symbols, including coonskins, pepper pods, etc. Hence the sobriquet "Coon Killer." Savannah *Republican*, November 19, 1851; Milledgeville *Southern Recorder*, December 2, 1851; Macon *Georgia Citizen* quoted in Augusta *Chronicle and Sentinel*, December 3, 1851; Athens *Southern Banner*, December 4, 1851; Augusta *Chronicle and Sentinel*, December 10, 1851.

[37] Milledgeville *Southern Recorder*, December 2, 1851; Athens *Southern Banner*, December 4, 1851.

[38] Athens *Southern Banner*, December 4, 1851.

years. They were not to be content with this role. The great Union triumvirate of Toombs, Stephens, and Cobb had no intention of sitting on the sidelines during the presidential contest of 1852. As a result they began studying during the late months of 1851 the chances of aligning their followers with one of the national parties. The prospects were hardly promising. National Whiggery was about to strangle from its efforts to swallow the Compromise of 1850. Nobody recognized better the impotence of the Whig party than the impetuous Toombs. Shortly after his election to the United States Senate late in 1851, he declared in his acceptance speech before the Georgia legislature that the Constitutional Union party had "greater reason to expect . . . support from the Democratic party of the North than from the Whig." [39] Returning to Washington a few weeks later to resume his duties in the House, Toombs was punished by his prompt removal from the ways and means committee. Neither he nor his close friend Stephens attended the Whig caucus, nor would either support that party's choice for Speaker.[40] By mid-December it was clear that if Constitutional Unionites were to join national Whiggery they would have to do so without the help of Toombs and Stephens, who by this time appeared to have been utterly unwhigged.

The prospects of aligning the Constitutional Union

[39] Cole, *Whig Party in the South,* 214 ff.; Athens *Southern Banner,* November 20, 1851. Toombs was elected in November, 1851, to take Senator Berrien's seat. However, Berrien's term did not expire until March 4, 1853. Hence Toombs served two sessions in the Lower House after his election to the Senate. His election provoked considerable opposition among Southern-rights Whigs and Democrats. It was alleged that he promised to support the Democratic nominee for President in 1852 in return for Union Democratic votes in the race for the Senate. See Milledgeville *Federal Union,* November 11, 1851, for an unusually severe analysis of how Toombs came to win a seat in the United States Senate, and Athens *Southern Banner,* November 20, 1851, for a friendly view of the event.

[40] A. H. Stephens to Linton Stephens, December 10, 1851, in Phillips (ed.), *Correspondence,* 273.

party with national Democracy were even more discourag-
ing. Governor Cobb was *persona non grata* among his
former Democratic associates, now engaged in the task of
reorganizing the Democratic party in Georgia. The astute
operations of Johnson and his colleagues precluded the possibility of the Governor's leadership in this reorganization
effort. In Washington a well-directed campaign was under
way to discredit Cobb among Democratic party leaders
there. Managed by Congressman Joseph Jackson, former
Southern Rightist and recent appointee to the Democratic
national committee, this campaign was designed to prove
to national party leaders that Cobb did not represent the
real Democracy of his State and that it was he, in fact, who
in 1850 had disorganized the party in Georgia.[41]

While H. V. Johnson and Joseph Jackson were rehabilitating Georgia's Democracy in preparation for the presidential contest of 1852, Constitutional Union leaders were
speculating about their party's future. During the last
weeks of 1851, Stephens and Toombs kept Governor Cobb

[41] Robert Toombs to Howell Cobb, December 21, 1851, in Cobb MSS.;
A. H. Stephens to Linton Stephens, December 10, 1851, in Phillips (ed.),
Correspondence, 273; Athens *Southern Banner,* January 15, 1852. According
to the Milledgeville *Federal Union,* December 2, 1851, fourteen of the
State's sixteen Whig papers had supported Cobb's candidacy for governor,
while thirteen or fourteen of the State's sixteen Democratic papers had supported McDonald's candidacy. This issue also carried an interesting breakdown of the vote for governor. The figures presented would appear to convict Cobb of the charge that he was more Whig than Democrat. On the
other hand, it should be noted that the Milledgeville *Federal Union* was
bitterly anti-Cobb. The following is the breakdown of the 1851 vote as seen
by this journal:

Total votes cast for governor 96,221
Whig votes 47,000
Democratic votes 49,000
Democratic votes for McDonald 36,000
Whig votes cast for McDonald 3,000
Democratic votes for Cobb 13,000
Whig votes for Cobb 44,000
Total votes for Cobb 57,000
Total votes for McDonald 39,000

acquainted with political affairs at Washington. It has been observed how the Whig leadership in Congress purged both Stephens and Toombs. Aligning the Constitutional Union party with the national Whig party was therefore out of the question. That neither Stephens nor Toombs had much confidence in the national Democratic party is attested by their correspondence with the Governor.[42] The bitter intraparty fight then taking place in the high councils of the Democracy was disgusting to Stephens.[43] He wrote Cobb that the national Democratic party was the offspring of the "foulest of all coalitions . . .—Southern Rights men and Abolitionists." [44] Both Stephens and Toombs agreed that the Constitutional Unionists should hold a State convention to plot the party's course for the coming presidential campaign. This is precisely what they recommended to Governor Cobb in December of 1851.[45] Stephens, whose consistent loyalty to the Union was one of his most conspicuous traits, explained to the Governor that he wanted "a pure sound National Party—I care not by what name it is called." [46] His views were shared by other Constitutional

---

[42] A. H. Stephens to Linton Stephens, December 10, 1851, in Phillips (ed.), *Correspondence,* 273; *id.* to Howell Cobb, December 8, 1851, Robert Toombs to *id.,* December 21, 1851, and A. H. Stephens to *id.,* December 23, 1851, in Cobb MSS.

[43] On November 29, 1851, William Polk, Tennessee Congressman and brother of former President James K. Polk, presented a resolution to the Democratic Congressional caucus which became the subject of acrimonious exchanges both at Washington and in Georgia political circles. This resolution was designed to commit the party to "finality," that is, acceptance of the Compromise as the final solution to the slavery question. Milledgeville *Federal Union,* December 16, 23, 1851; Athens *Southern Banner,* December 18, 1851; Shryock, *Georgia and the Union,* 357.

[44] A. H. Stephens to Howell Cobb, December 5, 1851, and *id.* to Linton Stephens, December 10, 1851, in Phillips (ed.), *Correspondence,* 268, 271; Joseph Jackson to Savannah *Georgian* quoted in Athens *Southern Banner,* December 18, 1851.

[45] A. H. Stephens to Howell Cobb, December 8, 1851, and Robert Toombs to *id.,* December 21, 1851, in Cobb MSS.

[46] A. H. Stephens to *id.,* December 23, 1851, in Cobb MSS.

Unionists, most prominent among whom was the former Jacksonian Democrat, Hopkins Holsey. Like Stephens, he believed Unionists could expect little from the extremists, either North or South, who, he insisted, dominated the national Democratic party. Unlike Stephens, however, he declared specifically for a national Union party.[47]

Not all Constitutional Unionists were as indefinite as Stephens or as impractical as Holsey on the subject of their party's future. Directing the party was primarily Cobb's task. As Governor he was the leading Constitutional Unionist. At this time he was getting considerable advice from what was known in political circles as the "Macon Regency," a sort of brain trust which had replaced the "Athens Junto" of earlier days.[48] Perhaps the most prominent figure in the Macon Regency was James A. Nisbet, whose paper, the Macon *Journal and Messenger,* served as a sounding board for numerous projects which must have originated with the Governor and his trusted advisers. After some reconnaissance work by the leading figures of the Constitutional Union party, the *Journal and Messenger* came forward in mid-January with a plan of action.[49] The crux of the plan was a suggestion that the party send delegates to the Democratic national convention which was to meet in Baltimore. Approximately a week later, on January 19, this suggestion was adopted at a State meeting of Constitutional Unionites when plans were made for a spring convention which was to name the delegates who were to go to Baltimore. The charge was quickly made by Cobb's enemies that this first Constitutional Union convention of 1852 was

---

[47] Athens *Southern Banner,* December 25, 1851.

[48] *Ibid.,* January 29, 1852. It was customary for editors to use such labels as these. Sometimes more picturesque names were employed, as for example, in the case of the Milledgeville circle of advisers, which was known as the "Bullfrog Regency." The Milledgeville *Federal Union* belonged to this particular brain trust.

[49] Macon *Journal and Messenger,* January 14, 1855.

a Cobb-controlled gathering.[50] Such a charge was probably
a fair one in view of the fact that the Governor would seem
to have succeeded in heading his party toward the gates of
national Democracy. Whether the gates would be open was,
of course, something else. H. V. Johnson and Joseph Jackson could be counted on to do their best to keep them
closed.

The Whig element of the Constitutional Union party
generally advised against the action taken by the meeting
of January 19. Among these former Whigs there was, however, no agreement on a program. Believing that a sound
decision would have to await the outcome of the national
conventions, many former Whigs counseled watchful waiting.[51] The *Southern Recorder,* formerly the Whig spokesman of Georgia, advocated a national Constitutional Union
party, while the *Chronicle and Sentinel* reported in February that A. H. Stephens favored a restoration of the old
parties of pre-Crisis days.[52] Within the Democratic wing
of the Constitutional Union party there was a somewhat
similar division of opinion. A small minority denounced
both national parties and, along with the *Southern Recorder,* insisted that the only guarantee of Southern rights
was a national Constitutional Union organization.[53] It may
be said, however, that Governor Cobb spoke for a majority
of the Democrats among Constitutional Unionites. He had
a program. His plan was to transfer the Constitutional
Union party into the national Democratic party. If successful, this would have made the Constitutional Unionites

[50] Milledgeville *Federal Union,* January 27, 1852.

[51] A. H. Stephens to Howell Cobb, January 26, 1852, in Brooks (ed.),
"Howell Cobb Papers," *loc. cit.,* 53–55; Augusta *Chronicle and Sentinel,*
January 21, 28, 1852; Athens *Southern Banner,* January 29, 1852; Savannah
Republican, February 5, 1852.

[52] Milledgeville *Southern Recorder,* May 9, 1852; Augusta *Chronicle and
Sentinel,* February 7, 1852; Milledgeville *Federal Union,* March 16, 1852;
Savannah *Republican,* February 5, 1852.

[53] Milledgeville *Federal Union,* April 6, 20, 1852.

who chose to follow Cobb the Democracy of Georgia. But
the Governor had waited too long. Perhaps his easy victory
over McDonald in October and the subsequent election of
Toombs to the United States Senate had led him to believe
he was invincible. Whatever the cause, the delay until January was to prove fatal. Governor Cobb was to find himself
fighting a rear-guard action, never an enviable spot for a
politician. While the Governor was waiting, H. V. Johnson
and Joseph Jackson were acting. They were determined
to head the delegation that went to the Democratic party's
Baltimore convention. As already pointed out, to Congressman Joseph Jackson had fallen the task of convincing
the party leaders at Washington that Georgia's Governor
was not a good Democrat.[54] Perfidious Cobb, remonstrated
Jackson, must be kept out of the national Democratic party.
That these efforts were bearing fruit is attested by the
appointment on December 30, 1851, of this former Southern Rightist to the Democratic national committee.[55] By
this act rejuvenescent Georgia Democracy was admitted to
the councils of the national party. Moreover, at the annual
Jackson Day Dinner in January, 1852, Stephen A. Douglas,
already emerging as the leader of the movement to preserve
the *"entente cordiale* between planter and mixed farmer,"
gave little comfort to Governor Cobb and his cumbersome
Constitutional Union party when he declared the Democracy the true party of the Union.[56] Former Southern
Rightists now engaged in rehabilitating Georgia Democracy lost little time in turning the Douglas utterance to
their advantage. Insisting that the Illinois Senator had endorsed their performance, they continued to denounce
Cobb as a renegade.[57]

[54] See page 48.

[55] Athens *Southern Banner,* January 15, 1852, for story on Jackson's appointment.

[56] Quotation from Binkley, *American Political Parties,* 201.

[57] Milledgeville *Federal Union,* January 20, 1852. The Milledgeville *Fed-*

The Governor struck back at the efforts to slam in his face the door of national Democracy. His first thrust was to mail a copy of the January 14 issue of the *Journal and Messenger* to Washington "before the ink was dry." [58] It will be recalled that this was the issue which contained the Macon Regency's suggestion to send Constitutional Union delegates to the Democratic national convention. Further, it has been observed how this plan was adopted at the Constitutional Union meeting of a few days later. Late in February, Governor Cobb made a hurried trip North. He stopped off in Washington long enough to receive what he described as a cordial welcome and to predict disaster for fire-eaters, doubtless having in mind national committeeman Joseph Jackson, who was indeed a special source of annoyance to His Excellency. [59] From the nation's capital the Governor hastened to New York, ostensibly to float a State bond issue in that city's money market. Few Georgia Democrats of Southern-rights livery were so naïve as to put their trust in the bond-issue story. The more skeptical openly accused their Governor of having gone to New York to do some bartering with the "injins" of Tammany in the interest of an "open door" at the forthcoming Democratic national convention. [60] Cobb had scarcely left Washington when Representative Elijah W. Chastain delivered a speech before the House which, it was alleged, had been prepared by the nimble Governor. [61] Chastain explained that Cobb

---

eral Union, January 27, declared: "If the Constitutional Union Democrats think they can force themselves into the National Democratic Convention, with their heavy burden of Whiggery hanging to their skirts, on the ground that they are the party in the majority, and will be counted by the Democracy, they have sadly mistaken the body they have to deal with."

[58] *Ibid.,* January 20, 1852.

[59] Howell Cobb to his wife, March 2, 1852, in Brooks (ed.), "Howell Cobb Papers," *loc. cit.,* 45.

[60] Milledgeville *Federal Union,* March 23, 1852; A[rthur] Hood to Howell Cobb, July 5, 1852, in Cobb MSS.

[61] Milledgeville *Federal Union,* March 16, 1852,

was tired of the Constitutional Union party and that he was now ready to act with the Democratic party.[62] A few weeks later Representative Junius Hillyer made a plea on the floor of the House in favor of sending Constitutional Union delegates to the Democratic national convention.[63] Chastain and Hillyer had been elected to Congress in 1851 as Constitutional Unionites. Before the Crisis of 1850 both had been Democrats.[64] They were now, with Cobb, engaged in the difficult task of returning to the party of their first choice. H. V. Johnson and Joseph Jackson could be counted on to resist Cobb and his colleagues until they were certain Georgia Democracy would never again be threatened with an experience like that of 1850. The best Cobb could hope for was a share, perhaps a very small share, in the management of Georgia's restored Democracy. But first he must do penance.

At the close of February, 1852, the Georgia party picture, while still in a state of considerable fermentation, may nevertheless be said to have included two rather well-defined factions and three inarticulate agglomerations. The former were really rival Democratic groups, vying to convince national party leaders of their orthodoxy. Among the latter were Union Whigs, some Union Democrats, and Southern-rights Whigs. Comprising approximately 40 per cent of the voters in the gubernatorial contest of 1851, the Union Whigs of early 1852 were bewildered.[65] Some of them favored a restoration of the old Whig party of pre-Crisis days; others advised awaiting the outcome of the national party conventions; and a few of them were seemingly satisfied to go along with Governor Cobb. The Union Democrats, it would appear, oscillated between the Cobb program and the somewhat impractical proposal of a na-

[62] Speech quoted in Savannah *Georgian*, March 12, 1852.

[63] Athens *Southern Banner*, April 8, 1852.

[64] Milledgeville *Federal Union*, July 15, 1851.

[65] *Ibid.*, December 2, 1851.

tional Constitutional Union party. Persistent in their contempt for H. V. Johnson and Joseph Jackson, former Southern Rightists, Union Democrats finally acted with Governor
Cobb in the presidential contest of 1852. Southern-rights
Whigs were the smallest of these agglomerations. Naturally
suspicious of the efforts of Johnson and Jackson, former
colleagues in the Southern Rights party, some of the
Southern-rights Whigs were to act independently in the
forthcoming election. These five groups complete the roster
of Georgia factions as of the eve of the presidential campaign of 1852. They were the product of the reaction
against Constitutional Unionism which began with the
gubernatorial contest of 1851. By March of 1852 the reaction had passed through its first stage. In this process the
Crisis party design had been dissolved. Five factions had
come to replace the Constitutional Union and Southern
Rights parties. To accommodate the exigencies of a presidential campaign, minor revisions in the over-all picture
were to be made, yet Georgia was to put up a total of five
electoral tickets, which may be said to have represented
the precampaign factions.

IV

FACTIONS

IN 1852 Franklin Pierce was elected President of the United States. The campaign which preceded his election may be said to have completely disencumbered Georgia's parties. In November, 1851, H. V. Johnson and Joseph Jackson had buried the Southern Rights party. Its place was to be taken by what came to be known as the "Regular" Democratic party. Marching to distant drums, political architects of the Regulars were ready by February, 1852, to align their creation with national Democracy. Meanwhile the Constitutional Union party had begun to break up. As a result its Whig and Democratic factions were set adrift. Disagreement within each of these groups produced further fragmentation. Consequently Georgians were to be offered a total of five electoral tickets in 1852. The Regular and Union Democrats, soon to be known as Supplementals, were each to present a slate of electors. Former Whigs of the Constitutional Union party were to offer two electoral tickets, while a few extreme Southern-rights men were also to enter a set of electors. How these five factions squared off for battle, what weapons they chose, and the success they attained comprise the main themes in Georgia's party development of 1852.

During the early months of 1852 Georgia's political leaders were getting ready for the presidential contest. Democrats were especially active. Their journals reported numerous local gatherings in the interest of a reunion of Regulars and Supplementals.[1] It will be recalled that Gov-

---

[1] Savannah *Georgian,* February 13, 1852; Milledgeville *Federal Union,* February 9, 17, March 2, 1852.

ernor Cobb was particularly anxious to restore the old
Democracy in whose management he once had had a major
share.[2] Former Southern Rights leaders had, however, acted
first. Many of them were to be reluctant in forgiving the
Governor for his behavior in 1850 and 1851. Nevertheless
when representatives of Regular Democracy met in a State
convention at Milledgeville on March 31, they must have
been conscious of what appears to have been a strong impulse for peace between the two party factions. The Milledgeville gathering selected delegates to attend the party's
Baltimore convention, which was to meet on June 1. It also
prepared an electoral ticket. Union Democrats were recognized by assigning a place on the electoral slate to Robert
W. Flournoy, a Union Democrat of Washington County.
He had been among the first to speak for a reunion of the
factions. His presence on the electoral ticket was hardly a
major concession to Union Democrats, however. Before
the campaign was very old they were to make themselves
clear on this niggardly treatment by the Regular convention of March 31. Union editors thought the convention's
failure to endorse the Compromise of 1850 was an unfortunate omission, some of them excitedly charging the
Regulars with a secessionist plot. One of Georgia's factions
had now put itself in the presidential race of 1852. In spite
of subsequent clamor from Union Democrats for a modification of the electoral ticket, Regulars stubbornly held
to their decision of March 31. With many of them it was
either "rule or ruin" the reorganized Democracy.[3]

On April 22 Constitutional Union representatives assembled in Milledgeville to consider what their party might
do in the forthcoming presidential contest. A spirited
debate followed the introduction of a resolution to send

[2] See page 16.
[3] Milledgeville *Federal Union*, March 16, April 6, 1852; Savannah *Geor-gian*, February 13, 1852; Savannah *Republican*, April 3, 1852; Milledgeville *Southern Recorder*, April 6, 1852.

delegates to the Baltimore Democratic convention. Judge James Jackson, a Union Democrat of Walton County, defended the resolution. He was supported by Augustus H. Kenan, astute Baldwin County Whig. Charles J. Jenkins, Richmond County Whig, ably assisted by Francis Cone, Judge Thomas W. Thomas of Elberton, Absalom H. Chappell, and others, declared such action would lose the Constitutional Union party the support of Webster and Fillmore Whigs. Jenkins therefore insisted on aloofness. He was speaking for A. H. Stephens. Stephens had hopes for a new national party and favored either Webster or Fillmore as its candidate for the presidency. The general outlook for national Whiggery was distressing. The breach in the party was characterized as "wide and deep" by United States Senator William Dawson. In a wire to the convention, Senator Dawson urged the delegates to avoid both national parties. The resolution to send delegates to the Democratic national convention was rejected; and after an expression of faith in the Compromise of 1850 the delegates adjourned with their eyes fixed on Baltimore, where both national parties were to hold their nominating conventions in June. The month of June, 1852, was to be a critical one. Few party leaders, however, either in Georgia or at Washington, suspected that there was anything more at stake than the prospect of public plunder. Hence the stage was being set for the "Artful Dodger," whose principal occupations were to assure mediocrity in high places and to share in the distribution of the patronage. Among Georgia's foremost party leaders only A. H. Stephens and H. V. Johnson would seem to have been doing any very serious searching for answers to the riddle of human affairs. Cobb's anxiety to return to the Democratic party compelled him to forego much of his earlier independence, while Toombs was sorely tried with the necessity of deciding whether it was to be Stephens' or Cobb's coattails he would ride.[4]

Disappointed at the refusal of the Constitutional Union convention to appoint delegates to the Democratic national convention, Union Democratic delegates left the April 22 meeting. The following day they assembled in a convention of their own. They promptly appointed twenty delegates to represent them at the Democratic national assemblage. After adopting some resolutions insisting that they had always been true Democrats, they wound up with a ringing declaration in glorification of the Compromise of 1850. These Union Democrats were quickly labeled "Supplementals." They were Governor Cobb's men. He was anxious to have them accepted at Baltimore on June 1. Mindful of his obligation to the Governor, Toombs seems to have decided to act with Cobb. Later he changed his mind and, with Stephens, supported Webster for President.[5]

The events of April 22 and 23 might be considered as having begun the disintegration of the Constitutional Union party. Its Whig and Democratic elements had for the first time shown signs of estrangement. Born during the Crisis of 1850, the Constitutional Union party had, by putting Georgia on record in favor of the Compromise, saved the Union. Less than a year later it had elected Howell Cobb to the governorship. After April 23 it was simply awaiting a formal death sentence. Approximately a month later the *Federal Union* editorialized that "there is now nothing left of the Union organization—its blossoms lie withered upon the earth; its perfume is lost, and the very

[4] Milledgeville *Southern Recorder,* April 27, 1852; Milledgeville *Federal Union,* April 27, 1852; Athens *Southern Banner,* May 6, 1852; see also George Fort Milton, *The Eve of Conflict: Stephen A. Douglas and the Needless War* (New York, 1934), 6, and Roy Franklin Nichols, *The Democratic Machine, 1850–1854* (New York, 1923), 197–220, 226. For an account of H. V. Johnson's efforts at this time see Flippin, *Herschel V. Johnson,* 34, 48.

[5] Milledgeville *Southern Recorder,* April 27, 1852; Athens *Southern Banner,* April 29, 1852.

memory of its existence will soon become as a dream of things that were, but are no more." [6]

The work of the April 23 convention was well received by Regular and Supplemental spokesmen. Both groups were certain that they would soon be reunited in a robust Democracy. Each, of course, expected to dominate this reestablished party. Among the more interesting designs for the future was that suggested by Supplemental Hopkins Holsey. This keeper of the Jacksonian tradition assured his readers that 8,000 Union Whigs of Cherokee were in the ranks of the Supplementals. They were anxious to act with Democracy and would certainly do so if Georgia Democrats would only assist in fashioning a healthy national party. An *entente cordiale* between Southern farmers and Northern labor offered the only hope of arresting the "unjust exactions of Northern capital." The economic royalists of Yankeeland, asserted this spokesman of the common man, were the real enemies of the South. Factory workers in New England and Pennsylvania were, on the other hand, the natural friends of Southern interests. Both groups had a common enemy. Finance capitalism with its vast empire of paper credits was exploiting alike the Southern farmer and the Northern workingman. Whiggery had always been unsound, he continued, for its Northern wing had ever been the cat's-paw of finance capitalism. During the thirties and forties Southern Whigs had too often held the South while their Northern colleagues had fleeced it. Here was a blueprint for a sane national party, argued Holsey.[7]

The Supplementals were not likely to be a docile group. As Constitutional Unionists they had shared in two suc-

[6] Milledgeville *Federal Union*, May 25, 1852.

[7] *Ibid.*, April 27, 1852; Athens *Southern Banner*, April 29, May 27, 1852; that Jacksonian Democracy was primarily a program which appealed to Southern farmers and Eastern workingmen is convincingly presented in Schlesinger, *The Age of Jackson*, 126, 206, 236–41, 307.

cessive victories over the late Southern Rights party. When the *Southern Recorder* announced soon after the April 23 meeting that the Supplemental delegates were going to Baltimore on June 1 to purge national Democracy of the enemies of the Compromise, to force the adoption of the Constitutional Union creed and to dictate the presidential nomination, Regular spokesmen promptly retorted that Supplemental delegates had no constituency, that they were acting on their own, that they were really not Democrats and that if they hoped to behave in the manner described by the *Southern Recorder,* they had better stay at home. Nothing daunted, Supplemental delegates prepared to go to Baltimore and share equally with Regulars in the Democratic convention's deliberations. "Our ultimatum," wrote Thomas D. Harris to Governor Cobb," . . . is to be allowed to go in with equal privileges and cast 5 of the ten votes." [8] Such was the state of feeling between rival Democratic factions as their respective delegations entrained for Baltimore.[9]

National party leaders decided that Georgia Democrats should settle their difficulties in their own way. Hence both Regular and Supplemental delegations were admitted at Baltimore. There were twenty-one Regulars and seventeen Supplementals. John H. Lumpkin, one of the Supplemental delegates, wrote Governor Cobb that a majority of the Regulars preferred the nomination of Stephen A. Douglas, the Illinois Senator. Most of the Supplementals, he thought, favored Lewis Cass of Michigan, while a few Regulars were working for the nomination of James Buchanan of Pennsylvania. Lumpkin further explained that a combination

[8] Thomas D. Harris to Howell Cobb, in Phillips (ed.), *Correspondence,* 298.

[9] Milledgeville *Southern Recorder,* April 27, 1852; Milledgeville *Federal Union,* April 13, May 4, 11, 25, June 1, 1852; Robert Toombs to Howell Cobb, in Phillips (ed.), *Correspondence,* 297; W. C. Cohen to Howell Cobb, April 29, 1852, in Brooks (ed.), "Howell Cobb Papers," *loc. cit.,* 50 ff.

of anti-Douglas Regulars with a few Supplementals threw Georgia's ten votes to Buchanan during the early stages of a long-drawn-out balloting contest. The Supplementals were determined to head off Douglas. James Jackson, another Supplemental delegate, thought the Illinois Senator might have received the nomination had Georgia's vote not gone to Buchanan. Since neither Douglas, Cass, nor Buchanan could get the necessary two-thirds majority, the nomination went on the forty-ninth ballot to Franklin Pierce. The selection of Pierce, whose supporters would have been content with the vice-presidential nomination, was a triumph for a type of mediocrity which was to plague the nation until 1861. The convention put the party on record as favoring the popular Compromise of 1850. It then adjourned with the hope that a weary nation had heard the last of the slavery issue.[10]

Supplementals appeared well pleased with what had taken place at the Democratic national convention. Writing from Baltimore, Dr. Richard Arnold, a Supplemental delegate from Savannah, explained that "our position as Democrats had been fully recognized by the National Democracy." Continuing, he pointed out that "we have united cordially with the Southern Rights delegates on terms of perfect equality." And concluding on a note of satisfaction, he declared, "The Convention have adopted as part and parcel of the Democratic Creed, the very position which was laid down in Georgia as the platform of the Union party." [11] Hopkins Holsey agreed with the Savannah physician, editorializing that national Democracy had put itself squarely on the Georgia Platform. This action, he reasoned, was a

[10] John H. Lumpkin to Howell Cobb, June 6, 1852, in Phillips (ed.), *Correspondence*, 299; James Jackson to *id.*, June 8, 1852, in Phillips (ed.), *Correspondence*, 300; Milledgeville *Federal Union*, June 15, 1852; Nichols, *The Democratic Machine*, 189–204. Douglas, it has been pointed out, gave Union Democrats no encouragement at the Jackson Day Dinner party.

[11] Richard Arnold to Miss Ellen Arnold [daughter], June, 1852, in Shryock (ed.), *Arnold Letters*, 60.

triumph for the Constitutional Union party. Even old-line Whig journals took occasion to congratulate the Democrats, both the *Southern Recorder* and the *Republican* expressing the hope that the Whig convention would do as well when it assembled a few weeks later. Making a pass at Cobb's coattails, Robert Toombs assured the Governor that all "sound" men in the South would support Pierce.[12]

Originally scheduled to hold their national convention in Philadelphia, the Whigs made a last-minute change of plans and shifted their meeting to Baltimore. They were to assemble there in mid-June to draft a platform and name Franklin Pierce's opponent. Assuming the leadership in a movement to resuscitate Georgia Whiggery, the *Southern Recorder* began to urge as early as May 25 a State meeting to select delegates to attend the Baltimore convention. Whigs of Georgia were exhorted to choose delegates who would go to Baltimore to nominate President Fillmore and nationalize the Georgia Platform. The response to the entreaties of the *Southern Recorder* was hardly encouraging. Robert Toombs and A. H. Stephens were utterly indifferent to national Whiggery. It will be recalled that months before, both had cut loose from their Whig moorings. Moreover, it was reported that the Augusta *Chronicle and Sentinel*, at one time the State's leading proponent of Whig doctrine, was likewise disinterested. Other traditional Whig journals reported as opposed to the supplications of the *Southern Recorder* included the Columbus *Enquirer* and the Washington *Gazette*. Hence it is not surprising that only sixteen counties were represented when the Whigs convened on June 7 at Milledgeville. The convention quickly developed into a listless affair. Taking their clues from the *Southern Recorder,* the delegates endorsed the

[12] Athens *Southern Banner,* June 17, 1852; Savannah *Republican,* June 8, 1852; Milledgeville *Southern Recorder,* June 15, 1852; Robert Toombs to Howell Cobb, June 10, 1852, in Brooks (ed.), "Howell Cobb Papers," *loc. cit.,* 53.

Georgia Platform. Although Daniel Webster was not entirely overlooked, they expressed a preference for Millard Fillmore's nomination for President. After selecting thirty representatives to attend the party's national convention, the gathering broke up. Toombs and Stephens were, of course, not in attendance, nor was Senator William Dawson. All three were reported as offended by the presumptuous behavior of a handful of journalists and their satellites.[13]

Hopkins Holsey, the "Sage of Tugalo," made some interesting comments on party affairs during the month of June. "The political elements at the South are now in a perfect state of chaos," he reflected on June 17. In his opinion this state of chaos would cease with the adjournment of the Whig national convention. While Holsey was crystal gazing, the Whig assemblage was busy in faraway Baltimore. Whigs had always had difficulty with specific issues on the occasion of their quadrennial gatherings. Struggling valiantly in 1852 to swallow the Compromise of 1850, Whiggery was slowly dying from strangulation. Four years earlier the party's leaders had successfully performed their duty by nominating General Zachary Taylor. Their choice proved a happy one, for the party went on to victory in the fall balloting. Whether from tradition or desperation, the Baltimore convention seized the needle and, repeating the performance of 1848, inoculated Whiggery with another shot of gunpowder. This time the nominee was General Winfield Scott, "whose ineptitude as a campaigner marked a new low in candidates." [14] With the adoption of a platform embodying the Compromise principles of President Fillmore the convention's work was ended. Thus General Scott and Franklin Pierce were to campaign from identical

---

[13] Milledgeville *Federal Union,* June 1, 8, 1852; Milledgeville *Southern Recorder,* June 8, 1852; Sandersville *Central Georgian,* June 15, 1852.
[14] Quoted from Binkley, *American Political Parties,* 180.

platforms—platforms pledging both candidates to respect the popular "business man's peace" of 1850.[15]

Winfield Scott's nomination ended whatever chance there might have been of restoring harmony among Georgia's Whig factions. Many of the old-line party journals openly denounced the General. The *Southern Recorder* thought his prospects were gloomy. Charging that the nominee cared nothing for the platform, the *Republican* insisted the Baltimore convention had produced a "Seward lackey." The *Chronicle and Sentinel* was confounded. Its editor repudiated the nomination, but was careful to express approval of the platform. The *Journal and Messenger* pronounced Scott's selection a triumph of the South's worst enemies. Among old-guard Whig journals only the Macon *Georgia Citizen* was reported friendly to the nominee. Although Robert Toombs had already assured Governor Cobb that all "sound" Southerners would support Franklin Pierce, on June 23 he joined A. H. Stephens to announce in a letter to the *Chronicle and Sentinel* that he would abide by the decision of the Constitutional Union party's State convention. It was to convene on July 15.[16]

While Georgia Whigs generally favored President Fillmore's nomination, Winfield Scott was not to be completely abandoned. Senator William Dawson was reported to have promised the Baltimore convention that Georgia would not let the General down. The Senator hurried home to organize the Scott campaign. Many old-line Whigs finally joined Dawson's effort to restore their party. Among them was J.

[15] Athens *Southern Banner*, June 17, 1852; Savannah *Republican*, June 23, 1852; see Binkley, *American Political Parties*, 152–80, for an excellent account of the Whig party.

[16] Milledgeville *Southern Recorder*, June 29, 1852; Savannah *Republican*, June 23, 1852; letter of A. H. Stephens and Robert Toombs quoted in Augusta *Chronicle and Sentinel*, June 23, 1852; Milledgeville *Federal Union*, June 29, 1852; Macon *Journal and Messenger* quoted in Savannah *Republican*, June 24, 1852; Macon *Georgia Citizen* quoted in Milledgeville *Southern Recorder*, June 29, 1852; Cole, *Whig Party in the South*, 263–64.

M. Berrien. After the campaign to carry Georgia for Scott got under way, Berrien was quoted by the Savannah *Republican* as having declared that the Whig candidate for President was a man of independent views. Further, Berrien was reported to have said of Scott that, if elected, he would be unlikely to succumb to any "undue influence." Despite Berrien's plea, Georgians could not forget that four years earlier much the same argument had been used in behalf of General Zachary Taylor, who, once in the presidency, proved very disappointing. Consequently the Scott campaign was to flounder on a sea of frustration.[17]

Exactly one month was to elapse between the adjournment of the Whig national convention and the State Constitutional Union meeting of July 15. At this stage of the presidential fight only two factions could report noteworthy progress. They were the Regular Democrats and the Scott Whigs. The former, it has been pointed out, began preparations for the presidential campaign of 1852 immediately after the gubernatorial contest of 1851. They knew exactly what they wanted, and, more important still, they seemed to know how to get what they wanted. Months before Pierce's nomination they had prepared an electoral ticket which they stubbornly refused to withdraw. While not as far along as the Regular Democrats, the Scott Whigs went into action immediately after their party's national convention had adjourned. Two other factions were to make little progress until after July 15. They were A. H. Stephens' Whig friends and the Union, or Supplemental, Democrats. Stephens might have gone along with national Whiggery had either Fillmore or Webster, instead of Scott, received the presidential nomination. As things turned out he was not happy over what had taken place at Baltimore. While Supplementals were content with Pierce's nomina-

[17] Charleston *Courier* quoted in Milledgeville *Federal Union,* June 29, 1852; Cole, *Whig Party in the South,* 256; Savannah *Republican* quoted *ibid.,* 269.

tion, they were distressed by the manner in which Regulars had taken over what was coming to be recognized as the reorganized Democracy. Significantly, both of these unhappy factions were still attached to the rapidly fading Constitutional Union party. Thus that party's convention scheduled for July 15 was to be of particular significance to these two factions.

The fight to revise the Regular Democratic electoral slate reached its crescendo just before the Constitutional Union convention of July 15. Control of the Democratic State machine was at stake. A Pierce victory would provide enormous public plunder. The faction which controlled the electoral ticket would fall heir to the State machine. By a judicious dispensation of the public plunder the machine could look hopefully to the future. Thus the Regulars were indeed in an envious position. Before this backdrop Hopkins Holsey's wild effusions against the Regular slate are perfectly intelligible. Since most of the Regulars had been members of the late Southern Rights party, Holsey accused them of secessionist intentions. Threatening to act with the Constitutional Union party, the Athens journalist became increasingly defiant at a time when some of the more moderate Regulars appeared willing to revise the electoral ticket. Since Holsey was still recognized in some quarters as Howell Cobb's spokesman, many Regulars thought the Governor was determined to "rule or ruin" the Democratic party. Whatever chance there was of a compromise over the electoral ticket had vanished by mid-July. There would be no revision of the March 31 slate, assured the *Federal Union*. Holsey, the Governor, and all of those misguided Democrats who had recently wandered into the "mazes of Whiggery" could continue to act with the opposition, if they were not satisfied with the electoral ticket.[18]

---

[18] Savannah *Georgian*, June 16, 17, 22, 23, 1852; Milledgeville *Federal Union*, June 22, 1852; Athens *Southern Banner*, June 17, 24, July 8, 1852; J. B. Lamar to Howell Cobb, July 1, 1852, in Phillips (ed.), *Correspondence*,

In late June the call for the third Constitutional Union convention of the year was issued. It was to assemble at the State capitol on July 15. By mid-summer even the most faithful of the Constitutional Unionists were compelled to admit their party was little more than a memory. The Dawson Whig faction had by this time announced its support of General Winfield Scott. Although they had not made peace with the Regular Democrats, the Cobb, or Supplemental, Democrats were satisfied with Franklin Pierce. Of those who had in 1850 and 1851 acted with the Constitutional Union party, there remained one small Whig faction which was unattached on the eve of the July 15 gathering. To this faction belonged those who generally followed A. H. Stephens.[19] Expressive of Stephens' feelings at this time was a letter written by his friend Charles J. Jenkins to Peter W. Alexander, editor of the Savannah *Republican*. The editor published the Jenkins letter on July 1, just two weeks before the Constitutional Union convention assembled. Its contents are revealing. Reiterating Stephens' dissatisfaction with Scott's nomination, Jenkins proceeded to advise Unionists against supporting Pierce. Before he had concluded Jenkins asked for a disbandment of what was left of the Constitutional Union party.[20] Two days before the Constitutional Unionists met, Stephens an-

---

307; John H. Lumpkin to *id.,* July, 1852, in Phillips (ed.), *Correspondence,* 308–309; Nichols, *The Democratic Machine,* 159–60.

[19] Robert Toombs was hardly in an enviable position in July, 1852. His old friend A. H. Stephens, by nature an independent, was preparing a third-party project and wanted Toombs to help him. On the other hand, Governor Cobb and John H. Lumpkin had made possible Toombs's election to the United States Senate. They expected him to act with them in 1852. For the Cobb-Lumpkin view, see John H. Lumpkin to Howell Cobb, July 11, 1852, in Phillips (ed.), *Correspondence,* 310. See also Cole, *Whig Party in the South,* 264, for a discussion of how Stephens harnessed Toombs and drove him away from the Governor.

[20] Quoted in the Sandersville *Central Georgian,* July 13, 1852.

nounced that he favored a third nominee for President.[21] The day before the meeting the *Chronicle and Sentinel,* which at this time echoed Stephens' sentiments, declared it would support Daniel Webster for President. Webster, the editor continued, was to be nominated early in August at Philadelphia. He was to be the candidate of a national Constitutional Union party. In this manner was the warming pan prepared for Stephens' third party, more commonly labeled the *Tertium Quid* project.[22]

Over a hundred delegates were on hand when the Constitutional Union convention opened at Milledgeville on July 15. Governor Cobb's men had a comfortable majority. The Governor's men had come to ratify the performance of the Supplemental delegation at the Democratic national convention. A minority of Whig delegates sought vainly to arrest the Cobb steam roller by offering an electoral ticket pledged to Daniel Webster for President and Charles J. Jenkins for Vice-President. The Governor's men had the votes, however, and put through a resolution in favor of an electoral slate pledged to Franklin Pierce. Thus did Cobb affix the Constitutional Union seal to the Supplemental performance at the Democratic national convention. Robert Toombs was reported by the *Federal Union* to have assisted the Governor in aligning the Constitutional Union party with the national Democratic party.[23] Cobb had now answered the Regular Democrats. He would use the Constitutional Union party against them in the race for control of the State machine. For a moment the battle lines were beginning to resemble those of 1850 and 1851. For a moment Governor Cobb gave promise of producing a Constitutional Union victory—the third in three years.

[21] See Milledgeville *Federal Union,* July 13, 1852.

[22] See Augusta *Chronicle and Sentinel,* July 14, 1852, for an elaborate discussion of plans for the *Tertium Quid* movement.

[23] See July 20 issue for an account of Toombs's behavior.

Actually, however, the situation was very different in 1852. Earlier, in 1850 and 1851, the dogma of the Union had generated enough emotionalism to assure a taut party organization. Constitutional Unionism had since become a brittle substance. The Scott Whigs had already deserted and had chosen their battle position. Of much greater significance was the behavior of the Stephens-Jenkins Whig bloc. Failing in their attempts to halt Cobb on July 15, this bloc withdrew from the convention. The next day they formally launched the *Tertium Quid* movement by making plans to meet in Macon on August 17. Although they were not ready to prepare an electoral slate, they repudiated both Pierce and Scott and expressed a preference for a Webster-Jenkins ticket. The *Tertium Quids* concluded their first meeting on a note of patriotism by accusing the national Democratic party of un-American activities. In keeping with the very best nativist procedure, they viewed with alarm what was described as Democracy's fraternizing with Louis Kossuth, the Hungarian *émigré*.[24]

Actually by mid-July the Constitutional Union party no longer existed in fact, although Governor Cobb was to hold on to its name until August 10. What had been in 1850 and 1851 a zealous party was now indeed only a memory. Its disintegration had produced three separate factions: Scott Whigs, the Governor's Supplementals, and the *Tertium Quids*. By midsummer each of these factions had decided to act independently in the presidential race. Well in the lead of these factions was a fourth, the purposeful Regular Democrats. Lacking the indubitable timidity of their rivals, the Regular Democrats entered the presidential race of 1852 shortly after the close of the gubernatorial contest of 1851. Still a fifth faction was to take up the chase.

[24] Athens *Southern Banner*, July 15, 22, 1852; Milledgeville *Southern Recorder*, July 20, 1852; Milledgeville *Federal Union*, July 20, 1852; Augusta *Chronicle and Sentinel*, July 28, 1852; John H. Lumpkin to Howell Cobb, July, 1852, in Phillips (ed.), *Correspondence*, 308–309.

Disgusted with what they described as the pusillanimity of all other factions, the extreme Southern rightists finally organized the Southern Rights Association and nominated for President the venerable George M. Troup, former Governor of Georgia.

V

GUERRILLA

"WE have not enough votes in Georgia to elect them all," was the facetious comment of an editor on the plentitude of parties in the free-for-all presidential contest of 1852.[1] Describing the plethora of fragmentation which had overtaken Georgia Whiggery, the *Republican* pulled all the stops to announce that there were "Union Whigs and Southern Rights Whigs, Scott Whigs and anti-Scott Whigs, Pierce Whigs and anti-Pierce Whigs, stand-still Whigs or those who wash their hands of both candidates and will have nothing to do with either, and *Tertium Quids,* or those who go for a third candidate." [2] In spite of the variety of Whig groups, the campaign of 1852 did not produce the violence among Whigs that dominated the relations between Supplemental and Regular Democrats. Several factors tended to produce this contrast. In the first place, the two Whig factions of 1852, Scottites and *Tertium Quids,* had recently been allies in the Constitutional Union party, while Supplemental and Regular Democrats had been aligned against each other in the bitter fights of 1850 and 1851. Added to this was the prospect of public plunder. While Whigs were certainly just as eager as Democrats to divide the spoils, yet a sort of despondency had enveloped their party and Whigs generally seemed to lack the self-confidence that permeated the Democracy. Anticipating the perfume of victory, rival Democratic factions plunged into battle with reckless abandon.

[1] Sandersville *Central Georgian,* August 24, 1852.
[2] Quoted in Cole, *Whig Party in the South,* 264.

In the event no electoral ticket received a popular majority, the law provided for the legislature to decide the issue. With two Pierce tickets already in the field, with a Scott ticket soon to appear, and with the *Tertium Quids* threatening a fourth for a third candidate, Regular Democrats were growing uneasy in late July. The legislature was still controlled by those who had been elected as Constitutional Unionists, a fact which was hardly comforting to the Regulars. It was natural then for them to flood the State with arguments against the legislature's choice of the electors. In the first place, it was alleged that the voters alone were the proper arbiters in presidential contests. Moreover, it was asserted that the legislature did not properly reflect public opinion. And finally, it was argued that to convene the legislature for the purpose of choosing the State's electors would be costly.[3]

Early in August Governor Cobb sent up a trial balloon on the subject of the Pierce electoral tickets. In a letter to Orion Stroud which was widely circulated in the State's press, the Governor declared he could not support the Regular slate. He could not support it, he explained, because Supplementals had been refused a part in its construction. Always the politician, Cobb held out the olive branch by offering to withdraw the Supplemental ticket and submit the fight over Pierce's candidacy to arbitration. Two journals, generally friendly to the Governor, rebuked him for his Stroud letter. They were the *Southern Banner* and the *Journal and Messenger*. Hopkins Holsey of the *Southern Banner* lashed Cobb sharply. There would be no compromise from him, he assured his readers. As long as the fire-eaters kept their ticket in the race it would be war, war to the bitter end.[4]

[3] Milledgeville *Federal Union*, July 27, August 10, 1852.

[4] Howell Cobb to Orion Stroud quoted in Athens *Southern Banner,* August 12, 1852; Milledgeville *Federal Union*, August 17, 1852; Athens *Southern Banner,* August 12, 19, 1852. See also Savannah *Georgian* quoted

In concluding his letter to Orion Stroud, Governor Cobb expressed the opinion that Pierce would carry the State in spite of the pair of Democratic electoral slates. Not all Union Democrats shared Cobb's sanguine expectation. Several of the Governor's closest friends warned him that some of the Union Whigs who had agreed to act with the Supplementals were now anxious to join the *Tertium Quid* cause. Among these Union Whigs were some, insisted the *Republican,* who wished to be formally released from their pledge to support the Supplemental slate. This was the atmosphere which produced on August 10, just a week before the *Tertium Quid* meeting, the *Address of the Executive Committee, To the Constitutional Union Party of Georgia.* By this document the Supplemental electoral ticket was withdrawn and the demise of the Constitutional Union party was formally acknowledged. Union Whigs who had loyally clung to the Governor's Supplemental movement since its inception in the guise of the Constitutional Union party were now free to act with the faction of their choice. Likewise Union Democrats no longer needed to feel obligated to the Governor. They too were free to do as they pleased.[5]

Meanwhile Whig factions were busy polishing their best weapons. "The fact that he [Scott] comes forward under the auspices of Mr. Seward of New York and Governor Johnston of Pennsylvania . . . is enough," wrote P. W. Alexander of the *Republican,* "to damn him to utter defeat

---

in Milledgeville *Federal Union,* August 31, 1852, for unfriendly views of Cobb's action as expressed by those presumably in accord with the Governor's efforts to get control of the State Democratic machine.

[5] H. R. Jackson to Howell Cobb, August 7, 1852, and J. B. Lamar to *id.,* August 10, 1852, in Phillips (ed.), *Correspondence,* 316; see Savannah *Republican,* August 11, 1852, for evidence of the Whig desire to withdraw the Supplemental ticket; *Catalogue of the Wimberley Jones De Renne Georgia Library* (Wormsloe, 1931), II, 545; H. V. McMillen to Howell Cobb, August 18, in Cobb MSS.

in this section of the Confederacy." [6] In spite of rather widespread Whig disapproval of General Scott, his Georgia friends had resolved not to lose by default. By mid-July Senator William Dawson had issued the call for a State convention to prepare a Scott electoral ticket. The convention was scheduled to meet in Macon on August 4. By late July there was a perceptible drift towards a fusion of Scottites and *Tertium Quids*. Sensing this drift, Scott leaders changed their convention date to August 18 so they would be in Macon when the *Tertium Quids* gathered in that city for their August 17 meeting. Suddenly reanimated by the prospect of victory, Whiggery was preparing to converge on Macon from three directions: from the Scott camp, from the *Tertium Quid* stronghold, and from the ranks of those who had stayed with the cadaverous Constitutional Union party until the funeral oration was pronounced on August 10 by that party's executive committee.[7]

The press accounts of what took place at Macon in mid-August warrant the inference that a sincere effort was made to unite the Whig factions behind a single electoral ticket.[8] Except for a merger of the late arrivals from Constitutional Unionism with the *Tertium Quids,* the Macon peace effort proved abortive. Scott men made it plain, however, that their differences with *Tertium Quids* were over men, not principles. Failing to compromise on a single ticket, the rival factions went into their prearranged conventions and prepared separate electoral slates. The Scott men naturally put up a slate pledged to their idol, while the

[6] Savannah *Republican,* July 1, 1852.

[7] Athens *Southern Banner,* July 15, August 10, 1852; Milledgeville *Federal Union,* August 3, 17, 24, 1852; Augusta *Chronicle and Sentinel,* August 4, 25, 1852; Savannah *Republican,* August 17, 1852; Milledgeville *Southern Recorder,* August 24, 1852; Sandersville *Central Georgian,* August 17, 24, 1852; *Address of the Executive Committee, To the Constitutional Union Party of Georgia.*

[8] Milledgeville *Southern Recorder,* August 24, 1852; Sandersville *Central Georgian,* August 24, 1852; Augusta *Chronicle and Sentinel,* August 25, 1852.

Tertium Quids ratified the National Constitutional Union party's nomination of Daniel Webster for President and prepared an electoral ticket in his behalf. Webster's running mate, J. W. Kennedy of Pennsylvania, declined the nomination and the *Tertium Quids* named Charles J. Jenkins, Richmond County Whig, as their candidate for Vice-President. There were now three electoral tickets in the race, a fourth having been withdrawn a week earlier by the Constitutional Union party's executive committee.[9]

The *Address of the Executive Committee, To the Constitutional Union Party of Georgia* was promptly followed by a second *Address* prepared by the Democratic members of the late Constitutional Union party's executive committee.[10] It was intended as a guide for Franklin Pierce's friends in the recent Constitutional Union party. They were the folks, it will be recalled, who, acting as Supplementals, had sent a delegation to the Democratic national convention. Later they had put a Pierce electoral ticket into the race. On August 10 it was withdrawn. Known as Supplementals, they were the followers of Governor Cobb. Since the genesis of the *Tertium Quid* movement of July 16, these Supplementals were composed mainly of Union Democrats. It would seem that those Whigs who still clung to them after July 16 left to join the *Tertium Quids* after August 10. Nevertheless the Supplementals were still a factor to be

[9] Milledgeville *Federal Union*, August 24, 1852; Milledgeville *Southern Recorder*, August 24, 1852; Savannah *Morning News*, August 9, 1852; Augusta *Chronicle and Sentinel*, August 25, 1852; Sandersville *Central Georgian*, August 17, 1852. J. W. Kennedy was nominated on the second ballot. On the first ballot Charles J. Jenkins received 23 votes for the vice-presidential nomination at the National Constitutional Union party's Philadelphia convention. Three other Georgians were under consideration for the vice-presidential nomination. They were Governor Cobb, Robert Toombs, and A. H. Stphens.

[10] The complete title of this second pronouncement was *Address of a Portion of the Executive Committee to the Union Democracy and Union Whigs, friends of Pierce and King*. The King referred to in the title was William Rufus King of North Carolina, Pierce's running mate.

reckoned with. A judicious use of this faction might conceivably enable Cobb to capture the State Democratic machine. This was precisely what the Governor had in mind when by the second *Address* his followers were notified to select delegates to attend a meeting scheduled for September 18 in Atlanta.[11]

As already pointed out, July and August were filled with an abundance of political happenings. In this confusing picture it will be recalled that the following events bulk large. On July 15 the Constitutional Union delegates assembled in Milledgeville. When the Cobb men raised the Supplemental Pierce electoral ticket, the Stephens-Jenkins bloc bolted. The next day they formally launched the *Tertium Quid* movement by issuing the call for the Macon convention of August 17. Meanwhile Senator William Dawson ordered a gathering of Winfield Scott's Whig friends. They, too, met in Macon, the day after the *Tertium Quid* conclave. According to prearrangement, the Scottites and *Tertium Quids* put up electoral slates for Winfield Scott and Daniel Webster. On August 4 Governor Cobb wrote his Stroud letter, which served as a sort of prologue for the withdrawal on August 10 of the Supplemental ticket. The *Address* which lowered the Supplemental slate was promptly followed, it will be recalled, by a second *Address* ordering a meeting for Atlanta on September 18 of all those former Constitutional Unionites who were interested in Pierce's candidacy. It will be noted that when the Scottites adjourned on August 18, a total of four electoral tickets had been offered. They were the Regular Democratic slate which was put up on March 31, months before Pierce's nomination; the Supplemental Democratic ticket which was put up on July 15 and withdrawn on August 10; the *Tertium Quid,* or Webster, ticket prepared at Macon on August 17; and the Scott ticket which was entered on

11 *Ibid.*

August 18. Against the background of this calendar of events, what took place between the adjournment of the Scottites on August 18 and the meeting ordered for Atlanta on September 18 is comparatively easy to follow. Actually it may be said that the events of this month belong to one or the other of two major developments. They were the final phase of the quarrel over the Regular ticket of March 31 and a *rapprochement* between Whig factions (*Tertium Quids* and Scottites) which was to carry them just short of agreement on a single electoral ticket.

For Regular and Supplemental Democrats the month which preceded the Atlanta gathering was a time of great concern over the electoral ticket of March 31. Secret plots and genuine peace overtures abounded. Each faction faced numerous possibilities. The Regulars could insist on holding fast to their electoral slate. Or, they could agree to withdraw it with as much grace as they could muster and with Supplemental assistance prepare a compromise ticket. The Supplementals faced three possibilities. They could accept the Regular slate. They could try to force the Regulars to withdraw their ticket and demand a voice in the construction of a single slate of Pierce electors. Or, they could mortgage their future by offering another Pierce ticket and thereby threaten to throw the choice of electors to the State legislature, where Cobb would be in a position to make a deal such as he had made to send Robert Toombs to the United States Senate.

That some of the Governor's friends were determined to go the limit in behalf of a compromise electoral ticket is attested by the suggestion of John E. Ward, a leading Savannah Unionite. Writing Cobb on August 24 from a place he described as not far from Franklin Pierce's residence, Ward confided that it would be better for the State to go for Scott than to have the Regulars cast the electoral vote. He requested the Governor to write him urging the desirability of withdrawing the Regular slate as the first step in the preparation of a compromise Pierce ticket. Ward would take the Governor's letter to Pierce and urge the Democratic nominee to write both Cobb and former Governor C. J. McDonald, a leading Regular, emphasizing the desirability of harmony among Georgia Democrats. If McDonald rejected Pierce's plea, as Ward prophesied he would, then there was a possibility that the Democratic nominee would repudiate the Regular slate.[12] Whether Cobb wrote the letter Ward requested is unknown. He did, however, reiterate his intention not to support the electoral ticket of March 31 because it had not been prepared by the joint action "of our friends and the Southern Rights men." [13] That Pierce ever seriously considered taking sides in Georgia Democracy's family fight is unlikely, if the neutral behavior of the Baltimore convention can be accepted as a test of the national organization's policy.

As the September 18 meeting approached, representatives of both the Supplementals and the Regulars expressed a desire for harmony. Just a few weeks before the gathering it was rumored that John H. Lumpkin, one of the Governor's closest friends, had deserted the Supplementals and was to support the Regular Pierce slate.[14] In Chatham County the *Georgian,* which had been the spearhead of the reorganization activities of the preceding November, was now working just as earnestly for peace between the factions. Late in August this journal published the call for a county Democratic mass meeting. When the gathering assembled on August 31 both Regulars and Supplementals were on hand. Speaking for the Regulars, Solomon Cohen urged a reunion of the factions. Two Supplemental leaders, H. R. Jackson and Dr. Richard Arnold, made similar pleas.

[12] John E. Ward to Howell Cobb, August 24, 1852, in Cobb MSS.

[13] Howell Cobb to Savanah *Georgian,* quoted in Milledgeville *Federal Union,* August 31, 1852.

[14] Milledgeville *Federal Union,* August 31, 1852.

Resolutions were promptly adopted announcing that Chatham County Democracy was at last reunited. Delegates were selected to attend the Atlanta meeting of September 18. They were specifically instructed to work for reunion when they got to Atlanta. Similar harmony meetings were reported for Baldwin, Henry, Jackson, and Walton counties.[15] Sensing the drift towards reunion, Governor Cobb wrote his wife in late August that ". . . there will be a regular love feast in Atlanta on the 18th Sept." [16]

One of the most conscientious devotees to party welfare was H. V. Johnson. Like the *Georgian,* he had been identified with the twice-defeated Southern Rights party. And like the *Georgian,* he had been in the forefront of the reorganization movement of late 1851 and early 1852. In fact, Johnson's relation to the Regular Democratic faction was much the same as Cobb's relation to the Supplementals. By midsummer Johnson had overcome the narrow partisan feeling which seemed to activate him during the months right after the gubernatorial contest of 1851. Yet no one was more closely identified with the genesis of the Regular faction than he. Furthermore, no one was better suited to accept the Governor's repeated request for compromise than he. Therefore when he offered on August 24 to give up his place on the Regular electoral ticket so that a representative from the Supplementals might be appointed, hope for peace between the factions ran high.[17] Within a short time three more Regulars offered their resignations. Peace within the Democratic household now seemed assured. Only a formal announcement was needed to end almost two years of internecine warfare. That was expected to come on September 18 from Atlanta. Even the dogged

[15] Athens *Southern Banner,* September 2, 9, 1852.

[16] Howell Cobb to his wife, August 27, 1852, in Phillips (ed.), *Correspondence,* 318.

[17] H. V. Johnson to the Democratic executive committee, quoted in Milledgeville *Federal Union,* August 31, 1852.

Hopkins Holsey stopped aiming his biting phrases at the
Regulars and actually eulogized Johnson for his "noble
acceptance" of the Governor's olive branch.[18] On September 2, H. L. Benning, Southern rightist of long standing,
wrote Cobb from Columbus that ". . . there seems to be
an universal feeling in favor of conciliation so far as we
in this region are concerned." [19] The Governor's "love
feast" now seemed a certainty.

Those Democrats who had risen on the tiptoe of expectancy were rudely jolted on September 7 when the *Federal
Union* announced that to alter the electoral ticket of March
31 would weaken Pierce. Within a week the Regular Democratic executive committee announced its intention not
to tamper with the ticket.[20] Such a course would dissatisfy
too many voters, it added. How the Regular executive committee arrived at its decision is not entirely clear. Several
considerations are worth noting, however. In the first place,
it has already been pointed out that many Southern rightists
were reluctant to forgive Governor Cobb for his behavior
in 1850 and 1851. They could not forget that he had dis-
rupted the Democratic party. A few of them like H. V.
Johnson and H. L. Benning were, it has been observed,
ready to bury the hatchet. Many of them, however, were
determined to make the Governor pay for his political
crime of bolting. Hence they refused to take down the
Regular slate. What seems to be a more plausible explanation, however, lies in the bold action of a handful of extreme
Southern rightists who felt the Regulars were on the verge
of compromise. Meeting in Columbus on September 2,
these fire-eaters paved the way for a regeneration of the
Southern Rights party. They nominated former Governor
George M. Troup for President and John A. Quitman

---

[18] Athens *Southern Banner,* September 2, 1852.
[19] H. L. Benning to Howell Cobb, in Phillips (ed.), *Correspondence,* 318.
[20] Milledgeville *Federal Union,* September 14, 1852.

of Mississippi for Vice-President. They demanded that Congress protect slavery in the territories. Pierce, they asserted, was unsound on both slavery and secession. They decided on an electoral ticket and made plans to co-operate with their brethren in Alabama and Mississippi.[21] Confronted with the Troup-Quitman threat, Regulars could hardly make concessions to the Supplementals. To have done so would have required a rear-guard action against the Troup-Quitman forces. Regulars saved themselves this embarrassing experience by announcing a few days before the September 18 meeting that there would be no change in the electoral slate which they had put up months before the nomination of Franklin Pierce.

Supplemental delegates gathered early for the Governor's "love feast." On September 17 they held a preliminary meeting in Atlanta's Parris Hall. Many wondered whether the events of early September presaged a renewal of Democracy's internecine war, already two years old. An air of despondency hung over the convention as anxious delegates went into session a day earlier than originally planned. They promptly tackled Georgia Democracy's foremost problem by appointing a committee to open negotiations with James Gardner, Jr., chairman of the Regular executive committee. The newly appointed committee was instructed to come to some sort of agreement with Gardner on the matter of a revision of the electoral slate. On the afternoon of the following day the convention reassembled to listen to H. R. Jackson's report on the progress of the committee's negotiations with Gardner. After reading the dispatch sent to the chairman of the Regular executive committee requesting a revision of the electoral ticket in the interest of party harmony, Jackson laid before the delegates Gardner's blunt refusal to honor the request. Hardly

21 Milledgeville *Southern Recorder*, September 21, 1852; Athens *Southern Banner*, October 7, 14, 21, 1852.

a diet for a "love feast." Expressing his disappointment at Gardner's response, Jackson proceeded to discuss the impropriety of putting up another Pierce slate of electors. This, he argued, would keep alive the fires of dissension. The time had come for peace between the Democratic factions, he continued. Concluding, he urged the adoption of his committee's majority report, which, he hoped, would end two years of internecine warfare in the Democratic family. Satisfied with Jackson's recommendations, the convention promptly adopted by a substantial margin the majority report.[22]

There was to be no "love feast," however. The convention's acceptance of the majority report was bitterly assailed by the Cherokee delegates. Utterly disgusted with the convention's "surrender," William B. Wofford led the Cherokee band from the hall. Meeting late on September 18, the Wofford following put up a competing Pierce ticket. In defending this "Tugalo" slate, Hopkins Holsey explained: "It claims no party allegiance whatever. It appeals to the judgment and the sympathies of all men who hate tyranny in whatever form it may present itself, and who at the same time desire to support Pierce and [William Rufus] King consistently with that feeling." [23]

The "Tugalo" crowd, as these men from Cherokee were called, lost no time in plunging into the fight. The Atlanta sessions were scarcely adjourned before Tugalo spokesmen were charging foul play. The Marietta *Union*, one of the few journals supporting the latest Pierce ticket, insisted a "plot was laid either by Gov. Cobb or among his friends in Chatham" to arrange the Atlanta convention so that Cherokee delegates would be outvoted on every question.[24]

---

[22] The official proceedings of the Atlanta convention were reported in detail by the Milledgeville *Federal Union*, September 28, 1852.

[23] Athens *Southern Banner*, September 23, 1852.

[24] Quoted in Augusta *Chronicle and Sentinel*, September 29, 1852, and Milledgeville *Federal Union*, October 5, 1852.

H. R. Jackson was selected, wailed the *Union,* to execute the "fix." That Jackson's enthusiasm for peace was activated less by principle than by a desire to share in the public plunder is betrayed by his correspondence with Governor Cobb. Shortly after the campaign was over he complained at length about a mysterious ailment which, he explained, might end his life at any moment. He wanted to provide for his wife and family, he continued. Concluding, he insisted on an appointment to diplomatic service. This the party owed him, he felt, as a reward for his faithful service at Atlanta and after.[25]

Jackson's behavior was, to be sure, symbolic of the tone of public morality in the fifties. The historian searches in vain for principled parties or factions in 1852. The struggle on both national and state levels in this year was for patronage and power. There existed a sort of moratorium on the discussion of public questions. The business community had set the pace. The "business man's peace" of 1850 must not be disturbed. Hence both Winfield Scott and Franklin Pierce, as already pointed out, were campaigning for the presidency on identical platforms. Georgia's five factions demonstrate the inefficacy of the party system when compelled to sustain itself on the struggle for patronage and power alone. Former Governor George M. Troup's refusal to take seriously his own candidacy for President after agreeing to accept the nomination has diagnostic significance. Nominated, as already observed, by the Southern Rights party, he declared in his letter of acceptance that he preferred Pierce to himself.[26] How brittle the substance of parties had become under the impact of the struggle for patronage and power. By comparison with Troup's behavior, Governor Cobb's is slightly less ingenuous, but just as symbolic. That he was involved in a plot as charged by the disappointed Marietta *Union* is not borne out by his

[25] H. R. Jackson to Howell Cobb, November 27, 1852, in Cobb MSS.
[26] Quoted in Athens *Southern Banner,* October 21, 1852.

correspondence with J. B. Lamar, his Macon kinsman. Writing Lamar from Atlanta after Gardner's reply had been read to the Parris Hall gathering, the Governor strangely reasoned that while a second Pierce ticket was impolitic, yet he desired a second ticket and would see that it was entered.[27] Thus was the five-act drama of the electoral tickets started towards the final curtain.[28]

Hopkins Holsey's mid-June forecast that Georgians would promptly restrain themselves once the national party conventions had done their work turned out to be more wishful thinking than sound political prophecy.[29] Contrary to Holsey's prognosis, as the last lap of the presidential contest approached, Georgia presented five entries. This was an odd contrast to the thirties and forties, when the bitter struggles over the bank and tariff had divided Georgians into evenly matched Democratic and Whig parties. Then principles had vied with plunder for popular enthusiasm.

The incantations of a few old-line Whig journals demonstrate the moral erosion of the early fifties. The *Southern Recorder* urged Scott Whigs and *Tertium Quids* to avoid "unnecessary acerbity of temper." [30] Later it exhorted both Whig factions to behave in a spirit of gentlemanly toleration, hopefully concluding with "that which is impracticable at this moment, may be found both practicable and pleasant, as well as efficient, when we meet to decide the matter in the legislature." [31] This journal as well as the *Republican* posted both the Scott and Webster electoral slates on its masthead.[32] The latter had originally defamed Scott but soon surrendered completely by announcing that:

[27] Howell Cobb to John B. Lamar, September 18, 1852, in Phillips (ed.), *Correspondence*, 320–21.

[28] John P. Hale, New Hampshire Free-Soiler, was nominated on a Free Democratic ticket, which, of course, had no support in Georgia.

[29] See page 64.

[30] Milledgeville *Southern Recorder*, August 24, 1852.

[31] *Ibid.*, August 31, 1852.

[32] See Savannah *Republican*, August 24, 1852, and Milledgeville *Southern Recorder*, August 31, 1852.

"As it is, we say to the Whigs of Georgia, there is no reason, so far as regards his [Scott's] sentiments on the Compromise measures, why they should not cast their suffrages for Scott." [33] A few weeks before the election the *Chronicle and Sentinel* counseled Whigs to support the candidate of their choice. The selection of the State's electors was certain to fall to the legislature, continued the *Chronicle and Sentinel.* Press and party leaders were therefore urged to pledge their support to the Whig nominee receiving the largest popular vote. [34]

Not all Whigs joined the incantations of some of the party's most highly respected journals. Senator William Dawson, Augustus H. Kenan, A. H. Stephens, and Benjamin H. Hill were among the exceptions. Dawson and Kenan were enthusiastic Scott men, while Stephens, the father of the *Tertium Quids,* was devoted to Webster. Speaking from the same platform to a Morgan County rally in September, both Kenan and Stephens rang all the changes in behalf of their favorite candidate. Having weaned Robert Toombs away from Governor Cobb, Stephens was in an enviable position late in the campaign. Always a shrewd operator, Stephens was staking his political future on the magic name of Daniel Webster, who, incidentally, was advising his friends in New England to vote for Pierce. If the selection of the State's electors fell to the legislature, Stephens' *Tertium Quid* project would be in a position to pay off handsomely. A deal with the Governor would then be in order. Had not Cobb and Stephens made a deal ten months earlier which sent Robert Toombs to the United States Senate? Younger and less attracted to Whiggism, Benjamin H. Hill thought it would be "shameful if Georgia did not cast her vote for" the Democratic nominee for President. [35]

[33] Quoted in Cole, *Whig Party in the South,* 272.

[34] Augusta *Chronicle and Sentinel,* October 13, 1852.

[35] Milledgeville *Federal Union,* September 14, 1852; Philip S. Lemle,

The Tugaloes and Regulars had no such truce as prevailed within Whiggery. Therefore they provided Whigs with many ready-made blasts. Whig spellbinders hurled them in all directions to shake the morale of Democrats. For example, the fuss which the Marietta *Union* kicked up by charging Governor Cobb and H. R. Jackson with a conspiracy was given a big play in the columns of the *Chronicle and Sentinel*.[36] Whig editors also exercised their talents by firing away on the national level. Employing the standard Whig line of the thirties and forties, party spokesmen explained that Whiggery was the party of "prudence and discretion." Whiggism was respectable, "eschewing . . . the mad schemes of young America," went the argument. Democracy, on the other hand, was given to "wild and reckless adventure" ranging from Locofoco attacks on capitalism to intervention in the affairs of Hungary. To demonstrate the rash proclivities of the opposition the *Chronicle and Sentinel* carried a fictitious exchange between an "Honest Dutchman" and a Pierce elector. "Ish Sheneral Pierce," the Honest Dutchman inquired, "going for us to send de army to help Kossuth? Dat's vot Ise for." With reckless abandon the Pierce elector fired back that "General Pierce . . . goes for Kossuth and intervention, and when he's elected every despot in Europe will shiver in his shoes." [37]

It was the Democratic factions which provided the fireworks for the campaign of 1852. Tugalo spokesman wailed endlessly about Regular trickery. The Supplemental ticket had been withdrawn in August, they explained, with the

---

Webster elector, to Secretary of the Independent Whig Convention, September 10, 1852, quoted in Sandersville *Central Georgian*, September 21, 1852; Sandersville *Central Georgian*, October 5, 1852; Benjamin H. Hill to Howell Cobb, August 30, 1852, in Cobb MSS. See Schlesinger, *The Age of Jackson*, 481, for Webster's impressions of Pierce.

[36] See especially the issues for October 20 and 27.

[37] Milledgeville *Southern Recorder*, September 14, 1852; Augusta *Chronicle and Sentinel*, November 3, 1852.

tacit understanding that a compromise Pierce slate was to replace it. For this purpose the Atlanta meeting had been called, they continued. Instead of compromise at Atlanta there had been infamy and betrayal, charged the Tugalo men. To appease the Tugaloes, W. B. Wofford, leading Atlanta bolter and Tugalo elector, was offered a place on the Regular electoral ticket created by a resignation. Declining the offer with a blistering reply to James Gardner, Jr., the Regular executive-committee chairman, Wofford charged the "secessionists" with usurping the party's name. In the race since March 31, the Regular slate was premature, continued Wofford. Concluding, he denounced Gardner for offering at the eleventh hour a pittance.[38]

The Tugalo stand offered Hopkins Holsey a chance to make a magnificent fight against the effort to Calhounize Democracy. He seems to have had a clearer understanding of the social forces back of the guerrilla campaign of 1852 than most of his contemporaries. Writing in Athens, the "classic city," he was anything but an obscure editor. A true Jacksonian, he never missed an opportunity to fight those who would sectionalize the Democratic party. He could aim a devastating missile at the bank or the tariff, but the abolitionist crusade spiked his guns. Northern Jacksonians like David Wilmot, Gideon Welles, William Cullen Bryant, and Walt Whitman could join the newly organized Republican party and continue the fight they had begun as Jacksonians, but Southern Jacksonians like Hopkins Holsey were helpless. Once the battle to prevent the slave interests from getting control of the Democratic party was lost, the contest was over. This was the fight Holsey, Wofford, and their Tugalo followers were making. Nominally Governor Cobb was on Holsey's side, but his heart was not in the

[38] Edward H. Pottle to Hopkins Holsey, October 13, 1852, quoted in Athens *Southern Banner,* October 21, 1852. Pottle had been a member of the executive committee of the Constitutional Union party. James Gardner, Jr., to W. B. Wofford quoted *ibid.,* October 21, 1852; W. B. Wofford to James Gardner, Jr., quoted *ibid.*

fight. Apostles of Calhoun, the Regulars would restrain the North by presenting a united South prepared to act either in or out of the Union. Pierce was simply the vehicle, insisted Holsey, which would convey into power the fire-eaters. They would bide their time until the opportunity for secession was more propitious.[39]

Regular spokesmen adopted the strategy of treating all opposition, excepting the Troup effort, as Whiggism. Tugaloism was invented, asserted the *Federal Union,* to provide a political sanctuary for Cherokee Whigs. They had tasted victory in 1850 and again in 1851 when the Constitutional Union party won smashing victories at the polls. With the dissolution of that party Cherokee Whigs were homeless. Hence they had started an opposition "Democratic party."[40] "To go for Scott is to become a Sewardite." Thus had the *Republican* spoken soon after Scott's nomination. When this journal switched to Scott in October, the *Georgian* greeted the news by quoting its rival's July fulminations against the Whig nominee. Further, Regular Democratic leaders pointed out that when the South could not get Buchanan at Baltimore it forced the convention to take Pierce, while Southern delegates had voted almost unanimously against Scott for fifty-five ballots. Pierce was thus presented as the true champion of the South, and the Reg-

[39] The following interesting defense of Holsey appeared in the Savannah *Georgian,* October 8, 1852: ". . . if there is a Union Democrat whose feeling should be *tolerated,* that man is Col. Holsey. In the hottest of the recent contest, whenever the blows fell the fastest and heaviest, he was to be found, dealing them out, it is true, with a warrior's spirit, but receiving them in return, from every quarter. It is difficult for such a man to realize that the conflict is ended; still more difficult to feel at home with his recent antagonists. The attacks upon him have been continuous and personal. We do not wonder at his feeling." Athens *Southern Banner,* October 21, 28, 1852; Milledgeville *Southern Recorder,* September 21, 1852; Sandersville *Central Georgian,* September 28, 1852. For an interesting account of the origin of the Republican party see Binkley, *American Political Parties,* 206–34. See Schlesinger, *The Age of Jackson,* 477–79, for the part of Jacksonians in the organization of the Republican party.

[40] Milledgeville *Federal Union,* October 12, 1852; Athens *Southern Banner,* October 7, 28, 1852.

ular faction of the Democratic party as the only agency to which Southern rights could safely be entrusted. As for the *Tertium Quids,* they were in the fight for the sole purpose of making a kill in case the choice of the State's electors fell to the Constitutional Union–controlled legislature. Regular spokesmen warned that Georgians might have to be satisfied with General Scott, the agent of New York abolitionists, in case the legislature chose the electors.[41]

On October 24 Daniel Webster died. He was never a real contender for the presidency. His advice to New England friends to vote for Pierce betrays the Stephens ruse in using this celebrity's name to head the *Tertium Quid* venture. The *Chronicle and Sentinel,* leading *Tertium Quid* paper of the State, promptly replaced Webster's name on its masthead with the names of Millard Fillmore and John J. Crittenden. Loyal Webster followers were urged to "stand by the ticket." If successful, the Webster electors could choose either Fillmore or Crittenden. It is therefore a little misleading to say that Webster, though dead for nine days, polled over 5,000 votes in Georgia.[42]

Georgia divided some 60,500 votes among five electoral tickets as follows: Regular Democrats, 33,400; Scott Whigs, 16,000; Tugalo Democrats, 5,775; *Tertium Quids,* 5,225; Southern Rights, 1,000. Approximately 34,000 fewer votes were cast than in 1851. The Regular Democratic ticket polled 5,000 fewer votes than former Governor C. J. Mc-

[41] Savannah *Republican* quoted in Savannah *Georgian,* October 8, 1852; Milledgeville *Federal Union,* September 14, November 2, 1852. The practice of the presidential nominee stumping the country was new in 1852, and when Scott made a speaking tour through the Middle Atlantic states Democratic editors in Georgia were mortified. Scott was breaking a dignified precedent, they complained. Pierce, they continued proudly, stayed at home "like a good citizen." Besides, grumbled erudite Democrats, Scott's grammar was bad. See early October issues of the Milledgeville *Federal Union.*

[42] Augusta *Chronicle and Sentinel,* October 27, 1852. Certain myths associated with Webster are treated in Schlesinger, *The Age of Jackson.* On page 386 Professor Schlesinger quotes Walt Whitman as remarking that Webster was "overrated more than any other public man ever prominent in America."

Donald had received in his campaign against Howell Cobb a year earlier. Professor Arthur Cole estimates that "fully 20,000 Whig voters, or one-half of the party," stayed at home on election day.[43] At Brunswick the *National Intelligencer* reported that the polls were not even opened, "it being the deliberate opinion of the people that none of the candidates were worthy of support." [44]

The campaign of 1852 was a highly complex affair. The prevailing motif was the struggle for power among the State's ablest politicians. That the voters were apathetic was demonstrated by the comparatively small turnout on election day. Yet this was a significant contest—more significant than either the spirited contest of 1850, which produced the memorable Georgia Platform, or the heated gubernatorial fight of 1851, which resulted in Howell Cobb's election. The victory of the Regulars served to Calhounize Georgia Democracy. John Forsyth, Jr., editor of the Columbus *Times,* openly boasted that Southern rightists controlled not only the Georgia Democratic machine but every state Democratic organization from Virginia to Louisiana. From now on Jacksonians would either conform or be purged. Some like Governor Cobb preferred to conform; others like Hopkins Holsey were purged. The *Federal Union* promptly revealed the intentions of the victors when it declared: "Hereafter we see no necessity for divisions and parties in Georgia, or anywhere else at the South. If Mr. Pierce does all in his power, as we trust he will, to protect the constitutional rights of the South, it is our duty and our interest to support him." [45]

[43] Cole, *Whig Party in the South,* 274.

[44] Washington *National Intelligencer* quoted *ibid.;* Milledgeville *Federal Union,* November 16, 24, 1852.

[45] Milledgeville *Federal Union,* November 9, 30, 1852; Savannah *Georgian,* November 4, 1852; Columbus *Times* quoted in Athens *Southern Banner,* November 11, 25, 1852; A. H. Stephens to Linton Stephens quoted in Cole, *Whig Party in the South,* 234; Robert Toombs to J. J. Crittenden quoted *ibid.,* 273; Savannah *Republican* quoted *ibid.,* 281; December, 1852, issues of Milledgeville *Southern Recorder.*

VI

DEAD HEAT

SURROUNDING President-elect Franklin Pierce was an astute group of political architects. To them fell the task of building a party machine. In the North as in the South conservative Democrats had wrested control of party affairs from the Jacksonian forces. The Democratic party which was emerging from the struggle of 1852 was developing a striking resemblance to the Whiggery of the thirties and forties. The Democracy was rapidly becoming a "respectable" party. While Varina Howell could express genuine amazement in 1843 upon discovering that her future husband, Jefferson Davis, was "refined and cultivated and yet . . . a democrat," a decade later she would undoubtedly have been equally amazed to find Democratic leaders "unrefined and uncultivated." [1]

The Democratic machine must be built on the solid rock of respectability. Indeed this promptly became a prerequisite for membership in the political family of Franklin Pierce. What Georgia Democrats would Pierce adopt? When the subject of cabinet appointments was first under consideration, Governor Cobb was hopeful that the President-elect would reward some Union Democrats. That Pierce would offer the Governor a cabinet post seems to have been sincerely believed by no less a person than the Governor himself. Yet the advice Cobb was receiving from his friends in Washington and elsewhere hardly warranted such optimism. Except for the unrealistic offerings of Con-

[1] Eron Rowland, *Varina Howell, Wife of Jefferson Davis* (New York, 1931), I, 48; Nichols, *The Democratic Machine*, 197–220; Schlesinger, *The Age of Jackson*, 466–67.

gressman George W. Jones of Tennessee, the Governor's friends gave him the woeful story of the proscription in store for those Democrats who in 1850 had wandered off the straight and narrow path of party regularity. Early in January, Thomas D. Harris wrote the Governor from Washington that President-elect Pierce was to "make up his cabinet out of the extremes [Southern-rights and free-soil] of the party."[2] A few days later Senator Robert M. Charlton (appointed by Cobb to the unexpired term of J. M. Berrien) prophesied that Pierce would be prevented from appointing the Governor to a cabinet post because of the influence of Southern-rights Democrats.[3]

By mid-February the die had been cast. The South was awarded two places in the Pierce cabinet. Both went to Southern-rights Democrats. The appointment of Jefferson Davis to the War Department was no less a rebuke to Mississippi Unionists than Cobb's proscription was to Georgia Unionists. Then came the Pierce inaugural, announcing that the Democratic party had taken its seat on the Georgia Platform. The effect of the inaugural in Georgia was precisely as predetermined. Many former Constitutional Unionists, notably the Union Whig panel, proudly pointed to the new administration's endorsement of Fillmore principles. Cobb and a few of his friends saw through the subtle Pierce plan. Hopkins Holsey wondered how the new administration could harmonize the appointment of Davis with the President's pledge to "interpose a ready and stern resistance" when the threat to dissolve the Union appeared.[4] Philip Clayton of the Navy Department neatly summed up this wanton incongruity when he explained to his friend Governor Cobb that "thus we have the principles

[2] Thomas D. Harris to Howell Cobb, January 7, 1853, in Cobb MSS.

[3] Robert M. Charlton to Howell Cobb, January 11, 1853; Thomas D. Harris to *id.*, February 13, 1853; J. D. Frierson to *id.*, February 8, 1853, in Cobb MSS.

[4] Athens *Southern Banner*, March 17, 24, 1853.

and the fire-eaters the offices. . . ." [5] The paradoxical performance of the Pierce administration did not escape the taunts of its Georgia opponents. Blithely reminding Cobb followers they had been passed over by the patronage dispensers, the *Southern Recorder* chided Southern-rights Democrats because their President had accepted the principles for which the Constitutional Unionists had contended. That "respectable" Democrats were annoyed by such ironic thrusts was demonstrated when their spokesman, the *Federal Union,* sharply retorted that the Compromise of 1850 held no terror for it.[6]

No Georgia politician was more completely marooned on the occasion of the national Democratic party's return to power than Howell Cobb. He was indeed a man without a party. To the Constitutional Union party he was indebted for his position as Georgia's Chief Executive. It had vanished soon after his election in 1851. He had sought restoration to good standing in the Democratic party by supporting Franklin Pierce only to be denied a place in the latter's cabinet. Yet over a period of four or five years Cobb had a good average for a politician. Elected Speaker of the national House of Representatives in 1849, he returned to Georgia the next year to help save the Compromise of 1850. For his part in this performance he was rewarded in 1851 with the governorship. Cobb seems to have accepted his reverses of 1852 and early 1853 philosophically. Doubtless

5 Philip Clayton to Howell Cobb, March 7, 1853, in Brooks (ed.), "Howell Cobb Papers," *loc. cit.,* V (1922), 35–36.

6 James D. Richardson, *A Compilation of the Messages and Papers of the Presidents* (Washington, 1908), V, 197–203; Milledgeville *Southern Recorder,* March 15, 22, 29, 1853; Athens *Southern Banner,* March 17, 24, 1853; Macon *Journal and Messenger* quoted in Milledgeville *Federal Union,* March 15, 22, 1853; Milledgeville *Federal Union,* March 15, 22, 1853; Roy Franklin Nichols, *Franklin Pierce* (Philadelphia, 1931), 228, 277, 286; Greene, "Georgia Politics," *loc. cit.,* 194. Except for H. R. Jackson, who was appointed minister to Austria, Union Democrats were generally passed over. Jackson, it will be recalled, refused to support the Tugalo slate. Among the Pierce appointees were numerous Southern-rights editors.

he reasoned those now in control of the Democratic party had cause to suspect him. He had been a Jacksonian. The Democratic party's swing to the right caused many Northern Jacksonians to fraternize with the free-soil movement. Some of them, including former President Martin Van Buren and his son, had deserted the Democratic party in 1848 to lead the antislavery crusade. Cobb had been intimately associated with many of these Northern Jacksonians. Thus when he deserted the Democratic party in 1850, extreme Southern rightists unjustly identified him with the Van Burens and other free-soilers who, like Cobb, had once marched with General Jackson. A politician as shrewd and as ambitious as Howell Cobb could not escape the realization that he was now paying for his political sins.

Instead of grieving about his fate, the Governor promptly began a campaign of *rapprochement.* His good friend William Hope Hull opened this campaign for him. Late in March, Hull wrote a lengthy letter to James Gardner, Jr., editor of the Augusta *Constitutionalist,* purporting to explain Cobb's behavior during the late presidential contest. Gardner ran the Hull letter in his paper. Other journals copied it. Hull explained that the Governor had hoped to use the Atlanta meeting of the past September to restore complete harmony in Democratic ranks. When the plan failed he reluctantly followed many of his friends into the Tugalo camp. Gardner was reminded at this point that from then on Cobb had withstood the most vitriolic assaults without uttering a word of protest. Now, Hull concluded, the Governor was ready to fight the battles of Democracy as a private in the ranks.[7]

Cobb was bending the knee at an auspicious moment. It was soon enough after Pierce's cabinet selections to suggest to party leaders that here was a man whose heart was free

[7] William Hope Hull to James Gardner, Jr., quoted in Milledgeville *Federal Union,* April 5, 1853.

of vengeance. Moreover, the Democratic State convention was soon to meet. A nomination for Governor would have to be made. Thereafter a campaign would be necessary. Harmony in the ranks had a way of simplifying conventions and campaigns. It was worth a big price on the eve of what promised to be a heated contest. The Governor was playing his hand skillfully. Perhaps he would move up through the ranks rapidly. After all, he was the Governor; and while he had offered to serve as a private, yet such service was hardly commensurate with his rank. That Cobb personally directed his campaign for restoration to good standing as a Democrat is evident from his correspondence. On April 16 H. R. Jackson, the Savannah conciliator, informed the Governor that a letter had been prepared, as Cobb had directed, and delivered to R. B. Hilton, editor of the *Georgian*. Hilton ran the Jackson letter in a late March issue of his paper. Like Hull's effort, the Jackson communication explained that Cobb had worked industriously for a reunion of the party factions during the late presidential contest.[8]

Thomas D. Morris, a loyal Cobb partisan, set the stage for what was doubtless intended as the Governor's supreme effort to win forgiveness from the Democratic high command. Frustrated by the late reverses of the Union Democrats, Morris asked for guidance. How, inquired this loyal follower, were conscientious Union Democrats to behave in the future? The Governor responded with an adroit explanation, which numerous journals printed at about the same time the Hull and Jackson letters appeared. Pointing out that there had always been a division in Southern Democracy between the Jackson and Calhoun wings, Cobb explained that this condition need not preclude party harmony in the future. Morris was advised to forget the expe-

[8] H. R. Jackson to R. B. Hilton quoted in Savannah *Georgian*, March 29, 1853; *id.* to Howell Cobb, April 16, 1853, in Cobb MSS.

riences of the past few years. All Democrats of whatever
convictions must join the ranks and take the oath of party
allegiance. Party harmony was the first consideration. As
for the Constitutional Union party, its revival was out of
the question. There was no longer a necessity for it and
besides it never had a real national organization. Concluding, the Governor urged all Georgians to unite behind
President Pierce and forget partisan strife. Cobb's polemics
bore a striking resemblance to the more recent contentions
of the Southern-rights men. His genuflection complete,
Georgia's greatest Jacksonian had at last been "Calhoun-
ized." [9]

Cobb's careful pursuance of a deliberate program of
rapprochement set off an explosion in the Tugalo dominion. The Marietta *Union* was certain the Governor had
lost many friends by trying to conciliate his former enemies.[10] The reply to Morris was more than the high-
spirited Holsey could endure even at the hands of one who
had been his closest friend. The Athens editor was too well
grounded in Jacksonian notions to conform in the Cobb
manner. Boldly repeating his "Tugalo heresies," Holsey
charged that "in order to drag the Union democrats along
with him into a party organization with the Secessionists,
into which he seems resolved to plunge, reckless of every
antecedent passage in his political history, Gov. Cobb has
advanced some positions in his late letter that are false in
fact—false in *theory*—and totally *repugnant* to each
other." [11] Then followed two columns of biting phrases
which cut to ribbons the Governor's reply to Morris. That
Holsey announced his retirement a week after this outburst
is not strange. Whether he stepped down voluntarily or not
is of little consequence. He was out of step with the times

[9] Thomas D. Morris to *id.,* quoted in Milledgeville *Federal Union,* April
12, 1853; Howell Cobb to Thomas D. Morris, quoted *ibid.*

[10] Quoted in Augusta *Chronicle and Sentinel,* April 20, 1853.

[11] Athens *Southern Banner,* May 5, 1853.

and he must either conform or retire. His valedictory was an excellent summary of his difficulty. The recurring motif of the last years of Holsey's journalistic career had been the inexorable conflict between principle and expediency. He was admittedly a brilliant editor. His passing stilled the conscience of Andrew Jackson. No longer would it vex Georgia Democracy. James Sledge, the new editor of the *Southern Banner,* would see to that.[12]

Georgia parties were described in the spring of 1853 by the Griffin *Jeffersonian* (Democratic) as having "fallen back into the old alignments" of the forties. The *Georgian,* too, thought the party pattern of pre-Crisis days had returned. Like the *Federal Union,* the *Georgian* claimed many Whigs of the Southern Rights party had joined the Democratic family. The former journal expressed the opinion on April 12 that the final blow to the Democratic schism would be dealt when the State convention met in June to nominate a candidate for Governor. Meanwhile Howell Cobb had ordered his followers to return to the Democratic party. Then came Hopkins Holsey's resignation from the *Southern Banner.* That the Athens editor's retirement practically ended over two and one half years of lethal warfare between Union and Southern-rights Democrats is attested by Dr. Richard Arnold's reflections. Writing to J. W. Forney of Philadelphia shortly after Holsey left the *Southern Banner,* Arnold complained that "Union Democrats labour under a great disadvantage in that we have neither a newspaper nor an Editor in whom we can fully trust." [13] After nearly three years of fratricidal warfare it was beginning to look as if Democrats were really going to end their differences and try out, as the *Federal Union* put it, the " 'Old Damascus' awhile on the sleek hide of Whiggery." [14]

[12] *Ibid.,* April 28, May 12, 1853.   [13] Shryock (ed.), *Arnold Letters,* 63.
[14] Milledgeville *Federal Union,* February 22, March 8, April 12, June 14,

Democratic strategists preferred fighting Whiggism to Constitutional Unionism. Memories of the terrible disasters of 1850 and 1851 were still vivid among Southern-rights Democrats, who, it has been pointed out, took over the party machine in 1852. On the other hand, a few Union editors had visions of a renascent Constitutional Union party. Courting the favor of Governor Cobb, on the one hand, and warning of the dangers of Southern-rights hegemony within Democracy, on the other, at least five Union journals were urging during the spring of 1853 a restoration of Constitutional Unionism—the *Southern Recorder,* the Marietta *Union,* the Rome *Courier,* the *Southern Banner,* and the *Chronicle and Sentinel.* Shocking reverses between early March and mid-June (when the Democratic convention met) ended whatever chance there might have been of revising the Constitutional Union party. It has already been pointed out how Governor Cobb's letter to Thomas D. Morris and Hopkins Holsey's retirement from the *Southern Banner* simplified the problem of discipline within the Democratic household. By the same token, the performances of Cobb and Holsey did irreparable harm to the Constitutional Union cause, particularly in Cherokee. Added to these reverses was the *Southern Recorder's* (Union Whig) failure in its own bailiwick of Baldwin County to sell the idea of reviving the Constitutional Union party. Instead A. H. Kenan succeeded in pledging Baldwin County Whigs to a reorganization of Whiggery. It may be said, then, that on the eve of the gubernatorial contest of 1853 Democrats had pretty well settled their family fight. They were now reasonably well united. Among Whigs there existed no such singleness of purpose. The presidential contest of 1852 had really produced more severe differences among Whigs than the issues raised by the fight over the Compromise of

1853; Griffin *Jeffersonian,* March 3, 1853; Savannah *Georgian,* March 3, 1853; Milledgeville *Southern Recorder,* April 5, 1853.

1850. For Democrats the recent presidential campaign served as a step toward reunion of the factions. Such was the party picture on the eve of the convention season in 1853.[15]

Among the Democratic delegates assembled in State convention at Milledgeville on June 15 were numerous Union Democrats. Most prominent among them were Governor Cobb, H. R. Jackson, and Junius Hillyer. After adopting the two-thirds rule the convention began balloting for a gubernatorial nominee. H. V. Johnson, who led throughout a moderately spirited contest, was nominated at the close of the fifth round. Thereafter the convention proceeded to draft a declaration of principles. One resolution reaffirmed the party's faith in the good old Jeffersonian doctrine of strict construction. Another praised the traditional principle of the low tariff. A third put the convention on record in the best Jacksonian manner by expressing hostility to the bank, the symbol of the business community's desire to rule. Union Democrats could take pride in the antibank declaration, but more to their fancy was a tersely worded resolution pledging Democracy to faithful observance of the Georgia Platform. Concluding, the delegates, to make it plain that they wanted no more of the slavery controversy, pledged their party to resist every effort to reopen this troublesome question.[16]

The choice of H. V. Johnson was a happy one. While it represented the determination of the Southern Rights leaders to hold on to the party machine, yet Johnson was not an extremist. True, he had suffered with other South-

---

15 Athens *Southern Banner,* March 17, April 21, 28, June 9, 1853; Milledgeville *Federal Union,* February 8, March 8, April 5, June 14, 1853; Milledgeville *Southern Recorder,* March 1, April 5, May 24, 1853; Augusta *Chronicle and Sentinel,* April 27, 1853; Willis Strickland to Howell Cobb, March 13, 1853, in Cobb MSS.; Junius Hillyer quoted in Athens *Southern Banner,* June 9, 1853; Greene, "Georgia Politics," *loc. cit.,* 196–97.

16 Milledgeville *Federal Union,* June 21, 1853.

ern Rights men the humiliating defeats of 1850 and 1851; yet, as already pointed out, Johnson's conciliatory attitude during the canvass of 1852 was anything but that of an embittered man. It is therefore doubtful whether anyone was better suited for the task of restoring good feeling between Democratic factions than H. V. Johnson. Long experience on the front lines of party affairs had hardened the Democratic nominee into a relentless foe. That he was to be an astute commander he demonstrated in his letter of acceptance when he observed that "on our restoration to health, we find ourselves strengthened, by the accession to our ranks, of many noble and patriotic Whigs, who, during our recent temporary alienation, acted with one or the other of the divisions of our party, but now rising above the influence of former associations, have not hesitated to affiliate with us." [17]

If the elements comprising Democracy's opposition could be fused into a single party, Johnson would have a hard fight on his hands. Scottites, *Tertium Quids,* and Tugaloes had polled a combined total of nearly 45 per cent of the votes cast in 1852. The problem was how to unite these mutually suspicious factions and use them against the Democratic party. The quandary of those who were looking for the answer to this problem was facetiously presented by a Democratic wag who understood how to get up a mischievous soliloquy. Entitled "A Webster Whig Soliloquizing," it appeared in the May 3 issue of the *Federal Union.*

> To give 'em up, or not to give 'em up,
> That's the question:
> Whether 'twere policy in Whigs to suffer

[17] H. V. Johnson's letter of acceptance quoted in Milledgeville *Federal Union,* June 21, 1853; Athens *Southern Banner,* July 7, 1853; Griffin *Jeffersonian,* June 30, 1853; Columbus *Times and Sentinel* quoted *ibid.;* Milledgeville *Federal Union,* June 21, 28. See also Flippin, *Herschel V. Johnson,* 54 ff.

The stings and arrows of the Scottites,
Or give up hope of catching Democrats,
Be Whigs, and *nothing else?* To part; to slope;
Ah me! if by this course, we could but end
The heartache, and a thousand breaches wide
In the Whig party— 'tis a consummation
Devoutly to be wished. To part; to slope;
To part! perchance to cave: aye, there's the rub;
For in that cave there's death, politically,
To every *Tertium Quid* who shuffled out
The Scott traces: There's a new Governor.
That makes a nice fat item in the race:
What Whig could bear to see "Disunionists"
And "Coffin regiment" boys, the "Nashville Waryurs,"
Upon the highest seats splurging a "finality,"
In the bright robes of office, chewing their quids,
Contemplating calmly us Whigs "shet out,"
I guess I'd spare myself that ugly sight,
With a bare bodkin? who should bear this odium,
Grunting, swearing 'neath oppression so abject:
But that the dread of something, (I know not what)
That oft discovered country—puzzles me so;
And makes a *Tertium Quid* bear present ills,
Rather than encounter those just ahead?
Thus conscience and our pockets make us quake,
And thus a man's resolution's lost.
Obscured by the heavier claims of *policy*;
And Whigs who otherwise had risen to place,
By truckling, lose the auspicious hour,
And *cave*, Jerusalem!!

On April 26 the *Southern Recorder* urged a "Gubernatorial Convention" to nominate H. V. Johnson's opponent. Carefully avoiding both the Whig and Union labels, this journal did its best during May and June to work up enthusiasm for the proposed convention. On June 22, just a week after the Democratic meeting, the Gubernatorial Convention of Republican Citizens gathered at the State capi-

tal. With A. H. Stephens lukewarm to the project, Robert
Toombs took charge of delegates from fifty-two counties
who were on hand to furnish him with sound effects.
Toombs was assisted by John W. A. Sanford, formerly a
Democrat. Elected to preside over the convention, Sanford
somewhat naïvely revealed what he and Toombs had in
mind when in his acceptance speech he told the delegates
that "we are here, not as we are teasingly told, to save the
Union again, *but to save ourselves.*" [18] In charge of the
committee on resolutions, Toombs prepared an interesting
political bill of fare which he built around the theme that
President Pierce's abolitionist and secessionist friends were
jeopardizing the Georgia Platform. Both parties were unsound, went the Toombs line. Whigs and Democrats
throughout the State were therefore urged to join with
him to save the Union. Thus did Toombs sprinkle the holy
water of Unionism on his latest project, to which, for the
present, he carefully avoided giving a name. The nomination of Charles J. Jenkins was further notice to Scottites
that *Tertium Quids* intended to manage the forthcoming
political show. "If it had not been for the name of the
thing," reflected one of the delegates, "it would have been
better to let Mr. Toombs select the candidate in the first
place, and not put us to the trouble of coming here for
nothing." [19]

The gubernatorial contest of 1853 exploded with greatest
force in Cherokee, traditionally the land of Unionism. Both
Johnson and Jenkins were prepared to bid high for up-

[18] Quoted in Milledgeville *Federal Union,* June 28, 1853.
[19] Milledgeville *Southern Recorder,* April 26, May 24, June 28, 1853;
Milledgeville *Federal Union,* June 28, 1853. The Milledgeville *Federal
Union* alleged on June 28 that Andrew J. Miller, a preconvention favorite,
was shelved for Jenkins because he had supported Pierce for President.
This charge was denied by J. M. Berrien. The Democratic journal at the
State capital further charged that Toombs was anxious to get the nomination for Jenkins so that his obligation to Toombs would preclude his be-
coming a rival.

country votes. The principals in this campaign had opposed each other before. In 1850 and again in 1851 Johnson had been intimately identified with the Southern Rights party, then and later accused of disunion notions, while Jenkins had worked with Cobb, Toombs and Stephens in the Constitutional Union party. In fact, some of his friends insisted Jenkins deserved the title "Father of the Georgia Platform." The Jenkins campaign rode into Cherokee astride the ghost of the Constitutional Union party looking for secession, the evil genius of an earlier day. "We want to see with what grace the Union Democrats will swallow the secession pill," thundered Augusta's *Chronicle and Sentinel.*[20] The Columbus *Enquirer* assured its readers that Johnson was a secessionist. This journal was equally certain Jenkins had saved the Union in 1850.[21] What apostasy, exclaimed Union Whig journals, for Johnson, a rank secessionist, to bait loyal Union Democrats who had acted with Jenkins in 1850 to save the Union.[22] "Reorganized Democracy is a cheat and a swindle," charged the Macon *Journal and Messenger*. It was a masked battery by which secessionists would conciliate Union Democrats, obtain a popular majority, and then agitate for disunion.[23] "The same party which struggled to elect McDonald is now striving," insisted the Rome *Courier*, ". . . to foist H. V. Johnson on the Compromise men of Georgia."[24] The *Southern Recorder* let the Democratic nominee speak for himself on the subject of Union Democrats. He was quoted by this journal as having said at Canton in 1852 that "they [Union Democrats] had to him an offensive odor . . . and in short time, *buzzards would not eat them, because of the mighty stench from their dead carcasses."*[25]

[20] Augusta *Chronicle and Sentinel,* June 22, 1853.

[21] Quoted in Augusta *Chronicle and Sentinel,* July 6, 1853.

[22] Milledgeville *Southern Recorder,* July 5, 1853; Augusta *Chronicle and Sentinel,* August 10, September 21, 1853.

[23] Quoted in Augusta *Chronicle and Sentinel,* August 10, 1853.

[24] Quoted *ibid.,* August 17, 1853.   [25] Quoted *ibid.,* September 21, 1853.

Jenkins' Unionism was not the only springboard from which he launched his Cherokee campaign. Back in 1836, as a member of the State legislature, he had been active in promoting a plan for a State-owned railroad. With the completion of the project in 1851, the State of Georgia found itself in possession of a railroad. "Breaking through the mountain barriers of Cherokee," this road, known as the Western and Atlantic, had joined Atlanta with the Tennessee River.[26] Georgia was thus drawn into the orbit of the rich Ohio country. The Western and Atlantic met with instant approval among the mountain folk of north Georgia. Doubtless the sudden fall in commodity prices was partly responsible for the popular acclaim an individualistic mountain folk accorded an ante-bellum project in socialism.[27] For example, salt, a highly prized article, was bringing as much as $2.50 per bushel before the State road was finished. Shortly after its completion the price dropped to seventy-five cents a bushel. Writing from Rome, the editor of the *Southern Recorder* assured his readers that north Georgians were grateful to Jenkins, whose statesmanship had brought them the State-owned railroad. Thus was Jenkins cast in two enviable roles in the Cherokee theater: "Father of the Georgia Platform" and "Father of the State Road." [28]

[26] Quoted from Milledgeville *Southern Recorder*, August 23, 1853.

[27] Georgians probably saw no difference in principle between a government-owned railroad and a government-owned post road or canal. Actually, there would appear to have been no difference as of 1851, which was before railroads gave promise of huge profits. Yet it is an interesting fact that Robert Toombs was decrying in 1853 the influence in American politics of "Red Republicans, Germans, and Jews." Whether Toombs thought the Western and Atlantic was "Red Republicanism," cannot be said with finality. It is assumable, however, that he did not, since his candidate for Governor was posing as the "Father of the Western and Atlantic."

[28] James Houstoun Johnston, *Western and Atlantic Railroad of the State of Georgia* (Atlanta, 1932), 8 ff.; *Acts of the General Assembly, 1836* (Milledgeville, 1837), 214–18; Ulrich B. Phillips, "A State Owned Railroad," in *Yale Review*, XV (1906), 259–82; Marietta *Advocate* quoted in Milledgeville *Federal Union*, September 20, 1853; Augusta *Chronicle and Sentinel*, August

The Jenkins offensive in Cherokee embraced still another feature. It has been observed how the Pierce administration divided the patronage between free-soilers and fire-eaters, leaving Union Democrats holding not "offices" but "principles." Generally popular in the mountain country, the Pierce administration was brought under withering fire by the biggest oratorical guns its enemies could swing into position. Robert Toombs, A. H. Stephens, and Warren Akin were particularly annoying. The national administration was generally represented by them as sound on all matters of Southern concern, except appointments. On this point it was held by the Jenkins forces to be vulnerable. In bringing it under fire they hoped to keep Union Democrats, their recent allies in the Constitutional Union party, from supporting Johnson. The Jenkins battery of spokesmen followed an adroit line. Warren Akin best summarized it at Cassville on September 15 when he explained before a Jenkins rally that while "they [the Jenkins party] disapprove of the free soil appointments of General Pierce, [they] do not array themselves against his entire administration policy." [29]

Union Democratic spokesmen were partially immobilized by the Jenkins tactics. Governor Cobb was a conspicuous victim until late in the campaign. Union Democrats simply could not answer the secession charge without drawing the fire of extreme Southern-rights Democrats. Even mild protestations against it by the *Southern Banner* and Johnson, undertaken to reassure the mountain people, were viewed with alarm by Southern rightists.[30] "I can't

17, 1853; Milledgeville *Southern Recorder* quoted *ibid.*, August 7, 1853; Milledgeville *Southern Recorder*, August 23, 1853.

[29] Warren Akin quoted in Augusta *Chronicle and Sentinel*, September 21, 1853; Milledgeville *Federal Union*, July 26, August 2, 1853; Athens *Southern Banner*, July 28, 1853; Augusta *Chronicle and Sentinel*, August 3, 21, September 14, 1853.

[30] Athens *Southern Banner*, August 18, 1853.

think," wrote John H. Lumpkin to Governor Cobb in mid-August, "that . . . any of the ultra crowd care much for Johnson's success." [31] Unabashed, Johnson and his confederates invaded Cherokee. They had some deadly weapons too. Who was Jenkins, they asked, that he should pose in north Georgia as the Unionite *ne plus ultra?* Was he not the author of the odious Alexander letter by which, on July 1, 1852, he had ordered his faithful Democratic allies in the Constitutional Union party to return to Democracy? Was the Alexander letter not the epitome of ingratitude? Had Jenkins not boasted that he was a Whig who had not been "democratized" by his associations with Union Democrats in the Constitutional Union party? Was not the current campaign really a race between "Pierce Democrats" and "Webster Whigs"? "Will Union Democrats hang on to Jenkins after he has dismissed them?" asked the Griffin *Jeffersonian* on September 8. And then, in unison, Democratic editors and stump speakers would teasingly cry out, importuning Toombs and Jenkins to label their handiwork. Of all Jenkins' woes none was more disconcerting than his nameless party. The Augusta *Constitutionalist and Republic* described his dilemma with the following metrical composition:

> Oh no, I never mention it,
>   That name is never heard;
> My lips are now forbid to speak,
>   That once familiar word.
>
> They bid me seek in change of scene,
>   The charms that others see;
> But the National Whig Party
>   Alone hath charms for me.
>
> From *Whig* to *Union* they hurry me,
>   To banish my regret;

[31] John H. Lumpkin to Howell Cobb, August 13, 1853, in Cobb MSS.

But had they loved as I have loved,
They never could forget.[32]

By mid-July it had become apparent to many Democratic leaders that Johnson's fate was in the hands of Governor Cobb. Panic-stricken Democrats rushed word to the Governor, then in New York, begging him for some sort of "demonstration" in Cherokee, where the Jenkins ground swell was reported to have reached alarming proportions. Cobb must save Johnson. The Democratic nominee, he was told, was expecting help from him. He must not fail.[33] The Governor was undeniably put in an awkward situation by this request for help. If he yielded to the urgent appeal of the Johnson managers, he would lose standing with many Union Democrats. Among them were many of his closest friends. On the other hand, failure to aid the party in its hour of distress might conceivably result in the election of Jenkins and a legislature which would do his bidding. Cobb could hardly expect such a legislature to support him if he chose to enter the fight in 1854 for the seat of United States Senator William Dawson. His good friend William Hope Hull advised against taking the stump for Johnson. Hull, it has been pointed out, had assisted the Governor with his spring campaign of *rapprochement*. Now he was advising Cobb to stand aloof. The Southern rightists were ungrateful, he warned. If Cobb were to save them with a speech in Cherokee, there was no assurance they would repay the debt by sending him to the United States Senate. Concluding, he asserted the Southern-rights crowd was

[32] This composition appeared in the Athens *Southern Banner,* July 21, 1853. See also Athens *Southern Banner,* June 30, July 14, 21, August 4, 1853; Milledgeville *Federal Union,* July 12, 19; Marietta *Advocate* quoted in Athens *Southern Banner,* September 8, 1853.

[33] H. I. [?] Tuckett to Howell Cobb, July 13, 1853; Arthur Hood to *id.,* July 18, 1853, both in Cobb MSS.

secretly anxious to drop Johnson. Why? Because he had
been too friendly with the Governor.[34]

The temptation to go out on the hustings was great,
too great, in fact, for Cobb to withstand. Despite Hull's
warning, he was on hand at Kingston, Cass County, on
September 9, prepared to deliver the *coup de grâce*. Explaining to the Democrats assembled in this small north
Georgia town that the Pierce administration deserved the
support of all Georgians, the Governor insisted he was bat-
tling for the same principles for which he and they had
fought in 1850 and 1851. The national administration, he
explained, had really assumed the true Union position.
There was but one course open to Union Democrats and
that was to return to the party of their original choice.
Concluding, the Governor warned that Jenkins was the
last man Union Democrats should support.[35]

Democrats generally appeared well pleased with Cobb's
offering at Kingston. Some of the extremists of the Southern-
rights wing were probably embarrassed. Former Governor
McDonald, the Columbus *Times and Sentinel,* and a few
others would fall in this category. On the other hand, the
Jenkins press naturally took umbrage at the behavior of
the Chief Executive. Two years before, the *Southern Recorder* had supported Cobb for Governor, but after the Kingston effort it pronounced him guilty of prostituting his
official power. Like the *Southern Recorder,* the *Chronicle
and Sentinel* had also supported Cobb in 1851. His Kingston speech provoked a blistering rebuke. "We, as Georgians," declared this journal, "feel that the escutcheon of
our noble state has been soiled, and that we have been
humbled in the dust by a *travelling* politician whose lust

[34] William Hope Hull to *id.,* August 16, 1853, in Phillips (ed.), *Correspondence,* 335.

[35] Athens *Southern Banner,* September 22, 1853; speech of Governor Cobb
quoted *ibid.*

for office is such that he will stoop to anything and any means to get it." [36] Appropriately the *Southern Banner* observed that Howell Cobb enjoyed the "distinction of having been, at some period or other, denounced by every political paper of the State." [37]

While a member of the State legislature in 1841, Jenkins had taken an active part in the passage of a law requested by some of his Augusta constituents. By this act Augusta's two-man Board of Aldermen, elected solely by those who owned property valued at $1,000 or over, was empowered to veto any action of the city council which was in any way related to raising or spending revenue. This legislation came to be known as the "Algerine" law, a derisive epithet which the followers of Rhode Island's Thomas Wilson Dorr applied to a punitive measure used in 1842 against Dorr and his reform party.[38] The Algerine law presented the Democrats with precisely the instrument they needed to prove to the wool-hat voters that Jenkins was an aristocrat, who, like the opponents of Dorr, was on the "side of power and property against the people." [39] "Apply his [Jenkins'] Algerine law to this county," wrote a Cherokee County correspondent of the *Federal Union,* ". . . and you would cut off probably three-fourths of the voters." [40] The Richmond County nominee was pictured as the "thousand dollar candidate" whose election would assure the adoption of a State-wide Algerine law. "We learn," exclaimed the *Southern Banner* in a moment of exaggeration, "that when

[36] Augusta *Chronicle and Sentinel,* September 14, 1853.

[37] Augusta *Chronicle and Sentinel,* September 21, 1853; Milledgeville *Southern Recorder* quoted *ibid.;* Athens *Southern Banner,* September 22, 1853.

[38] *Acts of the General Assembly, 1841,* 45–47; Milledgeville *Federal Union,* September 27, 1853; Augusta *Chronicle and Sentinel,* July 13, October 1, 1853; Milledgeville *Southern Recorder* quoted *ibid.,* July 13, 1853.

[39] Rome *Southerner* quoted in Augusta *Chronicle and Sentinel,* August 17, 1853.

[40] Quoted in Milledgeville *Federal Union,* August 16, 1853.

the law went into effect, they had two ballot-boxes in Augusta, one for the rich man . . . and another for the poor man. . . ." [41]

Democrats had a lot of fun with the Algerine law. The extent to which they carried their banter is illustrated by the following quip from James L. Seward, Democratic candidate for Congress in the first district: "If a man living in Augusta, at the time the Algerine law was in force, owned a Jackass, valued at one thousand dollars, he certainly could have voted. But suppose the Jackass had died the next year—the man could not have voted. Now, who voted in the first instance, the man or the Jackass?" [42] The De Kalb *Democrat* presented its readers with an Algerine arithmetic problem when it asked: "At this rate what is the fraction of a vote to which Dr. Franklin was entitled as he walked the streets of Philadelphia with his pocket stuffed with shirts and stockings, a roll of bread under his arm and one dollar in his purse?" [43]

The damaging effects of the Algerine law cannot be measured, but the *Federal Union* reported on September 13 that Jenkins cut short his stumping tour of Cherokee because of the chilly reception accorded his "aristocratic" notions. Toombs was quoted as having remarked that the "Algerine Law would beat Jenkins to h——l." [44] In spite of the widespread campaign against the measure the *Chronicle and Sentinel, Southern Recorder,* and other Jenkins journals defended it. Those who upbraided the authors and friends of the act were stigmatized as "Socialists" and "Red Republicans." Jenkins explained the law had not been designed to restrict the suffrage. It was intended, he explained, to impose a check on the city's financial administration. The

---

[41] Athens *Southern Banner,* August 11, 1853. See also Milledgeville *Federal Union,* July 26, September 6, 1853.

[42] Quoted in Milledgeville *Federal Union,* September 20, 1853.

[43] Quoted in Athens *Southern Banner,* September 8, 1853.

[44] Quoted *ibid.,* September 6, 1853.

Algerine law was not as pernicious as represented by its partisan assailants, for, as a matter of fact, it had been adopted by a Democratic legislature and approved by the Governor, who was none other than C. J. McDonald. The charges against the measure were equalled in extravagance only by the epithets manufactured by those who found themselves compelled to offer apologies for it.[45]

Except for the clash in Cherokee, the gubernatorial campaign of 1853 was a dull one. Democrats doubtless manufactured some excitement by their handling of the Algerine law. Among Jenkins followers there was some talk and more hope that Union and Southern-rights Democrats would continue their fight of the year before. However, Governor Cobb's decision to speak at Kingston shattered whatever hopes the Toombs-Stephens-Jenkins party might have entertained for continued strife within the Democratic household. In at least one respect the campaign was petty. Johnson's membership in the Swedenborgian religious sect was attacked. The *Southern Recorder* declared him anti-Christian and quoted at length from a commencement speech he had made at Wesleyan Female College to prove he was a "spirit rapper." The *Federal Union* answered the spirit-rapper charge with the clever explanation that Johnson, by nature a scientist, had indulged in the practice to inform himself on an "alleged phenomenon of physics." While there was some pettiness and a dash of humor, there was also a remarkable display of good sportsmanship. A reporter of the *Southern Banner* wrote from Cassville he "was pleased to see the kindest feeling existing between Judge Johnson and Mr. Jenkins; they are exceedingly social—travelling, eating and rooming together." [46]

---

[45] Augusta *Chronicle and Sentinel,* July 13, August 31, 1853; Milledgeville *Southern Recorder* quoted *ibid.,* July 13, 1853.

[46] Athens *Southern Banner,* September 8, 1853. See also Milledgeville *Federal Union,* July 26, August 2, 30, 1853; Macon *Journal and Messenger* quoted in Augusta *Chronicle and Sentinel,* September 14, 1853; Savannah

While the Jenkins followers did their utmost to perpetuate the Democratic schism, Democracy's high command
reciprocated by trying to keep *Tertium Quids* and Scottites
from reuniting. This they proposed to do by capitalizing
on the dissatisfaction of the Scottites. Collecting almost
three times as many votes in the late presidential race as
the *Tertium Quids,* Scottites were given little consideration
in either the selection of a gubernatorial candidate or the
preparation of a Congressional slate.[47] The Macon *Citizen*
and the Sandersville *Central Georgian,* both Scott journals,
scorched Toombs and Jenkins for deliberately proscribing
Scottites. The latter paper urged Scott men to organize and
run a "real Whig" for Governor.[48] Had anti-Jenkins Whigs
succeeded in their efforts to enlist the support of J. M.
Berrien and Senator William Dawson, they would have
created an embarrassing situation for the Toombs-Stephens-
Jenkins party. Dawson, however, wished to be re-elected
to the Senate in the fall. Therefore he could hardly afford
to fight the only Whig group which could boast an organization. Berrien, on the other hand, while a kinsman of Jenkins, remained something of an engima during the first half
of the campaign. He, too, wanted to be elected to the United
States Senate, declared the Albany *Patriot.* Consequently
he had made commitments to the Jenkins cause.[49]

Early in August the *Citizen* attempted to manufacture a
"real Whig" campaign. Expressing the opinion that thousands of Whigs would be pleased to vote for Berrien for

Georgian, September 9, 1853; Savannah *Republican* quoted *ibid.;* Milledgeville *Southern Recorder,* August 23, 1853.

[47] Milledgeville *Federal Union,* August 9, 1853.

[48] Sandersville *Central Georgian,* July 19, 1853.

[49] Quoted in Athens *Southern Banner,* August 19, 1853. According to the
Albany *Patriot* a deal had been made by which Jenkins was to get the
gubernatorial nomination and Berrien was to get support for Dawson's seat
in the Senate. Further, Berrien's son-in-law, Francis S. Bartow, was to get
the Congressional nomination in the first district.

Governor, this journal urged Scottites to cast a "complimentary" vote for the former Senator. Such action, it explained, would serve as a well-deserved rebuke to Toombs, Stephens, and Jenkins. The *Citizen's* proposal stimulated perceptible activity on the Scott front, which the eager Democratic press gleefully represented as presaging a Whig stampede away from Jenkins. Rumors were circulated that local Whig groups were on the verge of repudiating Jenkins.[50] Generally denied by the opposition press, such rumors were nevertheless cleverly exploited by Democratic editors, the *Federal Union* hopefully prophesying that these "mongrels [Toombs, Stephens, Jenkins, *et al.*] will yet be made to feel the indignation of the men they repudiated because they supported Scott." [51]

The threatened revolt of the Scottites never progressed beyond the stage of wishful thinking. On August 20, Berrien scotched it with a letter to the *Citizen* announcing that he preferred not to accept the "complimentary" vote his friends were planning for him.[52] Thereafter the Whig revolt against the Toombs-Stephens-Jenkins party amounted to no more than the vitriolic outbursts of a handful of disappointed Scottites. Most vocal among them was the Macon *Citizen*. Exasperated, it wailed that "the disaffected Scott Whigs—the justly indignant Scott Whigs—the *unjustly* 'spit upon' Scott Whigs who have any personal self respect left inside their utricles, will *let him* [Jenkins] *alone,* severely!" [53]

Despite the feeling that the contest was a dull one, a larger vote was cast in 1853 than in 1850 or 1851. Johnson

[50] Columbus *Enquirer* quoted in Milledgeville *Southern Recorder,* August 16, 1853; Milledgeville *Federal Union,* August 9, 16, 1853; Macon *Citizen* and Columbus *Enquirer* quoted in Augusta *Chronicle and Sentinel,* August 17, 1853; Macon *Citizen* quoted in Savannah *Georgian,* August 14, 1853.

[51] Milledgeville *Federal Union,* August 16, 1853.

[52] J. M. Berrien to Macon *Citizen,* August 20, 1853, quoted in Savannah *Georgian,* August 30, 1853.

[53] Quoted in Savannah *Georgian,* August 30, 1853.

pulled through with a slim majority of 510 of an approximate total vote of 95,000. The Jenkins forces blamed defeat on the Algerine law, the *Republican* complaining that it had turned between five and six thousand votes against them. The *Southern Banner* quite naturally claimed Governor Cobb's Kingston effort had repulsed the Jenkins invasion of Cherokee and saved Johnson from defeat.[54] Johnson was inclined to agree with the *Southern Banner's* appraisal, although publicly he ascribed his narrow margin of victory to the fact that hundreds of Cherokee Democrats had stayed at home on election day. They had been impressed, he asserted, by the "false charge of secession." [55] If the behavior of Senator Joseph Dunagan, "the boss of Hall county," was typical, then Governor-elect Johnson's belief that Cherokee Democrats had stayed at home on election day must be accepted as a valid explanation of his narrow margin of victory. Dr. Richard Arnold thought Johnson was "keen and devilish lucky," but "personally very unpopular." [56]

The most significant product of the campaign of 1853 was a frame of reference for the restoration of Democratic harmony. Democrats had emerged in possession of more than the governorship; they had captured six of the State's eight seats in the Congress of the United States. Of equal importance was Governor Cobb's example to those Union Democrats who still had misgivings about the Democratic party. President Pierce's plan of distributing the patronage

[54] Milledgeville *Federal Union*, November 29, 1853; Savannah *Republican* quoted in Athens *Southern Banner*, October 27, 1853; Athens *Southern Banner*, October 27, 1853.

[55] Quoted in Flippin, *Herschel V. Johnson*, 56; speech of H. V. Johnson to the citizens of Milledgeville quoted in Milledgeville *Federal Union*, October 18, 1853.

[56] Savannah *Republican* quoted in Savannah *Georgian*, October 11, 1853; Milledgeville *Federal Union*, October 18, 1853; Athens *Southern Banner*, October 13, 1853; Joseph Dunagan to Cassville *Standard*, January 28, 1854, quoted *ibid.*, February 9, 1854; Shryock (ed.), *Arnold Letters*, 78.

would seem to have been vindicated in the Empire State of the South. Governor-elect Johnson's task was to exploit the potential for party discipline which his election had done so much to accelerate. Since the architects of the Jenkins campaign were *Tertium Quids,* it may be assumed that they followed the Constitutional Union blueprint. In short, they had tried to revive the Constitutional Union party. Governor Cobb's performance scotched any hope the *Tertium Quids* might have had about reviving this party. As to Whiggery, it was dead nationally. The impotence of Georgia's Scottites (regular Whigs) eloquently testifies to this. Neither Berrien nor Dawson, Scott leaders of 1852, had dared to challenge *Tertium Quid* ascendency within Democracy's opposition. There simply existed no organization to hold Whigs together. That many individual Georgians experienced great difficulty in unwhigging themselves during the years after 1853 was superinduced by the persistence of a nostalgia rather than the existence of a party organization, either State or national.

Democratic harmony was shortly to be put to a severe test. Within a week after Johnson's election, party circles were astir with excitement over the choice of a candidate to oppose Senator William Dawson, the Whig incumbent. Again the key figure was Howell Cobb. Again he entered the fray with frightful handicaps. His decision to support Johnson's candidacy for Governor had embittered many former Union Whigs. It has been pointed out how such Union Whig journals as the *Southern Recorder* and the *Chronicle and Sentinel* reacted to Cobb's efforts in behalf of Johnson. They were not to forget easily. No sooner was the gubernatorial contest over than Governor Cobb's friends were advising him that in respect of Senator Dawson's successor, Union Whigs preferred "McDonald or *anybody*" over him.[57] At the same time, many Southern-rights

[57] R. F. Daniel to Howell Cobb, October 12, 1853, in Cobb MSS.; John T. Grant to *id.,* October 18, 1853, in Phillips (ed.), *Correspondence,* 337.

Democrats, taking their clues from Macon's *Georgia Telegraph*, acted as if they thought the real leader of Georgia Democracy was C. J. McDonald, not Howell Cobb.[58] Even a few Union Democrats were gathering around the embittered Hopkins Holsey to snub the Governor.[59] John H. Lumpkin, Cobb's Cherokee bellwether, revealed some interesting backstage play on the eve of the Democratic caucus which was to select Dawson's opponent. Writing from Rome in mid-October, Lumpkin informed the Governor he had been approached by a McDonald spokesman, who explained that neither Cobb nor McDonald was equal to the difficult task of holding together the fragile Democratic party. Of all Georgia Democrats, Lumpkin alone could perform satisfactorily as the party's leader. He must therefore make a determined bid for the Democratic nomination for Senator. His suspicions kindled, Lumpkin warned the Governor that this was a Southern-rights trick to immobilize him in the forthcoming Cobb-McDonald fight.[60] There was indeed very little in the Georgia picture to encourage Cobb. At Washington, however, things were different. There, according to Thomas D. Harris, the Governor had the blessings of President Pierce and his Secretary of War, Jefferson Davis. Both, continued Harris, expressed the hope he would be sent to the Senate.[61] Georgia's senatorial race was to be decided, however, by the Democratic caucus and the legislature, not by Pierce and Davis.

That Governor Cobb was approaching a crisis in his political career, as his friend John Milledge warned on November 1, was doubtless a fair appraisal.[62] But Cobb was used to crises. He had known little else since 1850. In fact, Cobb had averaged a major crisis every year since

[58] Greene, "Georgia Politics," *loc. cit.*, 205, 206.

[59] John B. Cobb to Howell Cobb, November 3, 1853, in Cobb MSS.

[60] John H. Lumpkin to *id.*, October 15, 1853, in Cobb MSS.

[61] Thomas D. Harris to *id.*, October 13, 1853, in Phillips (ed.), *Correspondence*, 326.

[62] John Milledge to *id.*, in Brooks (ed.), "Howell Cobb Papers," *loc. cit.*, 50.

1850. It might be reasoned that 1853 was to be different from other years, for by November Cobb had already weathered one crisis (the gubernatorial contest) and at the very time his friend Milledge was writing him, he was on the threshhold of a second. Approaching the end of his term, the Governor chose the occasion of his farewell message to dissipate any lingering doubts about his soundness on either state or Southern rights.[63] Doubtless the bold assertions of his final message were intended to throw the McDonald forces off balance and make his own bid for the nomination easier. When the Democratic caucus began its work a short time later, Southern rightists were on hand to help down Cobb. They were assisted by other groups which included the highly vocal Union Whig press and a few Union Democrats who were inspired by the turbulent Hopkins Holsey.[64] In spite of this formidable coalition the Cobb coterie plunged into the fight with reckless abandon. According to prearrangement, James Gardner, Jr., editor of the Augusta *Constitutionalist and Republic,* offered Cobb to the caucus. Gardner had been chairman of the Regular faction's executive committee in 1852. In this role, it will be recalled, he had stubbornly refused to compromise with the Cobb forces on the important matter of the electoral slate. Now he was Cobb's champion. He paid the former Governor a magnificent tribute for his recent unselfish labors in the Democratic party. Only by his nomination, pled Gardner, could Southern-rights Democrats prove the sincerity of their campaign pledges.[65]

Determined to break Howell Cobb, Southern rightists forced the nomination of C. J. McDonald on the seventh ballot.[66] Cobb's friends were bitterly disappointed by the

[63] *House Journal, 1853–54,* 8–33, for Governor Cobb's message.

[64] Milledgeville *Southern Recorder,* September 20, 1853; John B. Cobb to Howell Cobb, November 3, 1853, in Cobb MSS.

[65] Augusta *Constitutionalist and Republic* quoted in Athens *Southern Banner,* November 3, 1853.

[66] Milledgeville *Federal Union,* November 22, 1853.

action of the Democratic caucus. The behavior of the Southern-rights wing of the party was described as an act of deliberate treachery. The humiliation of the former Governor was execrated as the epitome of ingratitude. Union Democrats were now to be reduced to the status of "hewers of wood and drawers of water." [67] Cobb was urged to go to the State capital and protest against this base Democratic ingratitude. There were 20,000 vigilant Unionites in Georgia, boasted L. Q. C. Lamar, and they would be happy to have the former Governor organize them as his personal party. [68]

Cobb, however, stubbornly insisted that personal disappointment must not be permitted to disturb a precious party harmony. When invited by the friends of McDonald to address a Democratic caucus on December 19 in behalf of his successful rival, he cheerfully responded with a stirring appeal for understanding between the erstwhile estranged factions. [69] The *noblesse oblige* of former Governor Cobb won the plaudits of many who had lately denounced him as an unprincipled politician. He "has been dragged from private life," explained the Milledgeville correspondent of the *Chronicle and Sentinel*, "to which he had been consigned by the very persons now invoking his aid, to *re-unite* the Re-united and to *harmonize* the Harmonized." [70] His friend John H. Lumpkin expressed the conviction that the December 19 speech had made the former Governor the most prominent Democrat in Georgia. [71] But, like so many Union Democrats, Cobb was long on principles and short on offices.

[67] James W. Armstrong to J. B. Lamar, November 20, 1853, in Cobb MSS.

[68] *Ibid.;* L. Q. C. Lamar to Howell Cobb, December 3, 1853, in Cobb MSS.

[69] Thomas C. Howard to *id.*, December 3, 1853, in Phillips (ed.), *Correspondence,* 337; speech of Howell Cobb quoted in Milledgeville *Federal Union,* December 27, 1853.

[70] Augusta *Chronicle and Sentinel,* December 28, 1853.

[71] John H. Lumpkin to Howell Cobb, December 28, 1853, in Phillips (ed.), *Correspondence,* 338.

McDonald's difficulties were by no means ended with the action of the Democratic caucus. A combination of Whigs and Union Democrats put the upper house of the State legislature on record in favor of postponing for two years the election of a United States Senator. While the lower house refused acquiescence in this project, the behavior of the other branch of the legislature delayed the Senatorial election long enough to permit Cobb's friends to begin a frenzied campaign to get him back into the race for Dawson's seat. Hence, while the Athens leader was at Milledgeville on December 19 pleading with party leaders to give a demonstration of Democratic harmony by uniting to support McDonald, some interesting activities were taking place behind the scenes.[72]

Believing their favorite's chances were not really ended until the legislature had acted, Cobb's friends worked feverishly in his behalf throughout late November and most of December. Cobb would seem to have been unaware of this backstage play at the time of his Milledgeville plea for party harmony. Late in December, however, his friends apprised him of the deal they were trying to make. Jefferson Davis was to be replaced as Secretary of War by C. J. McDonald. Davis, who was to go to the Senate from Mississippi as part of the trade, was charged with the responsibility of inducing McDonald to throw his Southern-rights support to Cobb. The latter would then succeed McDonald as Dawson's opponent. All the elements of an excellent bargain were embraced in this proposal, which, if successful, would send Unionite Cobb to the United States Senate and Southern-rightist McDonald to the War Department.[73] That Cobb's friends were indulging in more than a mere flight of fancy is confirmed by Governor Johnson's corre-

[72] Milledgeville *Federal Union*, November 29, 1853.
[73] R. W. McCune to Howell Cobb, December 30, 1853, in Cobb MSS.; John H. Lumpkin to *id.*, January 18, 1854, in Brooks (ed.), "Howell Cobb Papers," *loc. cit.*, 148-49.

spondence with Cobb. Early in January the Governor informed Cobb of a rumor in Southern-rights circles to the effect that McDonald was soon to quit the Senatorial race. "You should be apprised of it," he concluded, "and shape matters as you would have them, if you can." [74] Lumpkin's correspondence also reveals the move that was on to send Cobb to the Senate. Writing late in December, he expressed the hope that Democratic leaders would reward the former Governor for his unselfish devotion to the party by sending him to the Senate.[75]

The anticlimactic efforts of Howell Cobb's friends to put him back into the race against Senator Dawson were ended in January when Southern-rights men dropped McDonald for Alfred Iverson of Columbus. The latter was then elected by the legislature to succeed the incumbent. Hardly a compromise selection, Senator-elect Iverson was characterized by the *Journal and Messenger* as a Southern-rights Democrat "not fierce enough for the latitude from whence he came." [76] Had the Constitutional Union legislature not elected Robert Toombs to the Senate in 1851, Southern-rights Democrats might not have put up such determined resistance against Cobb in the caucus fight of 1853–1854. Chosen two years before his term began, Toombs could not have been elected without the help of Howell Cobb, then Governor. Ironically, two years later Cobb was unable to get himself elected. The prospect of these two former Constitutional Union leaders in the Senate of the United States must have been disquieting to Southern rightists. Memories of the mischief they had

[74] H. V. Johnson to *id.*, January 10, 1854, in Brooks (ed.), "Howell Cobb Papers," *loc. cit.*, 146.

[75] John H. Lumpkin to *id.*, December 28, 1853, in Phillips (ed.), *Correspondence*, 338.

[76] Quoted in Griffin *Jeffersonian*, February 2, 1854. Senator-elect Iverson was a brother-in-law of John Forsyth, Jr., formerly the editor of the Columbus *Times*. Iverson did not take his seat in the Senate until 1855. It was customary to elect Senators two years in advance.

plotted in 1850, when they were in the House of Representatives together, were not easily forgotten. So Southern rightists were really fighting the ghost of the Constitutional
Union party in the Democratic caucus of 1853–1854. There
must be no repetition of the Cobb-Toombs-Stephens performance of 1850–1851. The best security against it was
to keep Cobb at home, or at least out of the Senate of the
United States. While the election of Iverson provided the
solution to reunited Democracy's first major family dispute,
the solution was hardly an even trade between Union and
Southern-rights factions. Southern-rights Democrats were
not yet ready to put their trust in Howell Cobb.

VII

DEMOCRATIC DRIFT

URING the three years following the Compromise of 1850, Georgians had gone to the polls annually to conclude a major political contest. Between the two gubernatorial campaigns (1851 and 1853) there had been a presidential election. These campaigns would seem to indicate the presence in Georgia, and the nation at large, of a strong feeling of conservatism underlaid by the sentiments of anxiety and uncertainty. In Georgia, as elsewhere throughout the land, there had been an overwhelming sense of the need for peace and quiet. This was the only guarantee of prosperity. Hence both State and national party leaders of the early fifties had adopted the dogma of "finality." These were the years which had brought about the collapse of Georgia's Whig party; the Democrats, however, had begun the slow and hard climb back to unity and strength.[1]

For the first time in many years Georgia had no State-wide election in 1854. As a result Democrats were given a chance to consolidate their recent gains. Since the Whig party had fallen apart at the seams, Democracy's opponents were to cut out the pattern for a new party in 1854. Labeled Know-Nothing, this new party suddenly posed a threat to Democratic supremacy. And finally, this was the year Stephen A. Douglas, Democratic Senator from Illinois, re-opened the slavery struggle with his Kansas-Nebraska Bill.

Immediately after Johnson's election, Democratic editors began a campaign to bring former Whigs into the Dem-

---

[1] Craven, *Coming of the Civil War*, 325; Arthur M. Schlesinger, "Tides of American Politics," *Yale Review*, XXIV (1939), 217–30.

ocratic party by urging all Georgians to support President
Pierce. By this plan the South was to achieve unity within
a party organization whose Northern segment was to keep
that section divided. In short, the South was to avail itself
of the advantages of a sectional party within a national
party controlled by Southerners. Here was a blueprint for
the protection of Southern rights by immobilizing potential Northern opposition. The editors of the *Federal Union*
and the *Southern Banner* kept up a steady plea for this plan
throughout 1854 in the face of frenzied efforts by Know-
Nothings to salvage the wreck that had once been the proud
Whig party. Generally both journals betrayed only the most
meager signs of optimism about the success of their plan.
As a matter of fact, there was often a note of pessimism, as,
for example, when the *Federal Union* gloomily predicted
on July 4 that former Georgia Whigs would oppose the
Democratic party in 1856 regardless of the presidential
nominee.

Old-line Whig editors generally admitted reunion with
Northern Whigs was not feasible. Further, both the *Southern Recorder* and the *Chronicle and Sentinel* acknowledged
the merits of the Democratic plan to protect Southern
rights. Two objections were generally raised against the
plan, however. In the first place, Northern Democrats were
not all sound on Southern rights. Too many of them were
free-soilers; and besides President Pierce had rewarded
many of these arrogant free-soil Democrats with Federal
offices. Southern support of such an administration was
preposterous, went the argument. Only those "truly National and Conservative men, whether they hail from the
North, South, East or West" deserved Southern Whig support, declared the *Chronicle and Sentinel*.[2] This was substantially the position of A. H. Stephens. Like most Democratic editors, he insisted on a national party. Unlike many

[2] Augusta *Chronicle and Sentinel*, August 30, 1854.

Democrats, however, Stephens, a consistent believer in the great dogma of the Union, did not want either "sectional men or sectional issues." He did want a party based on what he called "national issues and national principles." His part in putting the Kansas-Nebraska Bill through the House would warrant the belief that he considered this measure a specific procedure within the general framework of national issues and national principles.[3] The second objection to the plan advanced by the *Federal Union* and the *Southern Banner* was that it would reward only Democrats. They alone would get the offices. This was too much for many traditional Whigs, who favored the principle of Southern unity but were unwilling to pay the price of surrendering to Democrats control over the patronage.[4] In despair the *Federal Union* editorialized late in 1854 that "while the North is rallying for the battle, we are up to our ears in a petty dispute as to whether some minor Post Office at the North . . . is filled by a man who has not, some time in his past life, advocated Free Soil sentiments." "The most that southern men ask or expect of the North," reasoned the *Federal Union,* "is an observance of the constitution, and the compact with slavery solemnly entered into by the framers of that great instrument." To ask more, continued this journal, would be to say to the North that "you *shall* believe as *we* do about slavery, or we will cut loose from you." [5]

The campaign for Southern unity fell far short of its goal. Despite the advantages that would normally accrue from the absence of an election campaign plus the unifying effect

[3] A. H. Stephens to W. W. Burwell, June 26, 1854, in Phillips (ed.), *Correspondence,* 346.

[4] Milledgeville *Federal Union,* March 28, July 4, 11, 18, October 3, 24, 31, November 14, 21, 1854; Athens *Southern Banner,* June 15, 22, July 20, August 24, September 28, October 12, 1854; Augusta *Chronicle and Sentinel,* August 30, October 18, 1854; Milledgeville *Southern Recorder,* July 18, September 19, 1854.

[5] Milledgeville *Federal Union,* October 31, 1854.

of the sectional exchanges over the Kansas-Nebraska Bill, Georgians were not seriously considering a cessation of partisan politics. An analysis of the election returns of 1855 would warrant the conclusion that sometime after 1853 a strong Democratic trend got under way. By the end of 1855 Cherokee Democrats, long estranged from the mother party, were back in the fold. Moreover, many influential Whigs, including Robert Toombs and A. H. Stephens, had decided to unwhig themselves completely by joining the opposition. That the Democratic party gained some noteworthy adherents during 1854 cannot be denied. To say that Georgians were about to adopt a one-party system betrays a misunderstanding of the spirit of the age.

The late forties and early fifties had brought a heavy stream of immigration to the United States. Among the newcomers were many Irish Catholics and German liberals. The former settled down in the seaboard cities, where they promptly displayed an aptitude for rough and tumble politics. Many of the latter drifted into the old Northwest. Unlike the Germans who came to Pennsylvania in the eighteenth century, these nineteenth-century emigrants from central Europe were afire with a zeal for reform. Both groups quickly attracted attention. In fact, the impact of their arrival produced a hostile demonstration by the nativist Protestants who believed the American way of life was endangered. Popularly known as the Know-Nothing party, this new organization adopted the battle cry, "Americans must rule America"; its leading maxim became, "No papacy in the Republic." [6]

Georgia's political horizon first revealed the dim outline of Sam, as Know-Nothings were called, in June, 1853. Sam was presented to Georgians by Robert Toombs on June 22 at the gubernatorial convention which nominated Charles

[6] Carl Russell Fish, *Rise of the Common Man* (New York, 1927), 115; Carl Wittke, *We Who Built America* (New York, 1940), 482–97; Binkley, *American Political Parties*, 187–89.

J. Jenkins. Hoping to pump a little enthusiasm into a list-less gathering, Toombs singled out foreigners for several rounds of abusive epithets. The Pierce administration, he thundered, was an adjunct of *"German Jews, Red Repub-licans, and Infidel Scotch."* [7] Among the "foreigners" re-warded with Federal appointments was Pierre Soulé, a temperamental French emigrant, who was given the prom-inent post of minister to Spain. Taking their clue from Toombs, traditional Whig journals railed against Demo-crats and "foreigners" during the Johnson-Jenkins cam-paign. Carrying a letter over the signature "Examiner," the *Chronicle and Sentinel* rapped President Pierce's knuckles for "discriminating in favor of foreigners" in dispensing Federal patronage. Augusta's *Constitutionalist and Repub-lic* charged Toombs with authorship of the Examiner effort, while the *Georgian* printed the item at least twice, doubt-less to keep Savannah's Irish voters properly indoctrinated. Thus had Toombs prepared the way for Sam. He was hardly a stranger when the Macon *Journal and Messenger* announced in the spring of 1854 that a new party was shortly to be launched. The new organization was to be independent of old parties, continued the Macon paper. The *Federal Union* chided its colleague by reflecting that the proposed addition to the State's political family was to be some sort of a "Do-Nothing Party." [8]

Consistent with its notion of secrecy, the Know-Nothing party swept through Georgia during the summer and fall of 1854. With no place to go, former Whigs took the secret vows with reckless abandon. Searching for exits from frus-tration, many curious Democrats also joined this esoteric order. With secret dens springing up like mushrooms, Dem-

[7] Speech of Robert Toombs quoted in Milledgeville *Federal Union*, August 2, 1853; Milledgeville *Federal Union*, August 16, 1853.

[8] Savannah *Georgian*, September 30, 1853; Macon *Journal and Messenger* quoted in Milledgeville *Federal Union*, June 6, 1854; Milledgeville *Federal Union*, June 6, 1854.

ocratic editors sought to check Know-Nothing raids on their party's membership by charging that Sam had been spawned in the foul womb of Whiggery. The *Federal Union* charged in September that " . . . the Know-Nothings have managed to put the Whigs in office in most of the large cities, and this fact has encouraged the old Whig leaders, to look for higher game, through the great power of a secret society." Concluding, it challenged, ". . . come on with your new *alias,* gentlemen . . . then up with your new head, and whether it be Know-Nothing, Know Something, or something else, we are ready for you." [9] Later this Democratic organ insisted Whigs were "playing 'possum," but just before election the "old coon" would turn up "with perhaps a stripe or two extra around his tail, on the Know-Nothing order." [10] "Stay away from the secret dens of Sam," went the Democratic warning. This strange order, alleged Democrats, was made up principally of abolitionists who had sent Sam southward to "bore from within." [11]

Late in 1854 Howell Cobb expressed the opinion that Know-Nothings might succeed in taking over the decadent Whig party.[12] While many former Whigs objected to the secrecy and antiforeign pronouncements of the new party, there was a disposition among many of them to view the mysterious order as a possible source of relief from the threat of indefinite Democratic rule. Both the *Southern Recorder* and the *Chronicle and Sentinel* denied they were riding the "blind hobby" of the Know-Nothings.[13] Among former Whig journals the Athens *Southern Watchman* and the Macon *Citizen* were the first to declare unequivocally

[9] Milledgeville *Federal Union,* September 5, 1854.

[10] *Ibid.,* December 10, 1854.

[11] *Ibid.;* Griffin *Jeffersonian,* July 27, 1854.

[12] Howell Cobb to James Buchanan, December 5, 1854, in Phillips (ed.), *Correspondence,* 348–49.

[13] Augusta *Chronicle and Sentinel,* September 6, 1854; Milledgeville *Southern Recorder,* October 31, 1854.

in favor of Sam. The former exploded into the Know-Nothing camp early in 1855 with the blast that "God [must] protect this happy country from such *liberty* as these foreign Red Republicans or their American coadjutors and sympathizers would give it!" [14] The Union Whig press was inclined throughout 1854 and during the early months of 1855 to oscillate between neutral ground, on the one hand, and defense of Sam against Democratic editors, on the other.[15] Mindful of the *Tertium Quid* venture, former Whigs, despondent from repeated failures, were studying Sam carefully. The moment he demonstrated his mettle, many of them would arrange to adopt him.

On January 23, 1854, Stephen A. Douglas introduced in the Senate a measure for the organization of the territories of Kansas and Nebraska. All questions relating to slavery in these territories and the new states to be formed from them were "left to the people residing therein." [16] Attached to the bill was a section repealing the Missouri Compromise of 1820, which in principle, it was explained, had been repealed by the Compromise of 1850. The "object" of the Douglas measure "was neither to legislate slavery in nor out of the territories," but simply to "apply the doctrine of Congressional non-intervention." [17] In the lower house the Douglas bill was entrusted to William A. Richardson and A. H. Stephens, the latter exclaiming on May 22 when the act was adopted that: "The great struggle is over, Nebraska has passed the House." [18] Like Stephens, Robert Toombs

[14] Athens *Southern Watchman*, February 1, 1855. John H. Christy, editor of this journal, had edited the Athens *Southern Whig*.

[15] Savannah *Republican* quoted in Milledgeville *Federal Union*, January 20, 1855; Augusta *Chronicle and Sentinel*, October 11, 1854, February 21, 1855; Milledgeville *Southern Recorder*, October 17, 1854, February 21, 1855.

[16] *Cong. Globe*, 33 Cong., 1 Sess., Pt. I, 175, 221–22.

[17] *Cong. Globe*, 33 Cong., 1 Sess., Pt. I, 239–40. See also Albert J. Beveridge, *Abraham Lincoln, 1809–1858* (New York, 1928), II, 206; Craven, *Coming of the Civil War*, 325, 328; Milton, *The Eve of Conflict*, 126.

[18] Quoted in Milton, *The Eve of Conflict*, 143. See also Rudolph Von Abele, *Alexander H. Stephens* (New York, 1946), 141–45, and Richard M.

supported the Kansas-Nebraska Bill. In defending it on the Senate floor, he insisted the bill did not establish "squatter sovereignty," but rather provided for "popular sovereignty." The distinction was noteworthy. Squatter sovereignty permitted action on slavery in territorial days, while popular sovereignty held that such action came only with statehood.[19]

The real purpose of the Kansas-Nebraska Bill was the development of the Northwest. Its author, Stephen A. Douglas, believed the future of this region depended on railroads. After he moved to Chicago (1847) he became increasingly active as a railroad politician. Other railroad politicians began to threaten Douglas in the early fifties. One group was working for a transcontinental road with St. Louis as the eastern terminal, while farther south, Jefferson Davis, now Secretary of War, was promoting a Southern route. Douglas produced his Kansas-Nebraska Bill for the purpose of heading off his rivals and acquiring for Chicago the eastern terminal of the proposed transcontinental railroad. That he was content to permit the people to decide their domestic issues was good Western as well as New England doctrine. The bill was a logical answer to the demands of railroad politics. It was certainly not of Southern origin and, except for the explicit repeal of the Missouri Compromise, which would appear to have been a purely verbal triumph, realistic Southerners expected little gain from its passage.[20]

Two events promptly obscured the real purpose of the

Johnson and William H. Browne, *Life of Alexander H. Stephens* (Philadelphia, 1884), 277, for accounts of Stephens' part in the passage of the Kansas-Nebraska Bill.

[19] Augusta *Chronicle and Sentinel*, March 22, 1854; Horace Montgomery, "A Georgia Precedent for the Freeport Question," in *Journal of Southern History*, X (1944), 202.

[20] Craven, *Coming of the Civil War*, 326–32; Binkley, *American Political Parties*, 191.

Kansas-Nebraska Bill. Immediately after it was presented, the administration announced through its organ, the Washington *Union,* that support of the bill would be expected of all party members. Pierce had thus thrown the aura of partisanship about the bill. The day after Douglas introduced his measure the *National Era* printed the *Appeal of the Independent Democrats in Congress to the People of the United States.* A masterpiece of political adroitness, it rang all the changes on the anxieties of the Northwest. Douglas was represented as the tool of the power-mad slavocracy. He was determined to wreck the fondest hopes of the Northwest. Homesteads and railroads were about to be frozen out by the hated slave power. The *Appeal* was the swan song of a substantial group of Northern Democrats. Many of them had once followed Andrew Jackson. Now they looked to Salmon P. Chase, Ohio Democrat and author of the *Appeal.* He was unchaining an emotional drive unparalleled in American history. In this atmosphere there was no room for compromise. Excited men became willing to believe the worst about each other. Their impetuosity produced an intense sectionalism which underlaid a new party design. In this new design the sectional Republican party quickly became the prevailing motif. Combatting "Black Republicanism" naturally dulled the sharp edge of traditional Southern partisanship.[21]

Georgia's editors promptly endorsed the Kansas-Nebraska Bill. That it was conceived in the spirit of finality was the consensus of editorial opinion. While the debate raged in Congress many Georgia editors argued that the Douglas bill was consistent with the Georgia Platform. Others gave the impression they would be relieved by the repeal of the pernicious Missouri Compromise. In keeping with this ed-

[21] "The political shrewdness of the *Appeal* was matched only by its dishonesty," says Professor Craven on page 327. See also Beveridge, *Abraham Lincoln,* II, 184–85, 210; Schlesinger, *The Age of Jackson,* 477; Binkley, *American Political Parties,* 192–94.

itorial spirit, the legislature adopted resolutions reaffirming Georgia's faith in the settlement of 1850 and commending Douglas for his statesmanship. A. H. Stephens' half-brother, Linton, was active in putting pro-Douglas and pro-Pierce resolutions through the State Senate.[22]

Traditional Whigs scrutinized the Kansas-Nebraska Bill carefully. They were looking for flaws and their search was not entirely in vain. Had Douglas, they asked, hitched his measure to squatter sovereignty? (Squatter sovereignty would have empowered the territory to decide the slavery question.) While Congress was debating the bill, both the *Southern Recorder* and the *Chronicle and Sentinel* concluded he had not, the latter jubilantly citing Toombs's support of the measure as indisputable proof of its freedom from this hated doctrine.[23] Since many supporters of the Kansas-Nebraska Bill were to claim that they had been tricked, it is well to note these two purposeful journals believed at the time the measure was adopted that it was not tainted with squatter sovereignty. Still another objection to the bill was raised. Deploring the failure of Congress to restrict the elective franchise to natural-born and naturalized citizens, the *Southern Recorder* complained the Kansas-Nebraska Bill put a severe handicap on Southern institutions in the territories by permitting unsympathetic foreigners to vote.[24] While minor, nevertheless this complaint symbolized the sort of hysterical antipathy for foreigners which the nativist brand of American conservatism has tended to

[22] Milledgeville *Federal Union*, January 10, February 14, 21, May 30, 1854; Athens *Southern Banner*, January 26, February 2, 1854; Augusta *Chronicle and Sentinel*, February 8, 28, March 7, 22, 1854; Milledgeville *Southern Recorder*, February 28, March 7, May 23, 1854; Macon *Journal and Messenger* quoted in Milledgeville *Federal Union*, February 21, 1854; LaGrange *Reporter* quoted in Milledgeville *Southern Recorder*, May 23, 1854.

[23] Milledgeville *Southern Recorder*, March 21, 1854; Augusta *Chronicle and Sentinel*, March 22, 1854.

[24] Milledgeville *Southern Recorder*, May 30, 1854.

foster. This was the atmosphere which produced the comic
opera that was the Know-Nothing party.

If Georgia editors expected the Kansas-Nebraska Bill to
open new fields to slavery, they betrayed no such optimism
while the measure was before Congress. If, on the other
hand, editorial opinion accurately reflected popular feeling, then it must be concluded that Georgians generally
believed the Douglas measure to be one of wisdom. Party
lines tended to crumble in this atmosphere. Late in February the Union Whig *Southern Recorder* prophesied that
" . . . the South is likely to be almost, if not quite, a unit"
in supporting the Kansas-Nebraska Bill.[25] The principles of
the bill were sacred Union objectives, continued this journal. In conclusion it warned they must not be permitted to
hatch under a "secession" wing.[26] "But thanks to fortune,"
exclaimed the *Federal Union* a month later, "the South
is now united." [27] It was natural for Democratic editors to
exploit the Kansas-Nebraska Bill for partisan advantage.
They rejoiced at the support which former Whigs gave
the measure. This, contended enthusiastic Democrats,
amounted to a vindication of the Pierce administration.
Toombs, the Stephens brothers, and all Whigs who believed
in the principles of the Douglas measure were urged to join
the Democratic party. A fusion of these "Spartan" Whigs,
as they were called, with Southern Democrats and "sound"
Northern Democrats (Doughfaces) would create a coalition
which would secure Southern rights.[28] That Georgia Democracy profited from the Kansas-Nebraska Bill is assumable from the reflections of the *Southern Recorder*, a leading opposition journal. In midsummer it commended the
Democrats for "their almost unanimous support of the

[25] *Ibid.*, February 28, 1854.

[26] *Ibid.*, February 21, 28, 1854.

[27] Milledgeville *Federal Union*, March 21, 1854.

[28] *Ibid.*, March 7, 14, 28, April 18, May 23, 1854; Athens *Southern Banner*,
March 9, June 1, 1854.

Nebraska bill . . . ." Concluding, the editor boasted that ". . . Democrats have given an earnest of the sincerity of their acquiescence in, and even cordial support of, the compromise of 1850." [29] In mid-September the same journal announced it was ready for a fusion of the several political factions of the South.[30] The *Chronicle and Sentinel*, another traditional Democratic foe, had editorialized a few weeks earlier that while unity was desirable, it could be realized only on a truly "National and Conservative" ideology.[31] Since the early forties the national Democratic party had been progressively acquiring such a point of view. Where could Georgia's traditional conservatives of the former Whig variety find a more zealous guardian of their point of view than the Democratic party? Spartan Whigs took a realistic view and promptly joined the Democracy. However, many former Whigs could not cast aside the prejudices of a lifetime. Hence it is not strange that many Brahmins of Whiggery were willing to grasp the hand of that indiscreet character called Sam and follow him into Know-Nothing dens, where something was supposed to happen which would deliver the land, and the offices, from the Democrats.

29 Milledgeville *Southern Recorder,* June 27, 1854.
30 *Ibid.,* September 19, 1854.
31 Augusta *Chronicle and Sentinel,* August 30, 1854.

VIII

SAM CHALLENGES

A STRONGER Democratic party and the conviction that Sam offered the only practical means of checking this party constituted Georgia's chief gains from the emotional coloration of 1854. The following year was to be one of intense political activity in the South's Empire State. Scarcely had the new year begun when both the Democrats and Sam were challenged by a third party composed of the opponents of strong drink. Anxious to get the gubernatorial contest under way, eighty temperance delegates met in Atlanta on February 22. Declaring for repeal of the State's liquor-license system, they nominated Basil H. Overby for Governor on a Temperance ticket. The candidate was described by the *Federal Union* as a blend of Methodist preacher and lawyer whose political convictions were rooted in Southern-rights Whiggism and Know-Nothingism.[1]

The *Southern Banner* insisted Overby's nomination was another of versatile Whiggery's tricks.[2] This belief was strengthened when, less than a month after the Atlanta Temperance gathering, the *Southern Recorder* announced that "should our party fail to present a candidate opposed to 'grog-shops and crime,' and not in favor of 'wives and children,' we hereby and hereon pledge ourselves to go for Mr. Overby."[3] Grasping the Temperance movement with

[1] Milledgeville *Southern Recorder*, February 20, 1855; Milledgeville *Federal Union*, February 6, 27, March 6, 1855. See also Allen P. Tankersley, "Basil Hallam Overby, Champion of Prohibition in Ante-Bellum Georgia," in *Georgia Historical Quarterly*, XXXI (1947), 1–18.

[2] Athens *Southern Banner*, March 1, 1855.

[3] Milledgeville *Southern Recorder*, March 13, 1855.

one hand and frantically reaching for the shadowy figure
of Sam with the other, many old-line Whigs were desper-
ately trying to unwhig themselves short of joining the
Democratic party. Others swallowed their pride and
marched into the party they had recently opposed. The
behavior of Augusta's *Chronicle and Sentinel* reflected the
feelings which many traditional Whigs must have experienced in the spring of 1855. Gratified by the manner in
which Sam routed Democrats in the March New Orleans
city election, this journal proclaimed Sam's feat as the "most
complete and overwhelming victory over the democracy of
that city, who have scarcely ever before tasted defeat." [4] A
week later the *Chronicle and Sentinel* really had something
to boast about. Sam had come to Augusta to engage the
Democrats in a municipal contest. Electing eleven of the
city's twelve councilmen and winning the mayoral race by
a margin of two to one, Sam had finally demonstrated how
the more obstinate Whigs might continue the exciting game
of baiting Democrats. From this moment Overby's campaign was doomed to utter failure. Politically, its value was
to be that of a nuisance. [5]

As the time for the nominating conventions approached,
party leaders focused their attention on the Spartan twins,
A. H. Stephens and Robert Toombs. Both had acted with
the Democratic Pierce administration a year earlier on the
Kansas-Nebraska Bill. Neither had much standing among
old-line Whig colleagues in Washington. On the other
hand, the *Chronicle and Sentinel,* long the spokesman of
the Spartan twins, was tilting its lance in the direction of
Democrats. When the *Georgia Telegraph* (Democratic)
announced early in April that Toombs and Stephens were

[4] Augusta *Chronicle and Sentinel,* April 4, 1855.

[5] Savannah *Republican* quoted in Augusta *Chronicle and Sentinel,* April
18, 1855; Milledgeville *Southern Recorder,* April 24, 1855; Augusta *Chronicle
and Sentinel,* April 11, May 2, 1855; Augusta *Constitutionalist* quoted in
Milledgeville *Federal Union,* April 17, 1855.

opposed to the Know-Nothings, the *Chronicle and Sentinel* promptly countered with the explanation that while neither held membership in Sam's fraternity, both were nevertheless in complete accord with Know-Nothing principles.[6] Democratic journals promptly cited the *Chronicle and Sentinel's* performance to support the contention that Whiggery, prolific in new names and disguises, was temporarily screened behind its latest creation in buffoonery. Both Toombs and Stephens were scorched by outraged Democratic editors.[7] Regretting the abuse heaped on the Spartan twins for their alleged comradeship with Sam and convinced that neither was really a Know-Nothing at heart, the *Southern Banner* urged both of them to join the Democratic party.[8]

Early in May it was rumored Stephens was soon to declare against Sam. He was displeased with Sam's abolitionist proclivities, it was averred.[9] On May 9 "Little Aleck" started a chain reaction in Georgia politics by announcing in a letter to his friend Thomas W. Thomas that Know-Nothing ideology was antithetical to the precepts of the Founding Fathers. Although he was careful not to declare in favor of the Democratic party, he explained at length why he could not follow Sam.[10] Exactly one week after it had been written, the *Chronicle and Sentinel* published the Thomas letter. The editor appraised it as a "calm and dispassionate" review of the situation.[11] On the following day the *Southern Watchman* warned Stephens not to "be betrayed into the folly of running a tilt against 'Sam.' "[12]

[6] Quoted in Milledgeville *Federal Union*, April 17, 1855.
[7] Leading Democratic journals quoted in Athens *Southern Banner*, April 26, 1855.
[8] *Ibid.*   [9] Milledgeville *Federal Union*, May 1, 8, 1855.
[10] A. H. Stephens to Thomas W. Thomas quoted in Milledgeville *Federal Union*, May 15, 1855; Johnson and Browne, *Life of Alexander H. Stephens*, 294–96.
[11] Augusta *Chronicle and Sentinel*, May 16, 1855.
[12] Athens *Southern Watchman*, May 17, 1855.

A week later the *Southern Recorder* began an editorial on the Thomas letter with the proverb "Whom the Gods would destroy they first make mad." After completing a critical examination of the letter, the editor concluded his effort with an unequivocal declaration in behalf of Sam.[13] Not all traditional Whig journals shared the opinion of the *Southern Recorder* and the *Southern Watchman*. Despite a disposition to co-operate with Sam, both the *Journal and Messenger* and the *Republican* warned that failure to return Stephens to Congress would be disastrous to Southern interests.[14]

While the Thomas letter forced a number of traditional Whig journals to declare for Sam, it was also to serve as the signal for Stephens' Whig friends to let loose a series of broadsides against the secret Know-Nothing party. In Griffin they assembled shortly after their idol's pronouncement to adopt resolutions denying that Stephens had deserted Whig doctrine. These Griffin Whigs invited Democrats to join them in their effort to re-elect Little Aleck. Henry County Whigs ratified the stand Stephens had taken in the Thomas letter, and were subsequently urged by the *Federal Union* to join all "freemen" of whatever political faith in the crusade against the "dark lantern society." In Paulding County anti-Know-Nothing Whigs were reported as favoring immediate fusion with Democrats.[15]

Stephens followed his letter to Judge Thomas with a number of appearances in northeast Georgia. On May 28 he spoke to a crowd estimated at 2,000 from the steps of Augusta's city hall. After announcing his candidacy for re-election to Congress as an "Independent," he treated his

---

[13] Milledgeville *Southern Recorder,* May 22, 1855.

[14] Savannah *Republican* quoted in Augusta *Chronicle and Sentinel,* May 30, 1855; Macon *Journal and Messenger* quoted in Louis Pendleton, *Alexander Stephens* (Philadelphia, 1908), 144.

[15] Griffin *Empire State* quoted in Milledgeville *Federal Union,* May 22, 1855; Milledgeville *Federal Union,* May 26, 1855.

audience with an exposé of the Know-Nothing order.[16] At
an Oglethorpe County meeting the Athens *Southern Watchman* quoted Stephens as having declared that he had always
enjoyed the distinction of being on the right side of every
political issue. This was too much for editor John H.
Christy. Such a claim to infallibility, he scolded, amounted
to trespassing on the realm of Pope Pius IX. Little Aleck
would shortly be the recipient of a "bull with the longest
and sharpest horns," execrated Christy.[17]

Despite his antiforeign injunctions to the gubernatorial
convention of 1853, Robert Toombs was disposed to follow the course of action prescribed by his close friend
Stephens. While not a candidate, he had nevertheless been
at Augusta on August 28 where he echoed Little Aleck's
sentiments. A week later he wrote Tenant Lomax, editor
of the Democratic Columbus *Times and Sentinel,* setting
forth his reasons for refusing to act with Sam. Sam was an
insidious influence, explained Toombs. He had come to
the South for the specific purpose of keeping Southerners
divided. True sons of the Southland would abhor him like
a pestilence, concluded the Senator.[18]

Meanwhile Georgia Know-Nothings were busy setting
up their organization, drafting their liturgy, and populariz-
ing their dogma. More zealous at baiting foreigners than
most of its colleagues, the *Southern Watchman* published
an interesting version of the Know-Nothing initiation cere-
mony. While the editor may have leaned too far in the
direction of buffoonery, yet his account doubtless illustrates
something of the spirit of Know-Nothing liturgy and dogma.
". . . after he [the neophyte] has sworn to observe them

[16] Augusta *Constitutionalist* quoted *ibid.,* June 5, 1855; Johnson and
Browne, *Life of Alexander H. Stephens,* 294–96.

[17] Athens *Southern Watchman,* June 7, 1855.

[18] Augusta *Constitutionalist* quoted in Milledgeville *Federal Union,* June
5, 1855; Robert Toombs to Tenant Lomax, June 6, 1855, quoted *ibid.,* June
19, 1855; Augusta *Chronicle and Sentinel,* June 20, 27, 1855.

[Know-Nothing dogmas]," explained the *Southern Watchman,* "he is compelled to run a splinter—previously taken from a liberty pole—into the index finger of his left hand, and with the splinter and his own blood, he signs the Constitution and By Laws of the Order. Physicians on being admitted into the Order, are compelled to take an additional oath, to the effect that they will mistake strychnine for calomel in administering medicine to Dutch and Irish Catholics. Lawyers have to swear that they will abandon the habit of *lying* and *deception* in dealing with native born American clients. *Many Lawyers have left* the Order." [19]

On May 1 and 2 Georgia Know-Nothings held their first organization meeting. Three hundred robust agents of Sam assembled in a secret convention at Macon. They were reported to have made arrangements for local and district gatherings which were to nominate candidates for the bench, the legislature, and Congress. It was further reported that no action was taken, however, with respect to the forthcoming gubernatorial contest. Defending the meeting as one of "sobriety and intelligence," the *Southern Recorder* quoted a proslave resolution as evidence that the new party was not in league with abolitionists.[20] Democratic spokesmen denied that the convention had adopted a proslave resolution, the *Southern Banner* blistering the Know-Nothing party as a "monstrous abortion, lately dropped from the womb of Massachusetts abolitionism . . . warring against our institutions under the specious but delusive cry, that 'Americans shall rule America.' " [21] To the charge that the gathering was nine-tenths Whig, the *Southern Recorder* retorted that two of the State's lead-

19 Athens *Southern Watchman,* March 29, 1855.
20 Milledgeville *Southern Recorder,* May 8, 1855.
21 Athens *Southern Banner,* May 17, 1855.

ing Democrats, Howell Cobb and James Gardner, Jr., had attended.[22]

In mid-June Judge Francis H. Cone headed a delegation of Know-Nothings to the party's national council meeting in Philadelphia. As a foremost member of the pro-Southern committee on resolutions, the Georgia jurist was instrumental in getting the council to adopt the "twelfth resolution," the embodiment of the Southern viewpoint on slavery. Cone and his Georgia colleagues took the handiwork of the Philadelphia meeting to Macon on June 27 where the second Know-Nothing convention had gathered for a two-day session. Exhilarated by the opportunity to endorse the twelfth resolution, the convention nominated Garnett Andrews for Governor despite alleged pledges by some party leaders to forego a nomination. Sam's standard bearer was described by the Savannah *Journal and Courier* as having been a Unionite in 1850–1851 and a Tugaloite in 1852. The convention also adopted resolutions announcing the party's faith in the Georgia Platform, condemning Pierce's Kansas policy and approving the Kansas-Nebraska Bill, except the section enfranchising foreigners.[23] The Andrews nomination was a bitter disappointment to extreme Southern rightists. They had hoped to end partisan strife in Georgia and had actually proposed a plan toward that end. Know-Nothings were expected to co-operate by foregoing a nomination for Governor. Precisely what pledges their leaders had given the Southern Union Movement, as the Southern-rights project was now called, is uncertain. It was alleged, however, that Know-Nothing

[22] Milledgeville *Federal Union*, May 8, June 12, 1855; Milledgeville *Southern Recorder*, May 8, 1855.

[23] Athens *Southern Banner*, June 21, July 12, 1855; Athens *Southern Watchman*, June 21, July 5, 1855; Augusta *Chronicle and Sentinel*, July 4, 1855; Atlanta *Intelligencer* quoted in Milledgeville *Federal Union*, July 10, 1855; Savannah *Journal and Courier*, June 29, July 6, 1855.

leaders had agreed to a postponement of action on the gubernatorial fight.[24]

Meanwhile the Democratic party was preparing for the gubernatorial fight. Meeting in Milledgeville on June 5, the State convention renominated Governor Johnson on the first ballot. The delegates reaffirmed their party's faith in the Georgia Platform, emphasizing especially the resistance section. Northern Democrats who had fought for the enforcement of the fugitive-slave law and the passage of the Kansas-Nebraska Bill were commended. Homeless Whigs were invited to join the crusade against Sam's medieval notions. Both former Governor Cobb and Governor Johnson spoke to the convention. Cobb condemned the abolitionist agents in Kansas who by this time had made "Bleeding Kansas" a symbol which the newly organized Republican party was cleverly exploiting. The former Governor also offered a resolution favoring retaliatory legislation against those states which by their personal-liberty laws had successfully nullified the fugitive-slave law. The delegates adopted Cobb's resolutions. Democrats were now ready for the campaign of 1855.[25]

While Democrats, Know-Nothings, and Temperance leaders were disposing of the preliminaries to the gubernatorial fight of 1855, a group of Southern rightists launched an all-Southern movement. It has already been observed that the plea for Southern unity was frequently sounded during the debate over the Kansas-Nebraska Bill. It was repeated again and again in early 1855, the Atlanta *Intelligencer* and the Savannah *Republican* both strongly urging in May that Georgians cease their partisan quarrels

[24] Columbus *Corner Stone* quoted in Milledgeville *Federal Union,* July 10, 1855.

[25] Milledgeville *Federal Union,* June 12, 1855; speech of Howell Cobb quoted *ibid.;* Craven, *Coming of the Civil War,* 361.

before it was too late.[26] In response to this plea for unity a group of Southern rightists met in Temperance Hall, Columbus, on May 26 to consider a plan of action. Their labors brought forth the Southern Union Movement. It was largely the handiwork of James N. Bethune, editor of the Columbus *Corner Stone,* the only journal in Georgia whose agenda included a frank declaration in favor of secession. Georgia was to present a united front against those who would menace Southern rights. There must be a severance of the "entangling alliances" with Northern groups preparatory to a fusion of Georgia factions into an all-Southern party. Like Calhoun and the Southern Rights party of 1850–1851, the Southern Unionists insisted the ills of the South were hatched under the wing of intraparty bargains. Southern rights were thus on the perennial auction block of political expediency where they were consistently knocked down to the highest bidder.[27]

Editorial response to the Southern Union Movement presents an interesting study in semantics. Those journals which in 1850–1851 had supported the first Georgia drive for Southern unity scorched the Columbus declaration. To them the Southern Union Movement threatened to crack the Democratic machine, the bulwark of Southern rights. On the other hand, the Know-Nothing press was inclined to encourage these Southern Unionists, if for no other reason than to embarrass the Democrats. Most of these journals had rebuked the Southern Rights party in 1850–1851 for attempting precisely what the Temperance Hall group hoped to achieve.[28]

[26] Editorials quoted in Athens *Southern Watchman,* May 10, 1855, and Augusta *Chronicle and Sentinel,* May 30, 1855.

[27] Report of meeting quoted in Athens *Southern Watchman,* June 7, 1855. For a brief account of the Southern Union Movement, see Horace Montgomery, "The Solid South Movement of 1855," in *Georgia Historical Quarterly,* XXVI (1942), 101–12.

[28] Augusta *Chronicle and Sentinel,* May 30, June 20, 27, 1855; Milledgeville *Southern Recorder,* June 12, 1855.

The triumvirate's reaction to Georgia's second drive for Southern unity offers a glaring contrast to its behavior of five years earlier. Within a week after the Temperance Hall meeting, former Governor Cobb addressed himself to the Southern Union Movement. Southern unity, he agreed, was desirable. However, it must not be undertaken at the cost of scuttling the national Democratic party, which, he insisted, was the real defender of Southern rights. Cobb had now expressed the point of view of his party's high command. By doing so he had sounded the death knell of the Southern Union Movement.[29] The *Southern Recorder* complained that the former Governor's desire for national honors had compelled him to bind to the South this "body of death," as it characterized the national Democracy.[30] Both Robert Toombs and A. H. Stephens, the other members of the famous triumvirate, were inclined to avoid the Southern Union Movement, although the former in a letter to Tenant Lomax of the Columbus *Times and Sentinel* would seem to have favored more unity among Southerners. However, Toombs had been impressed by the manner in which many Northern Democrats (Doughfaces) had stood by the South during the fight over the Kansas-Nebraska Bill. To him the national Democratic party offered the only hope of defense against the South's enemies. Stephens, on the other hand, was a political maverick throughout the campaign of 1855. Avoiding Democrats, Know-Nothings, Temperance men and Southern Unionists, he reflected that he had his "own canoe to paddle, and every man in this campaign must 'tote his own skillet.' "[31]

29 Howell Cobb to Columbus Movement Committee, June 1, 1855, quoted in Athens *Southern Banner*, June 7, 1855.

30 Milledgeville *Southern Recorder*, June 12, 1855.

31 Macon *Journal and Messenger* quoted in Augusta *Chronicle and Sentinel*, June 20, 1855; Augusta *Chronicle and Sentinel*, June 20, 27, 1855; Milledgeville *Federal Union*, June 19, 1855; A. H. Stephens to W. W. Burwell,

A few days before the Democratic State convention met on June 5, John H. Howard, a Southern Union spokesman, addressed himself to Governor Johnson. In a letter to the Governor he urged the State's Chief Executive to declare in favor of a suspension of party lines and to appeal to Georgians for unity in the face of Northern aggression. Howard petitioned the Governor to call a State convention for the purpose of announcing the end of party warfare. The entangling alliances with Northern abolitionists must be dissolved, argued Howard. Assuring the Governor that Know-Nothings and homeless Whigs were anxious to co-operate in this all-Southern project, the Southern Union spokesman expressed the opinion that Johnson's acquiescence would guarantee him a second term. The issue of Southern unity was thus squarely put up to Governor Johnson. Renominated by the Democrats on June 5, Johnson disposed of the Howard plea three days later in his letter of acceptance. Following the Cobb line, the Governor explained that the Pierce program of alliances, not sectional unity, was the South's safest course. A race between North and South for sectional unity would result from the Southern Union Movement, declared Johnson. Clinching his argument, he showed that the South would lose such a race because the census returns were against her. In conclusion Johnson scorched the Know-Nothings for inspiring the Southern Union Movement.[32]

June 26, 1854, in Phillips (ed.), *Correspondence,* 346; James Gardner to Howell Cobb, June 12, 1855, in Brooks (ed.), "Howell Cobb Papers," *loc. cit.,* 154–55; speeches of A. H. Stephens at Augusta and Sparta, quoted in Milledgeville *Federal Union,* June 5, 17, 26, 1855; Johnson and Browne, *Life of Alexander H. Stephens,* 294–96; Robert Toombs to Tenant Lomax, June 6, 1855, quoted in Milledgeville *Federal Union,* June 19, 1855.

[32] John H. Howard to Governor Johnson, June 1, 1855, quoted in Milledgeville *Federal Union,* June 26, 1855; Governor Johnson's letter of acceptance quoted *ibid.,* June 12, 1855; Governor Johnson to John H. Howard quoted *ibid.,* June 26, 1855; Milledgeville *Federal Union,* June 12, 19, 26, 1855.

On June 16, which was about three weeks after their first meeting, the Southern Unionists met again in Columbus. Having failed in their effort to get Governor Johnson's support, they adopted a resolution requesting the Know-Nothings, who were scheduled to hold a State convention on June 27–28, to refrain from making a nomination for Governor. Grigsby E. Thomas delivered a spirited address declaring the Southern Union Movement was designed "to unite the South, *the whole South,* upon the great issues touching the existence of slavery in the territories. . . ." [33]

With the fate of the Southern Union Movement in their hands Know-Nothing delegates assembled in Macon on June 27 for their State convention. Torn between rival concepts of party discipline (Southern Unionism and entangling alliances), the delegates left no doubt as to their preference. They blithely nominated Garnett Andrews, who in 1850–1851 had marched away to battle in the army of Cobb, Stephens, Toombs, and Jenkins. He had aimed many thrusts at the heart of the first drive for Southern unity. Exasperated, the *Corner Stone* bitterly reflected that the Know-Nothing convention had chosen a "little union saver." "To nominate at all was unwise," editorialized Bethune; "to nominate Andrews was ridiculous." [34]

Those who were not sure what the Macon delegates had done when they nominated Andrews were orientated on July 16 by the candidate's letter of acceptance. Asserting that most Northern Democrats were unsound on the subject of Southern rights, he announced that Know-Nothing leaders had finally discovered the secret of building a truly national party. He assured Georgians that Northern Know-Nothings had at last renounced their antislavery disposition in return for Southern support of the party's antiforeign

[33] Report of meeting quoted in Augusta *Chronicle and Sentinel,* June 20, 27, 1855.

[34] Columbus *Corner Stone* quoted in Savannah *Journal and Courier,* July 6, 1855, and Milledgeville *Federal Union,* July 10, 1855.

program. Here was the familiar pattern of entangling alliances shrouded in the eerie cloak of Sam. As in 1850–1851 it suffocated the drive for Southern unity. Thus ended Georgia's second all-Southern attempt. Ironically the third attempt was to succeed in 1861 because the North had elected Abraham Lincoln to the presidency as the spokesman of the all-Northern Republican party.[35]

With the preparatory phase of the gubernatorial contest over and with the Southern Union Movement abandoned, Georgians were ready by mid-July to begin a steady diet of campaign arguments served from the stump and on the printed page. Three candidates were to assure a modicum of variety. However, since Overby's campaign was further weakened by the renomination of Johnson, one of the State's foremost temperance men, and since on the question of slavery there was general agreement among all contestants, the race resolved itself into a bitter personal feud between the Governor and Andrews, the Know-Nothing candidate. Since its thole was religion, the campaign was to be short on decorum and long on personal animus.[36]

"Let 'Americans rule America,'" entreated Garnett Andrews in his letter of acceptance on July 16, "and tried Georgia platform men rule Georgia."[37] These adroitly joined phrases were the epitome of the incantations of the American party, as Know-Nothings were now calling themselves. To the Democratic charge that the American party was really "un-American," Sam's apologists retorted that the Democracy was indubitably "anti-American." Thus "un-Americans" were vying with "anti-Americans."[38] By

[35] Garnett Andrews' letter of acceptance quoted in Augusta *Chronicle and Sentinel*, July 25, 1855.

[36] Milledgeville *Federal Union*, July 17, 1855; Augusta *Chronicle and Sentinel*, July 25, 1855; Tankersley, "Basil Hallam Overby," *loc. cit.*, 12.

[37] Milledgeville *Federal Union*, July 17, 31, 1855; Augusta *Chronicle and Sentinel*, July 25, 1855.

[38] Athens *Southern Banner*, June 28, 1855; Milledgeville *Southern Recorder*, August 14, 1855.

mid-September the American party had abandoned its secrecy, although Andrews was quoted as favoring its reten-
tion.[39] Throughout the campaign, religious bigotry and
personal animus transcended all other considerations. The
Governor and the triumvirate were the most popular tar-
gets of the American press. The *Southern Watchman* called
A. H. Stephens the "Pope's Nuncio," while a *Chronicle and
Sentinel* correspondent boasted that he could prove Little
Aleck was a "Polygamist in principle." [40] Toombs called the
editor of the *Chronicle and Sentinel* a "liar," the journalist
retorting that the Senator had said "he believed Herschel
V. Johnson a damn low down scoundrel, and that he would
vote for him if he knew he had stolen all the money out of
the Treasury of the State, or had caught him stealing a
sheep out of his pen." [41] Toombs countered through the
columns of the Democratic *Constitutionalist and Republic*
by explaining he could not continue the altercation because of the editor's "long and fathomless infamy." [42] The
latter concluded these bitter exchanges with the following
vitriolic blast: "This comes with admirable grace from a
man who, for fifteen years, has courted our friendship, and
during that whole period, has never omitted a convenient
opportunity to seek our companionship! Poltroonery could
not attain a lower depth." [43]

Running for Congress, former Governor Cobb was announced in the columns of the *Southern Watchman* as
"Don Lopez Howell, Bedini of the Sixth District,"
candidate of the "Foreign, Sag-Nichts-Erin-go-unum-E-
Pluribus-bragh" league.[44] The *Southern Recorder* gave vent

[39] Speech of Andrews at Augusta quoted in Milledgeville *Federal Union*,
August 28, 1855; Augusta *Chronicle and Sentinel*, September 19, 1855.

[40] Athens *Southern Watchman*, August 2, 1855; Augusta *Chronicle and
Sentinel*, September 26, 1855.

[41] Augusta *Chronicle and Sentinel*, October 3, 1855.

[42] Quoted *ibid*. [43] *Ibid*.

[44] Athens *Southern Watchman*, September 20, 27, 1855.

to its spleen with the following characterizations of the
Governor: "We believe that the spirit and temper of Herschel V. Johnson is better suited to the reign of terror and
the times of Robespierre, than the spirit of the present
age." In conclusion the Governor was accused of ferreting
out "with the keen scent of a Popish inquisition" every
man who was suspected of supporting the American cause
"and bringing him to the confessional and guillotine without pity or compunction." [45] In a moment of exasperation,
the *Federal Union* cried out with "we defy you to stand
before the looking glass, and repeat the whole Know-
Nothing ritual, and go through the Know-Nothing manual
exercise, without laughing in your own face." [46]

Aided by such erudite men of letters as Augustus B. Longstreet, Democratic spokesmen persistently charged Americans with advocating the practice of religious proscription.
To this the *Southern Recorder* responded with the explanation that since the Constitution was silent on the subject
of applying a religious test "to a candidate before the
people," a person or party could set up such religious re-
quirements as were desired.[47]

Georgians were spared the excesses which Sam's campaign of intolerance and bigotry produced in Louisville,
Kentucky. On Monday, August 6, there occurred in that
city an election riot. Having lost in North Carolina, Alabama, Tennessee and Texas, Sam was determined not to
let Kentucky slip through his fingers. In desperation he
sought to prevent the inevitable. The result was "Bloody
Monday," described by the Louisville *Times* as follows:
"The scenes on Monday were appalling beyond anything
yet witnessed in this Union. They were not exceeded by

---

[45] Milledgeville *Southern Recorder*, September 11, 1855.

[46] Milledgeville *Federal Union*, August 21, 1855.

[47] Milledgeville *Southern Recorder*, August 7, 1855. See also *ibid.*, September 4, 1855; Milledgeville *Federal Union*, September 4, 11, 18, 1855; John
D. Wade, *Augustus Baldwin Longstreet* (New York, 1924), 305–309.

the Jacobins of France under the most ferocious political tyrants. The city was for eighteen hours in the hands of a mob. The unfortunate Quinn . . . after he was shot, was thrown yet quivering and alive into the flames. . . ." [48] A correspondent of the *Federal Union* reported that twenty-five or thirty were killed and thousands of dollars worth of property destroyed.[49] The American party press dismissed "Bloody Monday" with the declaration that the rioting had been precipitated by the murderous hirelings of the Pope, the *Chronicle and Sentinel* explaining the incident proved the need for tightening up the naturalization laws.[50] Shortly after Louisville's "Bloody Monday" affair Garnett Andrews was quoted as having opened a speech before an Oglethorpe County rally with the remark that he was glad "to see so few foreigners in the audience." Their presence, he continued, might produce "riot and bloodshed." [51]

The campaign of 1855 impinged on slavery at a single point. Seeking to defend immigrants, Democratic editors asserted with some frequency that New England "fanatics" were opposed to foreigners, because they would not join in the "unholy crusade against the institutions of the Southern States, and the rights of the Southern people." [52] "Through Know Nothingism," warned the *Southern Banner*, "the Abolitionists of the North have offered the South the apple of discord." [53] Andrews enthusiasts, on the other hand, insisted the foreigner was behind the abolitionist movement. Therefore the immigrant was at the bottom of

[48] Quoted in Milledgeville *Federal Union,* September 25, 1844.
[49] *Ibid.*
[50] Athens *Southern Watchman,* August 16, 1855; Augusta *Chronicle and Sentinel,* August 15, 21, 1855; Milledgeville *Southern Recorder,* August 28, 1855.
[51] Quoted in Milledgeville *Federal Union,* September 18, 1855.
[52] *Ibid.,* July 24, August 7, 1855.
[53] Athens *Southern Banner,* September 27, 1855.

the great evil of sectional discord.[54] That over 90 per cent of the immigrants were free-soilers or abolitionists was the considered judgment of the *Chronicle and Sentinel*.[55] Created to ameliorate this condition, the American party proposed to fight for more stringent immigration laws and at the same time to prevent a recurrence of such foolish concessions to foreigners as those of the Kansas-Nebraska Bill. The section of this bill which enfranchised a foreigner on the strength of a mere declaration of his intention to become a citizen was inimical to Southern welfare. No true Southerner could subscribe to this folly, insisted Judge Eugenius A. Nisbet, one of the American party's most astute spokesmen. Nisbet's critique of the Kansas-Nebraska Bill set the style to which American party organs adhered in defending themselves against the charge that by objecting to this bill they were hurting the South's cause in the territories.[56]

Approximately six weeks before election day (October 1) the Democratic high command began a campaign which probably damaged Sam's morale. Lured into the secret fraternity from sheer curiosity, many former Whigs and Democrats quit the order in response to the Democratic invitation to do so. The *Federal Union* published the names of scores of these withdrawals. It also printed letters which many of these former colleagues of Sam addressed to the editor. A John W. Bassett of Houston forwarded the following impressions: "It [American party] is said by some to be a Whig trick and by others to be a Democratic trick, but I think it is a Yankee trick and that both Whigs and

[54] Milledgeville *Southern Recorder,* August 21, 1855.
[55] Augusta *Chronicle and Sentinel,* September 26, 1855.
[56] E. A. Nisbet to Milledgeville *Federal Union,* September 4, 1855; Milledgeville *Southern Recorder,* September 11, 1855; Macon *Journal and Messenger* quoted in Augusta *Chronicle and Sentinel,* September 26, 1855; Savannah *Republican* quoted in Milledgeville *Federal Union,* September 18, 1855.

Democrats have been caught by it." [57] Playing up the importance of these withdrawals, the *Federal Union* asserted two weeks before election day that American party leaders were "frightened at the numbers that are daily withdrawing, [and] have resolved to close their lodges, and thereby keep others from withdrawing." [58] Those who were still debating whether to break with Sam were advised on the election's eve by the State's leading Democratic paper to mail their resignations to the local council and "come out at once." [59]

None had worked harder to establish the enviable position accorded the Democratic party by the voters of 1855 than Governor Johnson. Winning by a vote of 54,476 to 43,750 for Andrews and 6,261 for Overby, Johnson now commanded a robust Democracy. Four years earlier he had started his party on the road which was to lead to this decisive triumph. A key figure in the bitter contests of 1852 and 1853, the Governor had replaced his latitudinarian viewpoint of 1850 with a national outlook. Encouraged by Spartan Whig support of the Kansas-Nebraska Bill in 1854 and the refusal of many Whigs to follow Sam, Johnson had come to believe that the hope of the South lay in a strong national Democratic party. By supporting the Kansas-Nebraska Bill when that measure was before Congress, the Spartan Whigs had made common cause with the national Democracy. The next year the "Anties" (Anti-Know-Nothing Whigs) also made common cause with the Democrats. Before the campaign of 1855 was over Charles J. Jenkins and "probably twenty thousand Whigs in Georgia locked shields with the Democrats to defeat it [Know-Nothing party]. . . ." [60] Sensing the drift of the Anties,

[57] Quoted in Milledgeville *Federal Union,* September 11, 1855.
[58] *Ibid.,* September 18, 1855.
[59] *Ibid.*
[60] James D. Waddell, *Biographical Sketch of Linton Stephens, containing a selection of his Letters, Speeches, State Papers, etc.* (Atlanta, 1877), 116.

Democratic leaders commended them by acclaiming their
"magnificent spirit" and "high intelligence." Hence Governor Johnson's stinging rebuke to J. N. Bethune and John
H. Howard for suggesting that an all-Southern party was
a normal reaction. The Democratic victory in the Congressional races was just as smashing as Johnson's triumph.
Counting A. H. Stephens' victory, the Anti-Know-Nothing–
Democratic fusionists captured six of the State's eight seats
in the lower house. Included in the new Congressional
delegation were Democrats John H. Lumpkin and Howell
Cobb, the latter winning in the sixth district by a two-to-
one majority. The Democrats also carried the legislative
fight by a substantial margin. "We have now," boasted the
Georgia Telegraph, "the strongest party, in point of intel-
lect, position and patriotism which has ever been known
in Georgia." [61] At no time since its organization was the
Democratic party so completely in charge of the State's
affairs.[62]

Though decisively defeated in the elections of 1855, the
American party showed up well in the big cities. Only Savannah failed Sam. Augusta, Milledgeville, Macon, Columbus, Griffin, Athens, and Atlanta turned in substantial
pluralities for American candidates. The *Federal Union*
charged the poor Democratic showing in these cities to the
presence there of a "spirit of abolitionism" and "prejudices
against German and Jewish merchants." [63]

American party organs were prompt with explanations
for their party's failure to stop Johnson. "Poor and ignorant
men," lamented the *Southern Watchman,* "whose hearts

[61] Quoted in Milledgeville *Southern Recorder,* November 20, 1855.

[62] Official returns of the election of 1855 quoted in Milledgeville *Federal Union,* October 16, 1855; speech of A. H. Stephens at Sparta, Georgia, quoted *ibid.,* July 17, 1855; Savannah *Georgian* quoted *ibid.,* October 23, 1855; Milledgeville *Federal Union,* July 24, August 14, September 11, October 16, November 20, 1855; Coulter, *Georgia,* 248; Phillips, *Georgia and State Rights,* 143–50.

[63] Milledgeville *Federal Union,* October 16, 1855.

throbbed for America and her sons, after being brutalized with liquor, were BRIBED to vote the Foreign ticket!" [64] Later the same journal wailed that Democrats won because of an unfortunate combination of "ignorance, foreigners, spoilsmen, and 'Little Aleck' since he 'went crazy.' " [65] Two other American journals, the *Chronicle and Sentinel* and the *Southern Recorder,* agreed that Sam's failure to capture more of the Whig vote had been fatal, the latter journal hopefully prophesying a quick ending to the honeymoon of Anties and Democrats in the scramble over spoils.[66]

A few weeks after the election of 1855 the *Federal Union's* astute editor recorded some pointed reflections on the state of the Union. In an editorial on "The duty and policy of the Democratic Party," he reasoned that the recent election returns proved Georgia was "an independent State, and not bound to obey the mandates of a Grand Council of the Know Nothings." Continuing, he emphasized that the "glorious victory over bigotry and intolerance was won by a happy fusion of the sensible man of both old parties." Concluding, he counseled newly chosen legislators to "remember that they were elected by the patriotic [voters] of both the old parties and [to] act accordingly." A week later the editor returned with a terse summary of what he considered the mutual obligations of both North and South. "In asking justice of the North," he began, "we must not expect or ask of Northern statesmen, that they should imbibe our sentiments, or our feelings on the subject of slavery." Explaining that such expectancy was unreasonable, he succinctly announced the North's obligation at an end when "they shall be willing to give us those rights which the constitution guarantees us; this we have a right

[64] Athens *Southern Watchman,* October 4, 1855.

[65] *Ibid.,* October 11, 1855.

[66] Augusta *Chronicle and Sentinel,* October 24, 1855; Milledgeville *Southern Recorder,* November 20, 1855.

to demand of them, and they have no right to refuse." [67]

Governor Johnson lost no time in making plans for cementing the fusion of Anties and Democrats. Two weeks after his re-election he wrote Howell Cobb requesting the latter to urge both A. H. Stephens and Robert Toombs to be on hand early in November for the opening of the legislature. None were better fitted than the Spartan twins, thought the Governor, for the task of helping with the formal induction of the Anties into the Democracy. Estranged from Stephens for some time, Johnson hoped Cobb would be able to put both Stephens and Toombs to work in the interest of the Democratic party. Little Aleck arrived early and on November 6 delivered a speech in the House chamber in which he upbraided the American party. While he did not openly announce his intention of becoming a Democrat, there was no other place for him to go. When the Anti-Know-Nothing–Democratic fusionists held their first caucus on November 8, the Spartan twins and many other former Whigs were on hand. Georgia's prince of political peace, former Governor Howell Cobb, was called to the chair. A. H. Stephens, his brother Linton, and Robert Toombs were assigned to the resolutions committee. Fulfilling the fondest hopes of Johnson and Cobb, Toombs chose this occasion to declare his views. The struggle in Congress over the Kansas-Nebraska Bill had convinced him, he explained, that the South's fate rested with the national Democratic party. He promised never again to fight Democrats and argued against prefixing the old party name with "Anti-Know-Nothing," as some were proposing. Completely unwhigged, Senator Toombs was not the type to conceal his new faith. The stage had been especially prepared for his explosive oratory. On to it he had rushed, thundering his "Democratization." His performance must have been supremely gratifying to

[67] Milledgeville *Federal Union*, October 16, 23, 1855.

Governor Johnson and Howell Cobb, the architects of the new Democracy.[68]

Reassured by the presence of so many prominent old-line Whigs, the caucus of November 8 drafted some blistering resolutions. The Union, it announced, was secondary to the "rights and principles it was designed to perpetuate." This verbalism suggests Georgians had discovered the aphorism that once "rights and principles" are provided with an institution, they often become lost in the tall weeds of procedures. The caucus also turned the "resistance resolution" of the Georgia Platform on the Kansas question with a sharply worded warning that rejection of the pro-slave Kansas constitution would be sufficient provocation for the disruption of the Union. This declaration was suggested by what Governor Johnson had said a few days earlier in his message to the legislature. "I there[fore] recommend you to provide by law," said the Governor, "for the calling of a State Convention, in the event of the rejection of Kansas, 'because of the existence of slavery therein [the constitution],' to deliberate upon and determine the time and mode of the resistance contemplated by the 4th resolution of the Convention of 1850." [69] Acting through her Governor and her majority party, Georgia had accepted the Republican party's challenge to keep slavery out of the territories. For the first time, the slavery issue was reduced to a comparatively simple verbalism. For this the Republican party was responsible. Conceived in an atmosphere of Calvinism and mid-nineteenth-century liberalism, this party was neatly laced with morality, the concept of "right" and "wrong," or "good" and "evil." By threatening the Union the Democratic caucus of November 8 was saying in effect that Georgia's neck was galled by

68 H. V. Johnson to Howell Cobb, October 15, 1855, in Cobb MSS.; Milledgeville *Federal Union*, November 13, 1855; speeches of A. H. Stephens and Robert Toombs quoted *ibid.*

69 Quoted *ibid.*, November 6, 1855.

the yoke of the conviction of "sin"—"sin" as understood
by crusading Republicans. Flushed with victory, Governor
Johnson and his party were rebelling against an artificially
imposed inferiority.[70]

With an eye to the presidential election of 1856 the
caucus prescribed three planks for the national Democratic
party platform. Failure to adopt them would cost the nominee the support of Georgia Democrats. They were an
unequivocal declaration in favor of the Kansas-Nebraska
Bill, a pledge to fight the Republican party's effort to restrict the extension of slavery, and, finally, a promise to
carry out the fugitive-slave law. When the *Southern Recorder* (American) reflected a few days after the caucus of
November 8 that it saw no reason "why the whole South
may not present a *unit* in the great Presidential struggle
of 1856," it was suggested for the first time that there might
possibly exist in Georgia an emotionalism strong enough
to sustain an anti-Union drive of dangerous proportions.[71]
The temptation is great to overemphasize the significance
of such events as the Democratic caucus of November 8.
It would be utterly erroneous to assert that henceforth
Georgians were in agreement on all matters pertaining to
public policy. One can say only that the fall of 1855 produced a perceptible restlessness among Georgians. As already pointed out, this display was provoked by the Republican party's effort to define sin as that which was not
Republican.

The *Southern Recorder's* reflections on the Democratic
caucus of November 8 were doubtless encouraging to Democrats. American party leaders, however, had no intention
of disbanding. After all Garnett Andrews had polled over
43,000 votes in the recent gubernatorial race. Moreover,

[70] Proceedings of the resolutions committee of the Democratic caucus
quoted in Milledgeville *Federal Union*, November 13, 1855.

[71] November 13, 1855. See also Milledgeville *Federal Union*, November 20,
1855.

the party had captured two seats in Congress, electing Robert P. Trippe and Nathaniel G. Foster. Further, Benjamin H. Hill had lost his Congressional fight by a mere sixty-eight votes. And finally, the party had piled up impressive pluralities in all the cities except Savannah. If there were any who believed the American party was to disband, they were suddenly disillusioned early in December when both Trippe and Foster came out against the Democratic candidate for Speaker. He was W. A. Richardson, who with A. H. Stephens had guided the Kansas-Nebraska Bill through the House. Instead of supporting Richardson, Georgia's two American representatives stuck to Henry M. Fuller, a Pennsylvanian who had been sent to Congress on an anti-Nebraska pledge, until the Democrats withdrew Richardson for James L. Orr of South Carolina, who in turn gave way to another South Carolinian, William Aiken. Meanwhile the Republicans put Nathaniel P. Banks into the coveted office and Georgia's Americans had trouble denying they had not helped with the act.[72]

Among American party journals none was more devoted to the party than the *Chronicle and Sentinel*. Urging Anties to quit the Democracy, this journal requested them to hold themselves in readiness for service in a revived American party. The task of reviving the American party was begun on November 9 when party leaders held a caucus at the State capital. With F. H. Cone, author of the proslave twelfth resolution, in the chair, the caucus declared the party an open organization and then proceeded to call a State convention for December 19–20.[73] According to prearrangement, one hundred and fifty delegates met on the evening of December 19 in Milledgeville. They listened to stirring appeals by Benjamin H. Hill and F. H. Cone.

[72] *Ibid.*, November 13, December 18, 1855, January 22, 1856; official returns for the election of 1855 quoted *ibid.*, October 16, 1855; *Cong. Globe*, 34 Cong., 1 and 2 Sess., Pt. I, 342.

[73] Proceedings quoted in Athens *Southern Watchman*, November 22, 1855.

On the following day the convention called the venerable Berrien to the chair. Resolutions were then adopted repudiating squatter sovereignty, glorifying the Georgia Platform and urging more stringent naturalization and election laws. After naming delegates to the party's national conclave the convention adjourned without making a concrete suggestion for treating slavery in the territories.[74]

The *Chronicle and Sentinel* thought the convention should have committed the party to a stronger antiforeign program, while the *Federal Union* thought the Kansas-Nebraska Bill had been given a "sideswipe" by a platform of "unmeaning generalities, or palpable contradictions." The deposition of Cone and elevation of Berrien was alleged to have been a scheme to set Georgia Americans right with the Northern wing of their party. The inertia of partisan politics was still powerful enough in 1855 to compel Georgia's Americans to adhere to the traditional pattern of entangling alliances. As long as this was so, Georgia would pose no very serious threat to the Union despite the behavior of the Republican party.[75]

[74] Proceedings quoted in Augusta *Chronicle and Sentinel,* December 26, 1855.

[75] *Ibid.;* Milledgeville *Federal Union,* December 25, 1855; John W. Duncan to Howell Cobb, December 21, 1855, in Cobb MSS.

IX

DOUGHFACE VICTORY

IF Georgians had wanted to concentrate on local matters during the fifties, they would have found it almost impossible to do so. Hence gubernatorial and other political contests were waged in the shadow of the slavery question. Once the Republican party had succeeded in making the question of slavery extension the slavery issue, Georgians suddenly realized the jagged juxtaposition of "sin." It has been observed how in November, 1855, vexed by the inexorable demands of morality, Governor Johnson and his party struck back by insisting upon fair play in Kansas. A few weeks later when the Thirty-fourth Congress began balloting for a Speaker, Georgians betrayed considerable anxiety. Approximately seventy-five Democrats stubbornly refused to desert their party's choice for Speaker. He was W. A. Richardson of Illinois. A friend of Stephen A. Douglas, Richardson had distinguished himself by his astute handling of the Kansas-Nebraska Bill in the Thirty-third Congress. One hundred Republicans steadfastly supported N. P. Banks, a Massachusetts free-soiler, while thirty-odd Americans tenaciously clung to H. M. Fuller, a Pennsylvanian who had been sent to Congress as an opponent of the Kansas-Nebraska Bill.[1]

Georgia's Congressional delegation split over the choice of a Speaker. The two Americans, N. G. Foster and R. P. Trippe, supported Fuller, while the remainder of the delegation stuck to Richardson. The State's journalists were similarly divided. Democratic editors bitterly assailed Fos-

[1] Milledgeville *Federal Union*, January 1, 22, 1856; *Cong. Globe*, 34 Cong., 1 and 2 Sess., Pt. I, 3 ff.

ter and Trippe, the *Federal Union* wailing that both would
have been repudiated had they announced during the campaign their intention of supporting for Speaker an opponent of the Kansas-Nebraska Bill.[2] Foster was a favorite
target for Democratic editors because of his outspoken
criticism of the Kansas-Nebraska Bill on the floor of Congress. In his maiden speech he bitterly castigated the "forty-
four doughfaces" (Northern Democrats) who had helped
put the Douglas measure through Congress. "The man you
sent to Congress to represent the interests of the South,"
complained the *Federal Union* in an editorial addressed to
Foster's constituents, "in his first speech on the floor of
Congress, made such an attack upon those Northern men
who voted for the Nebraska bill, as to call forth the praise
and commendation of Horace Greely [*sic*]." [3] What Greeley,
the high priest of the abolitionists, said about Foster did not
lose him the support of Georgia's American press. The
Southern Watchman, the Savannah *Republican* and the
Southern Recorder commended both American representatives, the latter journal scoffing at an administration which
was too weak to control the selection of a Speaker. Consistently opposed to that section of the Kansas-Nebraska
Bill which enfranchised foreigners (squatter suffrage),
Americans now added the charge that the bill provided
for squatter sovereignty rather than popular sovereignty,
which, of course, meant that the question of slavery could
be solved before statehood.[4]

Despite approval by a majority of the American press,
not all Georgia Americans were happy about the behavior

[2] Milledgeville *Federal Union,* January 8, 1856.

[3] Howell Cobb to his wife, February 2, 1856, in Phillips (ed.), *Correspondence,* 359; Milledgeville *Federal Union,* January 8, 15, 1856. See *Cong. Globe,*
34 Cong., 1 and 2 Sess., Pt. I, 68–69, for Foster's remarks.

[4] Athens *Southern Watchman,* January 10, 1856; Savannah *Republican*
quoted in Milledgeville *Federal Union,* January 22, 1856; Milledgeville
Southern Recorder, January 21, 1856, February 5, 1856.

of Foster and Trippe. Among the more apprehensive was State Senator F. H. Cone, the number-one party worker until his deposition on December 20. Early in January he called on his associates in the Senate to unite with the Democrats. Overwhelmed with a sense of urgency, Cone declared the hopes of the South would be dashed unless Republicanism was stopped. Americans and Democrats must forget their differences and unite at once. Soon it would be too late, he warned. As a gesture of sincerity, he eulogized President Pierce for the pro-Southern quality of his message to the Thirty-fourth Congress.[5] Georgia's Americans in Congress accepted Cone's counsel, but not until the Democrats had shelved Richardson for J. L. Orr of South Carolina. Orr withdrew in favor of William Aiken, another South Carolinian, who, despite Southern American support, lost to Banks by a half-dozen votes on February 2. In deserting Fuller for Aiken, Georgia's Americans demonstrated the wisdom of Senator Cone's appeal. However, they had waited too long, and, in the words of the *Federal Union,* "Fuller let Banks play 'leap frog' over his shoulders into the Speaker's chair. . . ." [6]

The election of a Republican Speaker was the signal for Democratic strategists to launch a drive for the purpose of heading off an American party nomination in the forthcoming presidential campaign. According to administration spokesmen the issue was now between free-soil Republicanism and the Democracy. There was no place, they argued, for the American party. When the *Organ,* the American party journal at the nation's capital, characterized Banks as an "American in the political sense," South-

5 Milledgeville *Federal Union,* January 22, 1856; *Senate Journal,* 1855–1856, 261.

6 Milledgeville *Federal Union,* April 8, 1856. See also *ibid.,* January 22, February 12, 1856; Milledgeville *Southern Recorder,* February 12, 1856; *Senate Journal,* 1855–1856, 261; *Cong. Globe,* 34 Cong., 1 and 2 Sess., Pt. I, 343; Richardson, *Messages and Papers of the Presidents,* V, 327–50.

ern Americans were promptly urged to join the Democratic party and even up the Republican absorption of North Americans. The success of this strategy was to be tested in the forthcoming presidential contest. It should be noted that two days after the election of Banks, A. H. Stephens announced that henceforth he would act with the Democratic party. Also, while the fight over Banks had shaken the faith of Cone, Foster, Trippe, and many other Americans in the soundness of their party, yet this was the occasion which produced the squatter sovereignty argument against the Kansas-Nebraska Bill. Americans were to employ this argument frequently during the coming months.[7]

With the speakership battle raging in the nation's capital, Georgia Democrats assembled in Milledgeville on January 15 for their second conclave since Governor Johnson's re-election. The delegates began where their colleagues of November 8 had left off. The mood of the gathering was reflected by H. M. Jeter, chairman of the resolutions committee, when he remarked that Georgia "has taken the lead in Southern resistance to the crusade of Northern fanaticism." In both North and South, concluded Jeter, Georgia's "leadership in this important and trying crisis" is acknowledged.[8] Sensing a precarious national situation, the convention invited the opposition to join in a concerted effort to sustain the rights of the South in Kansas. Those Congressmen who were then standing by Richardson were generously commended for their defense of the Southern cause. Convention leaders were careful to make those who lately had unwhigged themselves comfortable. Hence Linton Stephens' proviso to the resolution declaring for President Pierce's renomination was adopted. It read as follows:

[7] Augusta *Constitutionalist*, February 13, 1856; Milledgeville *Federal Union*, January 15, February 13, 1856.

[8] Quoted in Milledgeville *Federal Union*, January 22, 1856.

"Provided, He shall stand pledged to carry out the principles of our Platform in his administration and in his appointments to office." [9] Old-line Democrats who had consistently defended Pierce must have winced with the adoption of Stephens' addendum. It is apparent that there was developing within Georgia Democracy a highly competitive contest to make that party a veritable Southern fortress. The contestants were old-line Whigs and old-line Democrats. By vying with each other they were henceforth resolutely to advance Georgia Democracy toward the fateful decision to secede. The convention adjourned after naming delegates to the party's national convention, scheduled to meet in Cincinnati on June 2, and fixing July 4 as the occasion for the quadrennial ratification meeting.[10]

With the speakership fight concluded, the American party held its annual council meeting in Philadelphia. It has been observed how in 1855 F. H. Cone succeeded in getting the council to adopt the famous twelfth resolution. An unequivocal denial of the right of Congress to interfere with slavery anywhere, including the District of Columbia, the twelfth resolution had provided Southern Americans a suitable anchorage against the wild effusions of Democrats. Determined to even the score, the antislavery forces got control of the council in 1856. They repealed the twelfth resolution with dispatch, adopting in its place a squatter sovereignty declaration with a recommendation that voting in the territories be limited to natural-born and naturalized citizens. Despite its repeal of the twelfth resolution, the *Republican* and the *Southern Watchman* defended the council, the latter journal alleging that "platforms weren't worth much anyhow." [11]

Their council meeting over, Americans were now ready to hold their first nominating convention. On February 22,

---

[9] *Ibid.*   [10] *Ibid.*
[11] Athens *Southern Watchman*, March 13, 1856.

delegates met in Philadelphia to nominate a ticket for the forthcoming presidential campaign. For President, they chose former President Millard Fillmore; for Vice-President, former journalist Andrew Jackson Donelson. Bitter rivals during the Taylor canvass of 1848, both men had worked hard for the Compromise of 1850, one as President, the other at the helm of the powerful Washington *Union,* Democratic organ at the nation's capital. Here was a ticket designed to remind voters of happier days and to suggest that the country could have happiness again by electing the men who had done so much to produce the popular Compromise of 1850. There was additional magic in the ticket. Donelson was the adopted son of former President Andrew Jackson. William G. Brownlow, a Tennessee neighbor and friend of the vice-presidential nominee, announced soon after the convention had adjourned that it would be a good idea to print the "Andrew Jackson" part of the nominee's name in big letters and "Donelson" in small ones. The Democratic press converted Brownlow's suggestion into a campaign farce by running Donelson's name as follows: "ANDREW JACKSON donelson." [12]

While the American party convention was preparing for the campaign of 1856, crusading Republicans were holding their first national organization meeting in Pittsburgh. Beginning in July, 1854, free-soilers, anti-Nebraska Democrats, Conscience Whigs, nativists, abolitionists, and others had been busy with immense fusion meetings in Michigan, Illinois, Wisconsin, and New England. At Pittsburgh, on Washington's birthday, 1856, this vast concourse of restlessness was bolted to the antislavery impulse. Theories on

[12] Proceedings of American party's national convention quoted in Griffin *Empire State,* March 5, 1856, and in Athens *Southern Watchman,* March 6, 13, 1856; Augusta *Constitutionalist,* March 26, 1856; Athens *Southern Banner,* March 27, 1856; Athens *Southern Watchman,* March 13, August 2, 1856; Savannah *Republican* quoted *ibid.;* Milledgeville *Federal Union,* April 15, 1856; Beveridge, *Abraham Lincoln,* II, 357.

the genesis of the Republican party are legion. Indubitably early Republicanism was well irrigated with Yankee Calvinism and mid-nineteenth-century liberalism. Which of these dogmas the planter distrusted most is difficult to say. Certainly both annoyed him. It is therefore assumable that for Southern Americans the epitome of frustration was provided by an Ohio delegate to the Philadelphia convention who blithely wired the Republicans at Pittsburgh as follows: "The American party are now thoroughly united to raise the Republican banner. No further extension of slavery." [13]

On June 2, Democracy's delegates gathered in Cincinnati to nominate a presidential candidate. The three leading contenders were President Pierce, James Buchanan, and Stephen A. Douglas. Georgia Democrats favored another term for the President. The State convention had declared for him and the influential *Federal Union* thought he deserved a second term. Thoroughly unwhigged, both Stephens and Toombs were reported as favorable to the renomination of Pierce. Thomas R. R. Cobb, the Congressman's brother, expressed the opinion that sentiment in favor of the President was "universal." James Buchanan, the enigmatical Pennsylvanian, occupied an enviable spot, however. Serving as Minister to England during the bitter controversy over the Kansas-Nebraska Bill, he was peculiarly available. That Buchanan had Southern strength was the belief of one of Howell Cobb's friends, who wrote the Congressman two weeks before the convention that Cherokee Georgia was kindly disposed towards the Pennsylvanian. And with Southern-rights leaders, continued Cobb's friend, Buchanan was a special favorite. [14] The man from

[13] Quoted in Beveridge, *Abraham Lincoln*, II, 357, and Augusta *Constitutionalist*, March 1, 1856. See also Beveridge, *Abraham Lincoln*, II, 264, 356; William Starr Myers, *The Republican Party, A History* (New York, 1928), 62; Binkley, *American Political Parties*, 208.

[14] Beveridge, *Abraham Lincoln*, II, 386; Milledgeville *Federal Union*,

the Keystone State had still another advantage over President Pierce. Patronage had recently been withheld from Northern Democrats with pro-Southern records. These embittered Doughfaces were determined to block Pierce's renomination. The task of joining them with Buchanan's Southern supporters became the assignment of John A. Bayard of Delaware, Senator John Slidell of Louisiana, and other "accomplished politicians." Their "astute manoeuverings" gave James Buchanan the nomination on the seventeenth ballot.[15]

Georgians played a conspicuous part in the proceedings of the four-day Cincinnati convention. John E. Ward, the influential Savannah party leader, was chosen to preside. Governor Johnson was given more than passing recognition when on the first ballot thirty-one delegates supported him for the vice-presidential nomination. On the second ballot John C. Breckinridge of Kentucky was named Buchanan's running mate.[16]

The resolutions committee wove a platform around traditional Democratic ideology, urging respect for state rights, economy in government, a generous use of the veto, and opposition to the national bank and the tariff. Sectional parties were execrated and the preservation of the Union was acclaimed as the issue of paramount concern. The principle of Congressional nonintervention with slavery in the states, territories, or the District of Columbia was declared the basis of Democratic doctrine. Finally, the Kansas-Nebraska Bill was hailed as the special contribution of the party.[17]

June 10, 1856; T. R. R. Cobb to Howell Cobb, March 24, 1856, and William K. De Graffenried to id., May 13, 1856, in Cobb MSS.

[15] Beveridge, *Abraham Lincoln*, II, 387; A. H. Stephens to Thomas W. Thomas, June 16, 1856, in Phillips (ed.), *Correspondence*, 367–72.

[16] Proceedings of the Democratic national convention of 1856 quoted in Milledgeville *Federal Union*, June 17, 1856.

[17] *Ibid.*

With Millard Fillmore and James Buchanan already in the field, the youthful Republican party held its first national nominating convention at Philadelphia on June 17. Read to the delegates by David Wilmot of Proviso fame, the platform was a stinging declaration against slavery and the repeal of the Missouri Compromise as well as a red-hot challenge that Kansas must be free. To romantic John C. Frémont, Georgia-born "Pathfinder of the Rockies" and son-in-law of Thomas Hart Benton, went the party's first nomination for President. With Kansas now bleeding more freely, Republican delegates scattered to their homes determined to keep the burning issue of a "Bleeding Kansas" before the country until the voters started to the polls on election day. While Frémont had no Georgia following, his candidacy imparted to the presidential contest of 1856 its distinctive quality.[18]

Georgia's two parties quickly prepared to take under advisement the work of their respective national conclaves. Meeting in Milledgeville on Independence Day, Democratic leaders endorsed the work of the Cincinnati convention and named an electoral slate. The *Federal Union* declared the convention the biggest of its kind ever to assemble in the State. Suggesting a "be kind to the opposition" campaign, this traditional Democratic journal was especially pleased that no discourteous shafts had been aimed at the Southern Americans.[19] Four days later, Amer-

[18] Proceedings of the Republican national convention of 1856 quoted in Milledgeville *Federal Union*, June 24, 1856, and in Beveridge, *Abraham Lincoln*, II, 391–95; Allan Nevins, *John C. Frémont, the West's Greatest Adventurer* (New York, 1928), II, 492–519; Myers, *Republican Party*, 59–77; Binkley, *American Political Parties*, 217–18; Craven, *Coming of the Civil War*, 369; Savannah *Republican* quoted in Milledgeville *Federal Union*, June 24, 1856. The Savannah *Republican* declared neither free-soilers nor Democrats wanted peace in Kansas. Strife there made converts to Republicanism in the North, while in the South it provided Democrats a club with which to drive Americans into the Democratic ark.

[19] Milledgeville *Federal Union*, July 8, 1856; proceedings of the Democratic convention quoted *ibid*.

ican delegates gathered in Macon to consider the work of
their party's national leaders. Since a Fillmore electoral
slate had been prepared in mid-April, this July gathering
devoted all its time and talents to a study of the platform
which had been drafted at Philadelphia.[20] It has been observed how the national council scuttled Cone's twelfth
resolution on the eve of Fillmore's nomination, adopting
in its place what was generally recognized as a squatter-
sovereignty declaration. This was the act which had provoked the *Southern Watchman* to dismiss platforms as
unimportant. Putting the party squarely on record against
both Congressional and territorial control of slavery, the
Macon delegates took a position against Republicanism
identical to that chosen by the Democrats. Only by such
tactics could American party leaders prevent their followers
from breaking rank and stampeding into the hospitable
arms of the Democracy. With the life of their party at stake,
Georgia's Americans were compelled to vie with eager
Democrats as Southern-rights champions. In this contest
Democrats were to have the advantage of a national party
organization which was committed to the Southern position.[21]

Once the ratification conventions had done their work,
the embattled hosts were ready to carry their fight to the
voters. Democratic strategy called for five major tactical
operations. They were as follows: (1) to show that the
American party was splitting the South; (2) to demonstrate
how Fillmore's candidacy might throw the choice of a
President into the House of Representatives; (3) to identify
Fillmore with the abolitionists; (4) to undermine confi-

[20] B. H. Overby, Temperance candidate for Governor in 1855, was nominated as an alternate presidential elector, but was quoted by the Augusta
Constitutionalist, August 16, 1856, as having declared before the State
Temperance convention in Atlanta on July 23 that he "could not mix . . .
with the evils . . . attendant upon a political campaign."

[21] Macon *Journal and Messenger*, July 16, 1856; proceedings of the American convention quoted *ibid.*

dence in the American party by giving wide publicity to the desertions from that party; and (5) to employ out-of-state trends for whatever advantage they might suggest. American party leaders countered with the following: (1) Democrats were proponents of the "squatter twins" (squatter sovereignty and squatter suffrage); (2) the American party was the heir to sound Whig traditions; and (3) out-of-state trends pointed to a Fillmore victory. While this is a reasonably accurate picture of the party battle of 1856, yet there were many improvisations, some of which will appear, as specific aspects of the campaign are presented.

Employing an earthy turn of phrase, the *Empire State* put the case against the American party when it observed that "Fillmore men will 'hold' him [Democratic party] at the South, while the Black Republicans and Northern Know Nothings will 'skin' him at the North—at least they will try to do it." [22] The American ticket must be withdrawn, contended Democrats, so the South can unite against Republicanism. This was an obvious argument, easy to demonstrate and therefore liberally employed. Americans were obdurate, however, the *Southern Recorder* countering with the oblique thrust that the American ticket was the only truly national ticket in the race. If the American ticket were withdrawn, the contest would automatically become sectional. Frémont's election would then be inevitable.[23] Democrats developed a corollary for their argument that Fillmore was splitting the South. Mindful of how Americans had helped to elect a Republican Speaker in February, Howell Cobb, speaking to an Athens rally in July, warned that Fillmore's candidacy might throw the election into the House, where Americans and Republicans could easily unite to elect Frémont.[24] This

22 Griffin *Empire State,* June 25, 1856.
23 Milledgeville *Southern Recorder,* August 5, 1856.
24 Quoted in Athens *Southern Banner,* July 31, 1856.

approach was generously used and was usually concluded with the tocsin that a vote for the American ticket was a vote for Black Republicanism.[25]

Democrats did not stop with the accusation that Fillmore's campaign was hatched under the aegis of Republicanism. Contending that the Fillmore Club of New York was controlled by William H. Seward's "Woolly Heads," the *Federal Union* arraigned the opposition candidate as an abolitionist.[26] The former President was alleged to have confirmed this charge when he announced early in July at Albany, New York, that the repeal of the Missouri Compromise "seems to have been a Pandora's box, out of which has issued all the political evils that now afflict the country, scarcely leaving a hope behind." [27] Troubled by the persistent rumor that his party's nominee was an abolitionist, Congressman N. G. Foster addressed a personal inquiry to Fillmore.[28] If elected, interrogated Foster, what program with respect to slavery did the former President propose to follow? Fillmore replied by mailing an editorial from the Buffalo *Commercial Advertiser*. Entitled "Restoration of the Missouri Compromise," the editorial explained that it would require three years to restore the adjustment of 1820 because "the South has a large Democratic majority" in the Senate.[29] Democratic papers used the *Commercial Advertiser's* editorial and the "Pandora's box" speech as evidence of Fillmore's intention to set aside the Kansas-Nebraska Bill in favor of the Republican principle of Congressional intervention.[30]

---

[25] Milledgeville *Federal Union*, April 22, July 1, 8, August 19, 26, 1856; Augusta *Constitutionalist*, May 10, July 2, October 8, 1856; Athens *Southern Banner*, July 31, 1856.

[26] Milledgeville *Federal Union*, July 1, 1856.

[27] Quoted *ibid.*, July 15, 1856.

[28] Quoted in Athens *Southern Banner*, October 9, 1856.   [29] *Ibid.*

[30] Milledgeville *Federal Union*, July 15, 1856; Athens *Southern Banner*, October 9, 1856.

Georgia's Americans could hardly be expected to repudiate their party's nominee for the sake of maintaining a consistent attitude towards the Kansas-Nebraska Bill. Consequently such influential journals as the *Southern Recorder, Journal and Messenger,* and *Southern Watchman* began directing bursts of opprobrium at a measure which two years earlier they had loudly acclaimed as the epitome of their own creed.[31] While the presidential contest was still in its infancy the *Southern Recorder,* conveniently forgetting Whig encomiums for the Kansas-Nebraska Bill, wailed that "when introduced into Congress, as engrafted in the Nebraska bill, we looked upon it [squatter sovereignty] as a political scheme for political power. . . ."[32] Fulminating against the "squatter twins" (territorial control of slavery and foreign suffrage), the Fillmore press contended these evil demons were sired by the Kansas-Nebraska Bill. With Fillmore condemning the Kansas-Nebraska Bill for its repeal of the Missouri Compromise, with the American press denouncing the same measure because it had unchained the squatter twins and with Georgia Democrats flailing Fillmore as an abolitionist, Georgia's Americans would seem to have experienced an unprecedented exercise in frustration.[33]

Like many of his contemporaries, James Buchanan had a dubious record on the question of controlling slavery in the territories. At various times he had favored Congressional control, squatter sovereignty, and popular sovereignty. When he announced in his letter of acceptance that "the people of a Territory, like those of States, shall decide for themselves, whether slavery shall or shall not exist

31 See page 132.
32 Milledgeville *Southern Recorder,* April 29, 1856.
33 *Ibid.,* April 29, June 10, July 29, 1856; Macon *Journal and Messenger,* July 2, 30, 1856; James Buchanan to Thaddeus Sandford, August 21, 1848, quoted in Augusta *Constitutionalist,* August 13, 1856.

within their limits," he at once became the target for the American charge of favoring squatter sovereignty.[34] Since the Democratic nominee had not specified *when* the people of a territory were to make their decision, his Georgia followers had an escape. They laboriously explained that nowhere in his letter of acceptance had Buchanan conceded the right of territorial residents to act on slavery before they were ready for statehood. Therefore, they contended, their nominee had not committed himself to squatter sovereignty.[35] Nevertheless American journals struck back at Buchanan's Georgia defenders by quoting those Northern Democrats who claimed the Pennsylvanian had no intention of supporting the Southern position on slavery.[36] Concluding a typical thrust at the Democratic nominee, the *Southern Recorder* provided a terse summary of what had been for nearly a decade the Southern interpretation of local autonomy. "Southern statesmen," explained this journal, "contend that the people of a territory, *while in a territorial condition,* have no right to fix its conditions as regards slavery, much less prohibit it." [37]

It was in the sixth district that the tangled issue of local autonomy was most astutely resolved. In this district Cincinnatus Peeples, American candidate for elector, raised the question which was to be repeated two years later by Abraham Lincoln at Freeport. "Do you believe," he asked Junius Hillyer during a public debate, "that the people of a Territory, while in a territorial condition, and before they

[34] Quoted in Macon *Journal and Messenger,* July 2, 1856. See comments *ibid.;* Athens *Southern Watchman,* July 3, 10, 17, 1856; Milledgeville *Southern Recorder,* July 29, 1856. See also Montgomery, "A Georgia Precedent for the Freeport Question," *loc. cit.,* 205–206.

[35] Milledgeville *Federal Union,* June 17, 1856; Griffin *Empire State,* August 6, 1856; Athens *Southern Banner,* July 24, 1856.

[36] Milledgeville *Southern Recorder,* August 19, 26, 1856, for comments from several Northern Democratic journals.

[37] *Ibid.,* August 19, 1856.

form a State Constitution, have the right to legislate on the subject of slavery?" [38] Hillyer countered by showing that territorial legislation was necessary to enable the master to exercise the rights of ownership over his slaves as outlined by the Fifth Amendment to the Federal Constitution.[39]

Distrustful of Democratic views on local autonomy, the *Southern Watchman* declared Hillyer's position would endanger Southern rights. To concede a territorial legislature the right to enact laws to protect the slaveowner, continued this journal, was a double-edged sword. The right to protect was tantamount to the right to destroy. This, concluded an excited editor, was squatter sovereignty. Realizing the planter could not function in a legal vacuum, the editor promptly retracted his first interpretation of Hillyer's reply to Peeples. He now insisted that it was not the "right" but the "duty" of the territorial legislature to enact rules to protect slavery. Continuing his retraction, he pointed out that "the Constitution carries slavery into the Territories," and the territorial legislature possessed no power to legislate against the Constitution. In conclusion the editor gloomily reflected that "by 'changing the venue' to the Territories, our rights are determined where we are not represented, and by a people, not only not our friends, but blindly prejudiced against us! It is virtually leaving the whole question to arbitration, and suffering our antagonist to select the arbitrators!" [40]

It is impossible to determine how these verbal sallies of the embattled hosts affected the voters. This campaign was,

[38] Quoted in Athens *Southern Watchman*, August 28, 1856. Lincoln's inquiry was as follows: "Can the people of a United States Territory, in any lawful way, against the wish of any citizen of the United States, exclude slavery from its limits prior to the formation of a State Constitution?" Quoted in Beveridge, *Abraham Lincoln*, II, 655.
[39] Quoted in Athens *Southern Watchman*, August 28, 1856.
[40] *Ibid.*, September 4, 11, 1856.

however, not entirely conducted on the basis of verbal
maneuvering. Delegates to the Cincinnati convention had
scarcely returned to their homes when the optimistic
Federal Union brandished what was unquestionably the
most potent of the Democratic party's tactical weapons.
"Fully twenty thousand old line Whigs will vote for the
nominee of the National Democratic Party," was the hopeful prophecy of this journal.[41] Two weeks later sixty Muscogee County Americans won the plaudits of the Democratic press when they renounced Fillmore.[42] The stark fact
of desertions could not be nullified by sheer verbalizations.
Party leaders could not even fight a rear-guard action
against wholesale withdrawals. Appreciating the utter help-
lessness of the opposition, Democrats pressed their advantage eagerly.

The campaign of 1856 proved to be a turning point in
the lives of many prominent old-line Georgia Whigs who
had preferred breaking bread with Sam to boarding the
Democratic ark. For the first time the sectional struggle
appeared in bold relief. The nomination of Frémont had
injected into national affairs the simplicity of the "either-
or" frame of reference. Attending this simplicity there was
among Georgians, and Southerners generally, a vivid sense
of the necessity of escaping the stigma of "wrong," as defined
by crusading Republicans. Ironically, many of the more
zealous Republicans were "Heirs of Jackson." Frémont,
Thomas H. Benton's son-in-law, was identified with this
wing of his party. It is therefore not strange that old-line
Whigs, hardened in battle against "King Andrew," reluctantly unwhigged themselves. With heavy hearts they
boarded the Democratic ark, where once "Old Hickory"

---

[41] Milledgeville *Federal Union,* June 10, 1856.

[42] *Ibid.,* June 24, 1856; Augusta *Constitutionalist,* July 2, 1856; Griffin *Empire State,* July 2, 1856. The Milledgeville *Federal Union,* June 24, 1856,
also reported that two American newspapers declared for Buchanan immediately after the Cincinnati convention.

had commanded, but from where they were to renew their fight against the Blairs, Wilmots, Butlers, and other Heirs of Jackson.[43]

Among the first of the more prominent Whigs to repudiate Fillmore was Asbury Hull, a Taylor-Fillmore elector in 1848. Shortly after Frémont's nomination, he explained in a letter to the *Southern Banner* that "recent events and indications have forced upon me the conviction that if we receive justice at the hands of either party, it is, and will be the Democratic." [44] Hull's diagnosis was typical of the feelings of numerous old-line Whigs whose communications were published in the leading Democratic journals.[45] Late in August Charles J. Jenkins repudiated Fillmore. Somewhat evasive since 1853, this former *Tertium Quid* explained that in a fight between Black Republicanism and Buchanan, duty compelled him to abandon his political idol of former days. Concluding, he counseled, "I say let every southern electoral vote be cast for the Democratic nominee." [46] Dripping with invectives, the Fillmore press ascribed Jenkins' desertion to the "lashings" of the nefarious Toombs and Stephens.[47]

Caught in the drift to "Buck and Breck," E. A. Nisbet, one of the first Georgians to object to the foreign-suffrage section of the Kansas-Nebraska Bill, announced on September 1 his decision to support Buchanan. The election of the Pennsylvanian, he wrote in a letter widely circulated

[43] Binkley, *American Political Parties*, 217; Schlesinger, *The Age of Jackson*, 478–83.

[44] Quoted in Milledgeville *Federal Union*, July 15, 1856.

[45] See, for example, Augusta *Constitutionalist*, July 16, 1856.

[46] Charles J. Jenkins to Willis Willingham, August 28, 1856, quoted in Milledgeville *Federal Union*, September 9, 1856.

[47] Atlanta *Republican and Discipline* and Savannah *Republican* quoted in Milledgeville *Federal Union*, September 16, 1856; Milledgeville *Southern Recorder*, September 9, 1856; Macon *Journal and Messenger*, September 10, 1856.

by the Democratic press, transcended all considerations
of party ties. In closing, Nisbet justified his decision as
follows: "If Mr. Buchanan can defeat Frémont and Mr.
Fillmore cannot and if the success of Frémont will be followed by the dissolution of the Union, the case is fully
made out without farther [sic] argument. In a contest between the Union and my party principles—I go for the
Union." [48] Still another noted disciple of Whiggism was
to quit the Fillmore party. On October 20, F. H. Cone,
author of the ill-fated twelfth resolution, took his leave.
Bitter since he had been shelved during the reorganization
of the American party in December, 1855, he reminded
Fillmore apologists that their party had mired in the
squashy marshes of abolition. He was at a loss to understand how any true Southerner could continue to support
such a party.[49] Like other letters of resignation, Cone's
received wide circulation in the Democratic press.[50] Fillmore spokesmen could offer no rebuttal against the parade
to the Buchanan shrine of the Hulls, Jenkinses, Nisbets,
and Cones. Long recognized as among the most prominent
leaders of the Whig and American parties, they were an
irreparable loss.

With so many eminent members of the old Whig party
deserting Fillmore, the American cause in Georgia reached
a low ebb two months before the election. Rejoicing at
the misfortunes of the opposition, Democratic spokesmen
harassed a weakened foe with the taunt that the former
President would be withdrawn were it not for the neces-

[48] E. A. Nisbet to H. G. Lamar, September 1, 1856, quoted in Milledgeville *Federal Union*, September 16, 1856.

[49] F. H. Cone to James Hook, October 20, 1856, quoted in Augusta
Constitutionalist, October 22, 1856.

[50] See, for example, Augusta *Constitutionalist*, June 28, 1856; Griffin *Empire State*, July 9, 1856; Milledgeville *Federal Union*, July 29, October 14,
1856. The Griffin *Empire State*, July 9, 1856, announced that Hopkins Holsey, the old Jacksonian warrior, had declared for Buchanan.

sity of "saving a few county offices." [51] Whatever the merits
of the county-purposes argument, the fact remains that
Fillmore party leaders in Georgia fought on stubbornly to
the bitter end. To dull the cutting edge of desertions, the
American press trumpeted the effort to revive the national
Whig party and pretended to see in "out-of-state trends"
a drift to Fillmore in the nation at large.

After weeks of publicity the "National Whig Convention" gathered in Baltimore on September 17. According
to the *National Intelligencer*, old-line Whig journal in the
nation's capital, the object was to align traditional Whigs
in support of Fillmore "with a view to the ultimate reorganization of the National Whig party." [52] The convention
declared itself to be the product of a spontaneous rising of
Whigs who were pledged to a preservation of the Union.
Both Frémont and Buchanan were stigmatized as sectional
candidates, while Fillmore was acclaimed as the savior of
the Union in 1850 and its only hope in 1856.[53] Georgia's
American press hailed the event as one which, in the words
of the *Journal and Messenger*, would "give a new impulse
to the cause of Fillmore and the Constitution." [54] What
effect the Baltimore effort had on the former President's
chances in Georgia was perhaps best summed up by Charles
J. Jenkins, who, writing James Gardner, Jr., of the *Constitutionalist*, declared a short time after the event that Fillmore's campaign was progressively growing weaker.[55] No
Whig experienced greater agony in the process of unwhigging himself than A. H. Stephens; therefore, what he had to
say about the National Whig Convention is worth noting.

[51] Milledgeville *Federal Union*, August 19, 1856; Athens *Southern Banner*,
October 2, 1856; Augusta *Constitutionalist*, November 1, 1856.

[52] Quoted in Macon *Journal and Messenger*, October 1, 1856.

[53] Proceedings quoted *ibid.*, September 24, 1856.

[54] *Ibid.*; Milledgeville *Southern Recorder*, September 30, 1856.

[55] Charles J. Jenkins to James Gardner, Jr., quoted in Griffin *Empire State*,
October 15, 1856; Milledgeville *Southern Recorder*, October 14, 1856.

The occasion for his reflections on the Baltimore conclave
was a Democratic rally in Augusta in mid-October. Always
ready to verbalize, he declared it ridiculous to call on old-
line Whigs to rally to Fillmore. Then he blistered the former President as being "no longer a Whig, but an oath-
bound member of the Know Nothing Order." [56]
The "historic politics of maneuver" tended to dominate
the presidential race of 1856 in Georgia. Nowhere was it
more completely the master than in what has already been
described as the "out-of-state trends" campaign theater.
What rival editors were able to read into out-of-state trends
is not only an unmistakable exhibition of the intensity of
party spirit, but a compelling lesson in semantics as well.
Since many states were to elect governors and other local
officials as early as August, editors claimed to see trends
as early as the Fourth of July. With Missouri, Arkansas,
Kentucky, and North Carolina going Democratic and
Maine, Vermont, and Iowa turning in Republican victories in August and September, the die was cast. Both sides
agreed that the North, not the South, was to be the real
cockpit. American strategists, however, insisted that the
battle there was between Fillmore and Frémont, while
Democrats, on the other hand, argued that only Buchanan
could defeat Frémont.

August's returns from Missouri, Arkansas, Kentucky, and
North Carolina were a severe blow to American party leaders. They had been confident of success in several of these
states, notably Kentucky.[57] Embittered by the loss of these
four Southern states but somewhat encouraged by later
Northern returns, Georgia's Fillmore strategists launched

[56] Speech of Stephens quoted in Augusta *Constitutionalist*, October 18,
1856.
[57] Milledgeville *Southern Recorder* quoted in Milledgeville *Federal Union*,
July 29, 1856; Milledgeville *Southern Recorder*, August 5, 1856; Athens
Southern Watchman, July 24, 31, 1856; Macon *Journal and Messenger*, July
30, 1856; Athens *Southern Banner*, August 14, 1856.

a drive in the "out-of-state trends" theater for the purpose of holding their local lines, which, it has been observed, began to snap early in the contest. Hence shortly after the Southern reverses of August the *Central Georgian* (American) was quoted as pleased to report that "Frémont men are daily coming over to Fillmore [in Illinois] in order to beat Buchanan[,] their bitterest rival." [58] The *Federal Union* reported a Fillmore rally in mid-September at Eatonton to have "wildly" cheered Congressman Foster's announcement that Republicans had carried Maine, Vermont and Iowa.[59]

Inspired by Republican successes in three Northern states, American party spokesmen urged the South to unite solidly for the November election and with the help of New York's heavy vote return Fillmore to the presidency.[60] "Can the friends of Buchanan," inquired the *Southern Recorder* in mid-September, "point out a *single State north of the Potomac* to be depended upon for him?" [61] This was substantially the line followed by the *Journal and Messenger* as it urged Jenkins, Hull, and others who had "taken walks" to retrace their steps.[62] "It is in the power of the Union men of the South," exclaimed the militant *Southern Recorder,* "with the divided vote of the North, to elect Mr. Fillmore." [63]

As the campaign wore on news began to trickle into Georgia that Black Republicans and Americans were making deals in Pennsylvania and Indiana.[64] In both states local elections were scheduled for mid-October. The *Con-*

[58] Quoted in Milledgeville *Federal Union,* September 9, 1856.
[59] *Ibid.,* September 23, 1856.
[60] Milledgeville *Southern Recorder,* September 16, 1856; Macon *Journal and Messenger,* September 17, 1856.
[61] Milledgeville *Southern Recorder,* September 16, 1856.
[62] Macon *Journal and Messenger,* September 17, 1856.
[63] Milledgeville *Southern Recorder,* September 16, 1856.
[64] Milledgeville *Federal Union,* September 30, 1856; Athens *Southern Banner,* October 2, 1856; Griffin *Empire State,* October 8, 1856.

stitutionalist quoted the Keystone State's leading Democratic journal, the Philadelphia *Pennsylvanian,* as having predicted a general merger of Northern Americans and Republicans in the event of a victory for the fusionists in Pennsylvania's October election.[65] The *Empire State* wondered how "any man who has a drop of Southern blood in his veins"could continue to support Fillmore with the bald fact of ignoble fusion in Indiana and Pennsylvania in his eyes.[66] "If Mr. Buchanan is to be beaten in his own State," countered the *Republican,* "how can the *manner* in which it is done be made to affect the decision of the South upon the question, as to whether she should vote for him in the present crisis?" [67] To which the rival *Georgian and Journal* replied by labeling as "an insult [the] very suggestion [that] Georgia strike hands with one of the parties to that alliance [fusion]." [68] A Georgia wag thought the fusion ticket should read:

FOR PRESIDENT
COL. JOHN MILLARD FILLMONT
OF NEW CAROLINA

FOR VICE PRESIDENT
ANDREW JACKSON DAYTON
OF TENNE JERSEY.[69]

Throughout the entire contest Georgians of both parties kept an eye glued on Pennsylvania. Howell Cobb, who stumped the Keystone State, wrote Buchanan early in the race that in his opinion the November outcome "turns

[65] Augusta *Constitutionalist,* October 2, 1856. On November 1, the *Constitutionalist* quoted from nine Pennsylvania papers to prove the fusion charge.

[66] Griffin *Empire State,* October 8, 1856.

[67] Quoted in Athens *Southern Banner,* October 16, 1856.

[68] Quoted *ibid.*

[69] Quoted in Augusta *Constitutionalist,* September 20, 1856.

upon your October elections." [70] On the eve of these October elections the *Southern Watchman* announced that if "the Democracy were defeated in Pennsylvania on Tuesday, he [Buchanan] will probably be withdrawn at once." [71] October returns from Pennsylvania, and Indiana as well, were, however, gratifying to Georgia's Democracy. Both states went Democratic.[72] Immediately Buchanan spokesmen urged Fillmoreites to join them in defense of Southern rights.[73] However, American apologists were unyielding, the *Republican* insisting the Pennsylvania and Indiana results were in reality Southern defeats, because in both states the Democrats won by representing themselves as "abolitionized." [74]

Still another October result was heartening to the Democracy. This was in Savannah, where Sam's heirs could not break the Democratic habit. Utterly despondent, the *Republican* wailed that "just about the time the polls were closed and the Democratic victory announced in this city, the Moon veiled herself and went into eclipse." [75] To which the *Federal Union* blithely responded with the following: "Under the favor of the Moon Sam has performed a great many feats that he would not dare to expose to the light of the Sun." [76]

The *Southern Watchman* made a desperate last-minute appeal to old-line Whigs. Declaring the Pennsylvania and Indiana elections indisputable proof of the futility of Frémont's cause, this Athens journal argued that those Fillmoreites who had deserted their old favorite no longer had

---

[70] Howell Cobb to James Buchanan, July 27, 1856, in Phillips (ed.), *Correspondence*, 388; Griffin *Empire State*, October 22, 1856.

[71] Athens *Southern Watchman*, October 16, 1856.

[72] Griffin *Empire State*, October 22, 1856.

[73] Milledgeville *Federal Union*, October 28, 1856.

[74] Quoted in Athens *Southern Watchman*, October 30, 1856.

[75] Quoted in Milledgeville *Federal Union*, October 21, 1856.

[76] *Ibid.*

reason to support Buchanan. That the danger of Black Republicanism was chimerical had now been demonstrated. Those who had "taken a walk" could now come back where they belonged and register their preference for an old idol, former President Fillmore.[77] On the Democratic side there was a mixture of confidence and solemnity, with the *Federal Union* injecting, as election day arrived, a perceptible show of anxiety by observing, "The battle which is to be fought and won this day, will decide whether these United States shall be held together by a bond of Constitutional Union and Equality, or the North and South be divided into separate and distinct governments." [78]

Buchanan polled 56,000 votes to 42,000 for his opponent, with the Democrats again losing the third and seventh districts.[79] A glimpse of the entire Southern picture reveals that Buchanan narrowly escaped defeat. Had Fillmore been able to add Kentucky and Louisiana to his Maryland victory, the election would have been thrown into the Republican House of Representatives. Democrats were reluctant to forget how close to the precipice of disaster Millard Fillmore had led the South. Consequently the American party became the object of bitter attacks by the Democratic press during the weeks immediately after the election.[80]

Aware of the damage wrought by the postelection assault of the Democratic press, American party spokesmen set out to justify their late behavior. It was the Fillmore movement, grumbled the *Southern Recorder,* which had executed the downfall of the Black Republicans. Hence Buchanan owed Southern Americans a debt of gratitude for making possible his election.[81] Former President Fillmore's candidacy had

[77] Athens *Southern Watchman,* October 30, 1856.
[78] Milledgeville *Federal Union,* November 4, 1856.
[79] Returns quoted in Milledgeville *Federal Union,* November 18, 27, 1856.
[80] *Ibid.,* November 11, 1856; Griffin *Empire State,* November 19, 26, 1856.
[81] Milledgeville *Southern Recorder,* November 11, 1856; Griffin *Empire State,* December 17, 1856.

desectionalized the campaign, cracked the *Journal and Messenger*. Thus, boasted this Macon paper, the South's choice of candidates was elected.[82]

Georgia's Democracy ended the year on a note of conservative optimism. The *Federal Union* expressed the opinion that the election returns proved that a sectional party was incompatible with the political tastes of the American people. A united South could always command enough Doughface votes to assure victory in presidential contests, but, warned the State's leading Democratic paper, the national Democratic party must be maintained for the purpose of integrating the pro-Southern sentiment of the nation. There was no place in the national scheme of things political for such a violent party as the Black Republican order, continued the *Federal Union*. In fact, concluded this spokesman of Democracy, Republicanism had already spent itself, and "Hypos," as extreme Southern rightists were now called, were urged to cease making capital for the "snorts" of Horace Greeley.[83]

[82] Macon *Journal and Messenger*, November 12, 1856.
[83] Milledgeville *Federal Union*, November 25, December 2, 30, 1856.

X

DARK HORSE

DURING the six years which followed the Crisis of 1850, Georgia went through five heated election campaigns. There had been three gubernatorial contests and two presidential races. Except for 1854 there had been a contest every year. In 1851 former Governor C. J. McDonald, the Southern Rights party's candidate, was beaten by Howell Cobb, the Unionite. This had been a bitterly fought race, with Cobb winning by a decisive margin. The next year the presidential race between Franklin Pierce and Winfield Scott produced numerous splinter parties: Regular Democrats, Supplementals, Tugaloes, Scottites, and *Tertium Quids*. H. V. Johnson, Joseph Jackson, and James Gardner, Jr., brought the Regular Democrats successfully through this campaign. In 1853 Regular Democrats elected H. V. Johnson in a close gubernatorial contest. His opponent, Charles J. Jenkins, lost by slightly over five hundred votes. The following year saw a respite in party warfare. Yet 1854 was an important year. It produced the Kansas-Nebraska Bill and the Know-Nothing party, and it was in this year that the Republican party was begun. Georgians were to be vitally affected by each of these events. The next year, 1855, saw Georgians resume their political wars with H. V. Johnson defeating, in the gubernatorial race of that year, both Garnett Andrews, the Know-Nothing nominee, and B. H. Overby, the Temperance party's candidate. Johnson's second victory was more decisive than his first and was followed in 1856 by an even more decisive triumph for James Buchanan, the Democratic candidate for President.

Since Johnson's first election in 1853 the Democratic party had grown progressively stronger. This was due very largely to the collapse of the national Whig party. However, the "Heirs of Whiggery," the Know-Nothing and American parties, fought the Democrats stubbornly. The cement of county purposes was doubtless the most potent force in holding together Georgia's minority party during the fifties. This party's strategy was to picture the Democracy as unsound on national issues. This, it would seem, was considered the most effective way to influence voters. However, the Democratic party had the advantage of a strong national organization which was committed to the Southern view of things. Hence such prominent Heirs of Whiggery as the Stephens brothers, Robert Toombs, Charles J. Jenkins, James A. Nisbet, F. H. Cone, and Asbury Hull were convinced the national Democracy offered the greatest security against the rising crusade against slavery. Why, they reasoned, keep up the traditional fight against the Democracy?[1]

Georgia's political journalists betrayed the strain that was induced by incessant party warfare. Early in 1857, editors of two Democratic organs, the Savannah *Georgian and Journal* and the Atlanta *Examiner,* complained about the long campaigns they had been forced to endure.[2] Tired editors needed an "airing" in the country as well as a taste of the "mineral," apostrophized the *Georgian and Journal,* recognized for years as the leading Democratic paper of the coastal region.[3] The vigilant *Federal Union,* long the high priest of Georgia Democracy, smelled a rat. As to

[1] Augusta *Constitutionalist,* April 18, 1857; Milledgeville *Federal Union,* April 7, 1857.

[2] Milledgeville *Federal Union,* February 3, 1856; Savannah *Georgian and Journal* quoted *ibid.;* Atlanta *Examiner* quoted *ibid.* The Savannah *Georgian* had merged with the Savannah *Journal and Courier* and was at this time the Savannah *Georgian and Journal.*

[3] Quoted in Milledgeville *Federal Union,* February 3, 1857.

"minerals," this journal's editor was in complete accord with his Savannah colleague, confessing more than a modicum of comfort at the thought of being irrigated by "a plenty of the right 'ring.' " [4] As to a short campaign, however, the *Federal Union* countered stiffly in the negative and, with customary zeal, hastened to justify its stand. In the first place, contended its editor, party usage had established June as the month for opening political campaigns. Further, a long campaign would expose the duplicity of the American party. And finally, the Democratic party's new converts needed a long campaign to orientate themselves.[5] The proponents of a short campaign were not to be denied, however, and before it was over the squabble had involved practically the entire party press, the *Federal Union* reporting in mid-April that fourteen journals favored an early June date while nine preferred the convention to be held in mid-July.[6] When Fulton County Democrats adopted the Columbus *Times and Sentinel*'s compromise date, that of June 24, the way was paved for bringing to an end the obtrusive offerings of a set of febrile journalists. By early May most of them were reconciled to the compromise date.[7]

American party editors also had convention-date trouble. The Columbus *Enquirer* and the Augusta *Chronicle and Sentinel* wanted a short campaign. They proposed August 12 as a convention date. The Macon *Citizen* and the *Southern Watchman* objected to the August date and were gratified when their party's executive committee ordered the State convention for July 8.[8]

There were additional difficulties for American party

[4] *Ibid.*   [5] *Ibid.*, February 10, March 24, 1857.
[6] *Ibid.*, April 24, 1857.

[7] Proceedings of the Fulton County Democratic convention quoted in Milledgeville *Federal Union*, April 28, 1857. See also *ibid.*, June 16, 1857.

[8] Milledgeville *Southern Recorder*, June 2, 1857; Athens *Southern Watchman*, June 4, 11, 1857.

leaders. Some thought a new name would help the organization. Since 1852 the minority party had experienced
considerable difficulty in finding a suitable label. Numerous designations were suggested in 1857 for the "ghastly,
ghostly, Godless crew," as Sam's heirs were characterized
by the Richmond (Virginia) *Whig*.[9] The most frequently
mentioned of these suggested designations were "Peoples
Party," "Independent," and "Reform Party." [10] Poised for
a verse, the *Federal Union* taunted:

> You may change, you may *ruin* the name
> if you will,
> But the scent of the lantern will
> linger there still.[11]

Party magnates ruled against a change of name in 1857.

A few days after President Buchanan's inauguration,
the Supreme Court announced its decision in the Dred
Scott Case. The Court held that both squatter sovereignty
and Congressional intervention were unconstitutional.
Neither could therefore be employed in the future against
slavery in the territories.[12] As recently as 1856 Georgia's
American party leaders had charged the national Democracy with favoring squatter sovereignty. Robbed by the
Court of what had been their most glittering sword, the
heirs of Whiggery might have been more severely embarrassed had their national organization not instructed state
leaders to adopt such policies as local circumstances warranted.[13] Southern Americans were now freed of the abolitionist stigma which, it has been observed, inhibited the

9 Quoted in Milledgeville *Federal Union*, June 16, 1857.
10 Quoted *ibid.*, February 3, 1857.	11 *Ibid.*
12 Carl B. Swisher, *Roger B. Taney* (New York, 1835), 505–506 and Homer
C. Hockett, *The Constitutional History of the United States, 1826–1876* (New
York, 1939), 232–50, for accounts of the Dred Scott Case.
13 Proceedings of the American national convention quoted in Milledgeville *Federal Union*, June 16, 1857.

Fillmore apologists in 1856. Thus fumigated, Georgia's Americans promptly set out to prove their party a more zealous guardian of Southern rights than their opponents. Despite the action of the American party's national convention, Southern Americans most likely would have been helpless in their struggle to capture county offices had the Buchanan administration been more fortunate in Kansas.[14]

Soon after his inauguration President Buchanan announced that Robert J. Walker was to replace John W. Geary as Territorial Governor of Kansas. The new Governor, born in Pennsylvania and indoctrinated in Mississippi, was directed to urge Kansas antislavery leaders to join with their opponents to help form a state constitution. He was carefully instructed to assure a fair and honest election of delegates to the convention which was to prepare the state constitution. Governor Walker shared with President Buchanan the belief that the solution to the Territory's troubles lay in prompt admission to statehood. The Supreme Court had outlined the procedure a few weeks earlier in the Dred Scott Case. It was a reasonably simple procedure. The local constitutional convention, not Congress, had been empowered by the Court to decide the fate of slavery. If Governor Walker could have performed his projected operation in a vacuum, he doubtless would have sent a mission-completed report to Washington by midsummer. But Kansas was the nation's showpiece. The new Governor was not long in discovering that the showpiece was an ulcer of confusion. Shortly after arriving in the Territory he outlined his plan in an inaugural address. With lightning speed those who had axes to grind pounced on him. Republicans, Americans and antiadministration Democrats alike lost no time in casting the Mississippian in the role of a sycophant. Actually none of these groups

[14] Augusta *Constitutionalist*, April 18, 1857; Milledgeville *Federal Union*, April 7, 1857.

could afford to have Walker end the Kansas trouble. The woes of Kansas were grist for the mills of purposeful partisans whose objective was to defame the new administration at Washington.[15]

There were two groups in Georgia which were just as determined as the Republicans to discredit President Buchanan. They were the American party and a faction of Democrats. The latter played up the Kansas issue to weaken Howell Cobb's influence with the State Democratic machine. Cobb was now Secretary of the Treasury and, of course, therefore a part of the Buchanan administration. To stigmatize the administration as weakening in its defense of Southern rights would hardly react to Cobb's advantage. Encouraged by the *Constitutionalist,* anti-Cobb Democrats hoped this tactic would wreck Secretary Cobb's plan to have his friend, John H. Lumpkin, nominated for Governor by the Democratic convention when it met on June 24. American journals joined the *Constitutionalist* in vilifying Walker for his inaugural, charging the Territorial Governor with "presumptuous interference" and insisting that he had committed the Buchanan administration to an act of "vile treachery." [16] The following is the part of Walker's inaugural which set off these wild effusions: "There is a remedy, also, if such facts [violence, fraud, etc.] can be demonstrated, in the refusal of Congress to admit a State into the Union under a Constitution imposed by a minority upon a majority by fraud or violence. Indeed, I cannot doubt that the convention, after having framed

[15] Beveridge, *Abraham Lincoln,* II, 527; George T. Curtis, *Life of James Buchanan, Fifteenth President of the United States* (New York, 1883), II, 198; Craven, *Coming of the Civil War,* 387. For a brief explanation of the relations between Northern Americans and Republicans see Fred Harvey Harrington, "Frémont and the North Americans," in *American Historical Review,* XLIV (1939), 842–48.

[16] Augusta *Constitutionalist,* April 8, June 10, 1857; Athens *Southern Watchman,* June 25, 1857.

a State Constitution, will submit it for ratification or rejection, by a majority of the actual *bona fide* resident settlers of Kansas." [17]

Secretary Cobb was quick to sense the political capital which might be made of Walker's apparent endorsement of Congressional intervention. Writing A. H. Stephens, who was already disturbed by a fiery communication from Thomas W. Thomas, the Secretary of the Treasury explained on June 17 that Walker thought at the time of his inaugural that Kansas would soon enter the Union as a slave state and that "his [Walker's] object was to satisfy the other side." [18] In a second letter on the following day Cobb assured Stephens of Buchanan's "soundness," and, further, he declared the new President was unequivocally committed to a program of administering the Kansas-Nebraska Bill in conformity with the Supreme Court's latest opinion. Announced in the Dred Scott Case, this opinion had, it has been pointed out, declared Congressional intervention to be unconstitutional. Cobb conceded Walker's remarks had been unfortunate, but he carefully repeated his opinion of the preceding day as to their provocation.[19]

The indignation unchained in Georgia by Governor Walker did not spend itself quickly. Secretary Cobb's explicative letters to A. H. Stephens had little effect. American party journals continued to arraign the Kansas Governor, the *Southern Watchman* accusing him of being a free-soiler.[20] Meanwhile anti-Cobb factions were springing up within the Democratic party. Determined to head off the nomination of John H. Lumpkin, each faction had its favorite son. Most prominent among them were James

[17] Quoted in Augusta *Constitutionalist,* July 15, 1857.
[18] Thomas W. Thomas to A. H. Stephens, June 15, 1857, in Phillips (ed.), *Correspondence,* 400–401; Howell Cobb to *id., ibid.,* 401–402.
[19] *Id.* to *id., ibid.,* 402–403.
[20] Athens *Southern Watchman,* June 25, 1857.

Gardner, Jr., Hiram Warner, William H. Stiles, and Henry G. Lamar.[21] James Gardner, Jr., was probably the most widely known of these aspirants for the Democratic nomination for Governor. Active in political and journalistic affairs for many years, he had recently turned over the editorial department of the *Constitutionalist* to J. A. Nisbet, formerly of the *Journal and Messenger*. The blasts which the *Constitutionalist* hurled at President Buchanan and Governor Walker were hardly less stinging than those of the American editors. On the opening day of the Democratic convention, Nisbet lectured the President as follows: "No responsibility will attach to it [Democratic party] for the loss of Kansas to the South, and its admission as a free State, *unless that result is brought about through the influence of the Federal Administration.*" [22] Nisbet and his friend Gardner were making it as difficult as they knew how for Cobb and his friend Lumpkin.

On June 24, while Governor Walker's behavior in Kansas was still the subject of lively exchanges, Democrats met in Milledgeville for a three-day convention. A platform committee promptly reported five resolutions which the assemblage summarily adopted. The first two resolutions endorsed the Cincinnati platform on which President Buchanan had been elected the year before, while the third was a stiff rebuke to Governor Walker, who, according to this sharp asseveration, was violating the nonintervention provision of the Kansas-Nebraska Bill by actively directing in the interest of the free-soilers the settlement of Kansas. Since Buchanan had been elected on a pledge to execute faithfully the nonintervention formula, Walker's behavior, continued the third resolution, amounted to an act of party perfidy. In conclusion, the third resolution demanded

21 Herbert Fielder, *Life and Times of Joseph E. Brown* (Springfield, 1883), 86–87.

22 Augusta *Constitutionalist*, June 24, 1857.

that the President recall the renegade Democrat, whose behavior in Kansas was described as a disgrace.[23] This oblique
thrust at the Buchanan administration did not escape the
Central Georgian, which reflected that "they must . . . lay
hold of this *Bull* [Walker] by the horns for the sake of
State politics, but let the *Buck* [Buchanan] go free for the
sake of National politics. . . ."[24] Impetuous Democrats
had touched off an explosion with their third resolution.

As already pointed out, the race for the Democratic
gubernatorial nomination was a wide-open affair. On the
ninth ballot Gardner led Lumpkin, 172–127. On the
thirteenth ballot the vote was 151–149 in favor of Lumpkin. At this point Gardner's name was withdrawn. On six
of the next seven ballots Lumpkin led, but was unable to
amass the necessary two-thirds majority. With the convention deadlocked after twenty ballots, William Hope Hull
moved the appointment of a committee to end the stalemate. The motion carried and a committee composed of
three delegates from each of the eight Congressional districts was promptly chosen. Convening immediately to dis-
charge its duty, the committee decided to end the stalemate
by having each member cast a ballot for the Democrat he
preferred as the party's nominee for Governor. However,
before the first round of ballots was counted, Linton Stephens moved that Joseph E. Brown be named the committee's choice for the nomination. Stephens' motion was
speedily adopted. When the convention reassembled, it
unanimously ratified its committee's recommendation.[25]
"Through curiosity," relates Isaac W. Avery, "the ballots
[those cast before Linton Stephens' motion] were counted,

[23] Proceedings of the Democratic State convention quoted in Milledgeville *Federal Union,* June 30, 1857.

[24] Sandersville *Central Georgian,* July 8, 1857.

[25] Proceedings of the Democratic State convention quoted in Milledgeville *Federal Union,* June 30, 1857; I. W. Avery, *The History of the State
of Georgia from 1850 to 1881* (New York, 1881), 36.

and Alfred H. Colquitt was found to have had a majority of one." [26] Thus was Joseph E. Brown, an unknown
Southern-rights Democrat from Cherokee, unanimously
nominated for Governor. The revolt against Howell Cobb
had produced Georgia Democracy's only dark horse of the
fifties.[27] Writing his wife from Washington, Secretary Cobb
complained that the "course of the party in Georgia is to
me inexplicable." "They have lost all their good sense,"
he continued, and "seem bent on self destruction." "In
the history of politics," he mournfully concluded, "I have
never witnessed anything like it." [28]

During the two weeks preceding its State convention of
July 8 the American party's outlook for 1857 brightened
perceptibly. The impetuous Democratic convention's third
resolution constituted a neatly tailored campaign argument for Americans. They simply needed to quote it often
enough. A less oblique thrust at Howell Cobb and President Buchanan was the nomination by the Democrats of
Joseph E. Brown. Reanimated by Georgia Democracy's
double rebuke of "Cobbocracy," American party delegates
assembled in Milledgeville on July 8 for their regular
biennial nominating convention.[29] They promptly went
after President Buchanan and Governor Walker in a manner reminiscent of the Democratic gathering's frothy third
resolution. The Dred Scott decision, they boldly asserted,
was simply a judicial endorsement of the considered judgment of the American party. As a reward for his tireless
efforts in behalf of Fillmore's candidacy and because he
was probably the most prominent figure in his party, Benjamin H. Hill was nominated by acclamation. Once more

[26] Avery, *History of Georgia,* 36.
[27] Howell Cobb to John B. Lamar, July 10, 1857, in Brooks (ed.), "Howell
Cobb Papers," *loc. cit.,* 236.
[28] Howell Cobb to his wife, June 27, 1857, in Cobb MSS.
[29] Athens *Southern Watchman,* July 2, 1857; Savannah *Republican* quoted
in Augusta *Constitutionalist,* July 11, 1857.

Georgia was ready to wage a State contest in the crucible of national issues.[30]

Although only thirty-four years old, Hill was a capable performer on the stump. He was eloquent, enthusiastic and confident.[31] He lost no time in going after the Democrats. In his letter of acceptance, the American party's nominee scolded Governor Walker for his "interference" in Kansas.[32] Hill's blasts at the Kansas Governor were intended to bring both President Buchanan and Joseph E. Brown under the fire of his brilliant eloquence. Did Brown, he repeatedly asked, approve the action taken by the convention which nominated him? [33] If so, how could the Democratic nominee refuse to repudiate President Buchanan, who, he charged at La Grange, "does not only approve and sustain Walker, but *actually gave him* instructions"? [34]

Those Democrats who feared Brown would crumble before the withering oratory of his opponent were pleasantly surprised early in the campaign. Two years Hill's senior, Brown, like Hill, was a capable performer on the stump. Less sparkling than his opponent, Brown was equally enthusiastic and far more deliberate. He met the American nominee's attack by frequent slashes at Governor Walker. Brown's thrusts at the Kansas Governor were as sharp as

[30] Proceedings of the American party convention quoted in Milledgeville *Southern Recorder*, July 14, 1857; Phillips, *Life of Toombs*, 171.

[31] Haywood J. Pearce, Jr., *Benjamin H. Hill: Secession and Reconstruction* (Chicago, 1928), 22–31.

[32] Quoted in Milledgeville *Federal Union*, July 28, 1857.

[33] Savannah *Republican* quoted in Sandersville *Central Georgian*, July 23, 1857; Hill's letter of acceptance quoted in Milledgeville *Federal Union*, July 28, 1857; speeches of Hill quoted *ibid.;* Augusta *Constitutionalist*, August 1, 1857, and Sandersville *Central Georgian*, August 27, 1857.

[34] Quoted in Sandersville *Central Georgian*, August 27, 1857. Approximately a year later J. W. Forney declared in a speech at Tarrytown, New York, that Governor Walker had been instructed by the administration and that President Buchanan subsequently broke his pledge to sustain him. See Milledgeville *Southern Recorder*, September 14, 1858, and John H. Lumpkin to Howell Cobb, November 14, 1858, in Cobb MSS.

those of Hill, but abuse of President Buchanan was always scrupulously avoided. The Democratic nominee clung obstinately to the view that he could freely denounce Walker's interference in Kansas without questioning the integrity of the President.[35]

Not all Democrats cared to match Brown's objurgatory efforts against Walker. The *Federal Union,* for example, thought the third resolution had been hastily drawn.[36] That the Kansas Governor had "exhibited considerable vanity" was freely admitted by this paper, the State's leading Democratic prolocutor. However, it insisted that the proslavery element of the Territory was supporting him. Therefore to make an issue over Kansas was ridiculous.[37] Other Democratic journals joined the *Federal Union's* effort to cushion the shock of the third resolution. The Atlanta *Examiner,* for instance, declared that if American leaders were right in 1856, then Walker was right in 1857.[38] According to the *Southern Recorder,* the *Southern Banner,* reflecting Howell Cobb's view of the Walker mission, was even more dubious about the wisdom of the third resolution than either the *Federal Union* or the *Examiner.*[39] The latter two journals identified themselves with the so-called "Isothermalists," who with Governor Johnson believed the extension of slavery "for the sake of Southern aggrandizement" was impolitic and that slavery should be permitted "to work out its own destiny under the laws of climate, soil and pro-

[35] Brown's letter of acceptance quoted in Milledgeville *Federal Union,* July 21, 1857; speeches of Brown quoted *ibid.;* Augusta *Constitutionalist,* August 1, 1857; Savannah *Morning News,* August 14, 1857.

[36] Milledgeville *Federal Union,* July 14, 28, 1857; Augusta *Constitutionalist,* August 1, 1857.

[37] Milledgeville *Federal Union,* July 21, 28, 1857; Milledgeville *Southern Recorder,* July 14, 1857; Athens *Southern Watchman,* July 23, 1857.

[38] Atlanta *Examiner,* July 23, 1857.

[39] Milledgeville *Southern Recorder,* July 14, 1857; Howell Cobb to A. H. Stephens, September 12, 1857, in Phillips (ed.), *Correspondence,* 422.

duction." [40] Few of Georgia's public figures of the fifties had grown as much as Governor Johnson. Identified with extreme Southern rightists in 1850 and 1851, elected to the governorship in 1853, and re-elected in 1855, he had attained the sort of maturity which, had it been a more common asset among the nation's public men of the fifties, might have prevented the Civil War. The psychic violence which had been deliberately generated by "Bleeding Kansas" precluded the application of popular sovereignty, now called Isothermalism. The *Federal Union* appraised the situation perfectly when it declared early in 1856 that "the abolition hive is never so lively and happy, as when they see Southern men getting into a furious passion . . ." over their "rights." [41] Kansas was doomed to treatment within the framework of the orthodox abstractions of right and wrong.

Secretary Cobb was less subtle in his defense of Walker than the Isothermalists. He wrote A. H. Stephens frequently during the campaign, always assuring him that the Kansas Governor had done no injury to Southern rights. Cobb's political future was anything but encouraging in midsummer of 1857. With Hill and Brown vying to see who could turn the most graceful anti-Walker phrases, a Democratic victory would be only slightly less distasteful among party leaders in Washington than an American triumph. In victory or defeat, Cobb, it seemed, stood to lose. In a desperate effort to extricate himself from the incongruity created by the third resolution and by Brown's behavior

---

[40] H. V. Johnson to Jackson (Mississippi) Democrats quoted in Milledgeville *Federal Union*, January 20, 1857.

[41] *Ibid.*, February 5, 1856. The Griffin *Empire State*, September 3, 1856, carried an account of how two Georgians who went to Kansas were killed in the civil war there. The same paper carried on June 11, 1856, a report of the activities of J. W. White, a conspicuous proponent of emigration to Kansas.

on the stump, the Secretary of the Treasury requested
Stephens to round up party leaders during the State University's annual commencement exercises (then held in late
summer) to consider what might be done to save certain
party leaders from further embarrassment.[42] What trans-
pired at Athens is unknown. The *Chronicle and Sentinel*
was quoted as having charged that a "secret midnight council" had commanded Brown to ease up on Walker.[43] When
Hill repeated this charge, Brown promptly responded with
a vigorous denial.[44] Thomas W. Thomas accused Cobb's
clique of having taken under advisement during the commencement exercises a plan to run a third candidate. This
project was dropped, continued Thomas, only because it
was the considered judgment of Cobb's coterie that there
was not enough patronage to assure success.[45] Hence, in
the opinion of the *Southern Watchmen,* Brown was forced
"down the middle." Flanked by Cobbites and third resolutionites, he fulminated against Walker but spared the
President.[46]

Democrats who believed the third resolution to be a fair
appraisal of the Buchanan administration's stewardship
found an impulsive champion in Thomas W. Thomas, the
Elbert County jurist. This stormy petrel had been a Unionite in 1850–1851. In 1856 he had been a Buchanan elector.
A close friend of A. H. Stephens, Thomas was ably flanked
by two powerful journals, the *Constitutionalist* and the

[42] Howell Cobb to A. H. Stephens, July 23, 1857, in Phillips (ed.), *Cor-
respondence,* 408. Other letters from Cobb to Stephens dated July 21 and
September 12, 1857, *ibid.,* 406–407 and 422. For an account of the part
State University commencements played in politics see Coulter, *College
Life in the Old South,* 192.

[43] Quoted in Sandersville *Central Georgian,* September 24, 1857.

[44] Joseph E. Brown to James Gardner, Jr., quoted in Augusta *Constitutionalist,* July 25, 1857.

[45] Thomas W. Thomas to James Gardner, Jr., quoted *ibid.,* September 2, 1857.

[46] Athens *Southern Watchman,* September 3, 1857.

Times and Sentinel. The plain-spoken judge from Elbert
County insisted that the third resolution had been adopted
for the purpose of demonstrating the incongruity between
the Cincinnati platform, on which Buchanan had been
elected, and the performance of Walker in Kansas. It was
the opinion of Thomas that President Buchanan's stubborn refusal to dismiss Walker was evidence enough that
the national administration had repudiated the Cincinnati
platform.[47] Judge Thomas informed Brown privately that
he was disgusted with the candidate's letter of acceptance.
Continuing, he called on the Democratic nominee to
repudiate Buchanan for his Kansas policy.[48] To scotch what
seemed like a revolt against the Buchanan administration,
it has been observed how Howell Cobb brought about the
commencement caucus and how certain prominent Democratic journals adopted the Isothermal formula.[49]

Whatever hopes Hill might have entertained with respect
to detaching Thomas and the third resolutionites were
shattered when the volatile jurist announced on August
10 that he would stand by his party. "When I voted for
the third resolution," he explained, "I did not doubt
Walker would be removed." "Now would it be just . . .
in me," he inquired, "to desert Judge Brown because he
cherishes this hope longer than I find myself able to?"[50]
Disappointed at the refusal of Thomas to repudiate Brown,
some American party spokesmen charged that the Elbert
County jurist's demonstration had been a deliberate move
to permit dissident Democrats to vent their spleen without

[47] Thomas W. Thomas to James Gardner, Jr., quoted in Augusta *Constitutionalist,* July 25, 1857.

[48] Thomas W. Thomas to Joseph E. Brown, July 27, 1857, in Telamon
Cuyler Collection.

[49] Atlanta *Examiner,* July 23, 1857; Milledgeville *Federal Union,* July 14,
28, 1857; Milledgeville *Southern Recorder,* July 14, 1857; Howell Cobb to
A. H. Stephens, July 23, 1857, in Phillips (ed.), *Correspondence,* 408.

[50] Quoted in Augusta *Constitutionalist,* August 19, 1857.

quitting their party. Who, inquired the *Central Georgian,* was better equipped to open the spigots of psychic violence than the impulsive judge from Elbert County? [51] Whatever the merits of this appraisal, it is reasonably certain that the State University's commencement of 1857 was the occasion for some master plumbers to make plans for closing some pretty big spigots. With the Thomas declaration of August 10, the biggest of them was closed and the most serious threat to Brown's candidacy had vanished. Reassured by Thomas' refusal to bolt his party, leading Democrats denounced Hill's party as untrustworthy. A. H. Stephens, for example, taunted the opposition by quoting the record. In an open letter to the voters of his district, he wrote as follows: "If *tricksters* were the authors of it [Kansas-Nebraska Bill], they [Americans] were the tricksters backers. . . . Apart from this Walker business, no administration has ever in my day so fully met my cordial approval." [52] Like Stephens, the *Constitutionalist* went to the record to demonstrate the opposition's vacillation. By quoting two editorials from the *Chronicle and Sentinel,* the *Constitutionalist* would seem to have demonstrated that its rival was at least capricious. One editorial was dated February 28, 1854, and read as follows: "Our readers will require no apology for occupying so much of our space to-day with the *admirable* speech of Hon. A. H. Stephens, on the Nebraska question." The other, dated August 26, 1857, exclaimed as follows: "We denounced the Kansas Bill the moment we read it. . . ." [53]

The only local issue to enter the campaign of 1857 concerned the disposition of the State railroad. Something of an issue in the gubernatorial race of 1853, the Western and Atlantic had frequently broken into print as a result

[51] Sandersville *Central Georgian,* September 3, 1857.

[52] A. H. Stephens to the voters of the Eighth District, August 14, 1857, quoted in Phillips (ed.), *Correspondence,* 409–20.

[53] Augusta *Constitutionalist,* September 5, 1857.

of charges and countercharges with respect to how party leaders were using it to build up their political machines.[54] The *Southern Watchman* estimated in 1857 that State road patronage was worth 20,000 votes. Little wonder, it contended, that Democrats, in control of the State government since 1853, did not wish to sell the Western and Atlantic.[55] Charging that "Democrats put chalk marks on their hats, and rode free of charge," Hill proposed the sale of two thirds of the State road.[56] Brown, on the other hand, believed if the people wanted to sell their railroad, it was up to the legislature, not the executive, to act.[57]

Brown's vote of 57,000 exceeded President Buchanan's by 1,000, while Hill's 46,000 ballots surpassed Millard Fillmore's vote by 4,000. The Democrats retained their six-to-two advantage in the Congressional delegation.[58] It is significant that six of the eight Democratic candidates for Congress had formerly been members of the old Whig party, a fact which provoked the *Southern Recorder* to refer to the majority party as the "Bastard Democracy." [59] The flower of old Whiggery was at least sharing control of the Democratic party—hence the dearth of prominent figures in the American party. That Hill ran as well as he did was a tribute to his personal charm. The Savannah *Republican* thought he would have beaten Brown by

[54] Augusta *Chronicle and Sentinel*, August 29, 1855; Savannah *Republican* quoted *ibid.*, September 12, 1855; Louise Biles Hill, *Joseph E. Brown and the Confederacy* (Chapel Hill, 1939), 26–28; Pearce, *Benjamin H. Hill*, 30; Johnston, *Western and Atlantic Railroad*, 50.

[55] Athens *Southern Watchman*, November 13, 1857.

[56] Speech of Hill at Cool Springs quoted in Milledgeville *Federal Union*, September 22, 1857. Also speeches of Hill and Brown quoted in Savannah *Morning News*, August 14, 1857; Milledgeville *Southern Recorder*, September 22, 1857; Athens *Southern Watchman*, October 1, 1857; Pearce, *Benjamin H. Hill*, 30.

[57] Joseph E. Brown to Carrollton *Southern Democrat* quoted in Milledgeville *Federal Union*, September 22, 1857.

[58] Returns quoted *ibid.*, October 20, 1857.

[59] Milledgeville *Southern Recorder*, August 11, 1857.

20,000 votes had he worn the Democratic label.[60] That the majority party's label was an asset was generally conceded. Its national organization was construed as "safe." "The Democracy of Georgia," editorialized the *Morning News* in a postelection effort at analyzing public opinion, "interpret the National Democracy to be conservative of the *Constitutional rights of the whole Union.*" [61]

That Georgia Democracy was in complete control of State politics was demonstrated when the legislature met a few weeks after Brown's victory. The legislature promptly took up the matter of electing a United States Senator. It was necessary to choose a Senator at this time because Robert Toombs, although not seated until 1853, had been elected in 1851. While his term did not end until 1859, yet it had been six years since he was elected. Hence an election was in order in the fall of 1857. On the eve of the election an abortive attempt was made to put Benjamin Hill in the race against Senator Toombs.[62] Former Governor C. J. McDonald was also an aspirant. In Howell Cobb's opinion McDonald was making a futile attempt to fuse Southern-rights Democrats and Americans in behalf of his candidacy.[63] On November 7 the Democratic machine ground out the result. Toombs received 169 votes to 74 for Eli H. Baxter, the American candidate, while McDonald polled only 4 votes.[64]

A few days after Toombs was re-elected, the Democrats assembled at the State capital for their regular postelection convention. Former Governor Johnson, lately conspicuous for his moderate views, was called to the chair. A. H. Stephens and Senator Toombs were active participants, both

[60] Quoted in Milledgeville *Federal Union*, September 15, 1857.

[61] Savannah *Morning News*, October 13, 1857.

[62] Athens *Southern Watchman*, November 5, 1857.

[63] *Ibid.;* Howell Cobb to A. H. Stephens, October 19, 1857, in Phillips (ed.), *Correspondence*, 425.

[64] Athens *Southern Watchman*, November 12, 1857.

serving on the resolutions committee. The convention
pointed its verbalisms in the direction of Kansas. While
Buchanan's administration was warmly endorsed, Governor
Walker's recall was demanded at once. The moderate Isothermal view, which was really popular sovereignty, was
reiterated as the substance of Democratic dogma. Congress,
the convention resolved, had absolutely no authority even
to inquire into the manner in which a territory prepared
itself for statehood. There was a soberness about this Democratic gathering which reflected the feelings of H. V. Johnson, A. H. Stephens, and Howell Cobb. These were men
of moderate views. They were counting on the national
Democratic party to preserve the Union, and since this
party understood the Southern way of life, they believed
it would do what it could to protect that way of life. It
was in this spirit that the delegates called on Northern
Democrats to help realize the objectives of Georgia Democracy as understood by the convention of November,
1857.[65]

Demoralized by its late reverses and fragmentized by
the pulling and hauling of dissident groups, the American
party had little to offer after Hill's defeat. Some party leaders appeared to see an advantage in the absence of a national
organization. This precluded the necessity of appeasing
Northern colleagues. As a result, completely frustrated
American editors came up with strange jeremiads. The
Republican, for example, was quoted as having declared
in November of 1857 that ". . . we are 'Americans,' but
we had rather see the Sampsons of Democracy buried beneath the ruins of our glorious fabric, than by helping
to save the Union, help to save Democracy." [66] This was
strange language for a journal which for decades had been

[65] Proceedings of the Democratic party convention quoted in Milledgeville *Federal Union,* November 17, 1857.
[66] Quoted *ibid.,* December 1, 1857.

identified with the great dogma of the Union. The warp and woof of the Fillmore campaign had been Unionism, and among Georgians there was no more steadfast friend of the Union than Benjamin Hill. In their mid-December convention, Americans, like Democrats, continued to deride Governor Walker. When the Governor resigned on December 15, they were without an issue, while, on the other hand, the passing of Walker was followed by a rise in Democratic prestige. However, minority-party leaders professed to see a new ray of hope in the economic unbalance precipitated by the Panic of 1857. Mindful of what the Panic of 1837 had done to Jacksonian Democracy, American partisans prophesied evil days for their opponents.[67]

[67] Proceedings of the American party convention quoted in Milledgeville *Southern Recorder,* December 22, 1857; Macon *Journal and Messenger* quoted *ibid.,* December 29, 1857; Sandersville *Central Georgian,* October 22, 29, 1857.

XI

YOUNG HICKORY

UNLIKE Howell Cobb and H. V. Johnson, Joseph E. Brown looked upon Georgia Democracy as capable of acting independently of the national party organization. His election was to end the subordination of the State organization to national party interests. Thus during his regime strictly local matters frequently took precedence over national affairs. Since 1850 Georgians had lived in a political atmosphere heavily charged with national currents. Governor Brown was to provide a different experience—an experience which encouraged the independence and self-assurance that made it easier to snap the bonds of union in January of 1861. Unlike his two predecessors, Governor Brown was never to be very much concerned about appeasing Northern-interest groups for the purpose of holding together the national Democracy. Hence the national Democratic party was to grow more fragile and necessarily the great dogma of the Union was finally to succumb.

Few Democratic politicians doubted that their party had won in 1857 with a man who would have to be instructed in the duties of his office. It was assumed that because of his youth and inexperience Governor Brown would yield to the wishes of his seniors both in and out of the legislature. Therefore when the youthful Governor invoked the veto power to halt what he considered unwise legislation, he promptly became the target of wounded lawmakers who charged the Chief Executive with failure to show proper respect and deference for their views.[1]

[1] Fielder, *Life and Times of Joseph E. Brown*, 111.

An adroit politician, Brown understood the value of a whipping boy. From the ashes of economic conflagration, the legislature, acting on the recommendation of retiring Governor Johnson, brought forth the whipping boy the new Governor needed when it voted to legalize bank suspensions.[2] After sharply warning against suspension of specie payments in his inaugural, Brown had to reject the suspension act.[3] His veto message scorched the legislature in a manner reminiscent of President Andrew Jackson's assault on the Second United States Bank. He accused the banking community of a "high commercial, moral, and legal crime." Asserting that "all capital is the result of labor," Georgia's Young Hickory excoriated the lawmakers for conferring upon banks the privilege of defaulting on their notes. "If the suspension is legalized," he exclaimed, "it cannot be denied that the banks have triumphed over the people. . . ." Continuing, he objurgated that to legalize suspension would further depreciate bank notes and thereby work undue hardships on an already hard-pressed laboring class.[4]

The Democratic legislature overruled Brown's veto in December, 1857, and the suspension act became a law. Under it the banks were not required to resume specie payments until November 15, 1858.[5] No local issue of the fifties was to produce as much popular excitement as the suspension question. Governor Brown had cleverly dramatized the issue with his veto message. Before two months of his term had passed, the youthful Governor had eclipsed most of his seniors, and Georgians found themselves di-

[2] *Acts of the General Assembly, 1858,* 26–29.

[3] Governor Joseph E. Brown's inaugural address quoted in Atlanta *Intelligencer and Examiner,* November 13, 1857.

[4] Veto message quoted in Fielder, *Life and Times of Joseph E. Brown,* 121–22.

[5] *Acts of the General Assembly, 1858,* 26–29; Fielder, *Life and Times of Joseph E. Brown,* 123. Resumption came in May, 1858. Perhaps popular disapproval of the law hastened this action by the banks.

vided into "Brown" and "anti-Brown" parties. The Democratic press generally supported the Governor in his fight
against suspension, while the American party press generally sided with the banks.

Among the most outspoken opponents of Governor
Brown's antisuspension policy were the *Southern Watchman, Chronicle and Sentinel, Republican,* and *Central
Georgian.* All of these journals had supported Benjamin
Hill's gubernatorial candidacy. A few weeks before Brown
was inaugurated, the *Central Georgian* claimed a Democratic Congress had transferred the bulk of the nation's
specie to the upper Mississippi Valley for the purpose of
promoting railroad projects in that section. It was a Democratic trick, complained this journal, to promote free-soil
interests as well as railroads. Hard money had always been
a Democratic scheme, continued the *Central Georgian.*[6]
Protesting that hard money was reactionary, the editor advocated a plan to permit banks to issue notes against their
"general assets." This scheme, it was maintained by those
friendly to the banks, would inject a resiliency into the
State's credit money (bank notes) which was lacking in a
pure "specie," or "currency," program like that advocated
by the Governor.[7] It was the contention of the *Southern
Watchman* that suspension was the only way to keep specie
from going North.[8] The *Chronicle and Sentinel* insisted
that because Northern and Charleston banks had suspended, Georgia's banks were compelled to do likewise.[9]

Some of the supporters of the banking community ridiculed Governor Brown as a "country bumpkin" who was
naïve enough to suspect something "crooked" in a ledger

[6] Sandersville *Central Georgian,* October 22, 29, 1857.
[7] Many excellent editorials on this subject appeared in both the Sandersville *Central Georgian* and the Augusta *Chronicle and Sentinel* in late
1857 and early 1858.
[8] Athens *Southern Watchman,* November 19, 1858.
[9] Augusta *Chronicle and Sentinel,* January 28, 1858.

that balanced. The *Central Georgian*, however, appraised the Governor's behavior more accurately when it observed that there was "something to be gained by playing 'Old Hickory' in respect to banks. . . . So look bright, ye whitlings, who are watching out, to get on the blind side of the Governor; he has a sharp eye on both sides, and can see as far into a mill stone—i.e., a pecuniary difficulty—as any cashier to be found." [10]

Governor Brown's inaugural, his veto of the suspension act, and the subsequent attack on him by the banking community's press crystallized antibank sentiment throughout the State. In addition to strong editorial support from such journals as the powerful *Federal Union* and the *Intelligencer and Examiner,* the Governor's case profited immensely from countless demonstrations against the banking interests.[11] These demonstrations took the form of local indignation meetings. The following is a typical resolution adopted at these local gatherings: "Corporations are dangerous institutions, as they favor the interest of the few, by taking from the interest and pockets of the many." [12] In Clinch County the opponents of the banking interests adopted a resolution hailing Governor Brown as the new champion of the doctrines of Andrew Jackson.[13]

Alarmed at the extent and temper of these popular demonstrations, the banking community's press stigmatized them with the derisive epithet of Red Republicanism. They were inspired, exclaimed both the *Republican* and the *Chronicle and Sentinel,* by the Governor's satellites whose distorted minds could not possibly comprehend the

[10] Sandersville *Central Georgian,* November 19, 1857.

[11] Milledgeville *Federal Union,* January 5, 12, 19, 26, 1858; Atlanta *Intelligencer and Examiner,* December 10, 1857.

[12] Proceedings of the Cullondon, Georgia, antibank meeting quoted in Milledgeville *Federal Union,* January 26, 1858.

[13] Proceedings of the Clinch County antibank meeting quoted *ibid.,* February 16, 1858.

mysteries of property rights.[14] The wool-hat boys may not have understood the intricacies of suspension. Of one thing, however, they were certain. They had discovered a Young Hickory; and he gave promise of conducting a stubborn fight against the "economic royalists," whose behavior, it was believed, had somehow produced the economic purgatory of the winter of 1857–1858.[15]

The contest over suspension reopened the question of direct trade. Like other Southern states, Georgia had little direct trade with Europe. The bulk of her cotton was shipped to New York and then to Europe. Returning ships docked at Northern ports with their cargoes of manufactured goods which were then distributed throughout the South in the coastwise trade. This "cotton triangle" was a costly system because it involved high transportation costs as well as commissions to Northern middlemen.[16] It also imposed another penalty on the South by binding her to the highly sensitive Northern economy. Thus Southern economic life was subjected to the inquietudes of the business cycle, and when the Panic of 1857 broke, Georgia planters, like Northern business men, were caught in the benumbing coils of a depression.

Late in his second term Governor Johnson urged a committee of Savannah merchants and citizens to consider direct trade with Europe as a means of escaping from the clutches of a paralyzed Northern economy.[17] Throughout the State, planters gathered to take under advisement the Governor's recommendation. In Washington County such a gathering proposed a plan to ship cotton directly to Liverpool. It was contended that direct shipment would

---

[14] Augusta *Chronicle and Sentinel,* January 20, 1858.

[15] Issues of Milledgeville *Federal Union* for January and February, 1858.

[16] Harold Underwood Faulkner, *American Economic History* (New York, 1943), 322.

[17] H. V. Johnson to committee of Savannah merchants and citizens, in Georgia State Archives MSS.

not only speed up the movement of cotton, but that it would also ease the banking crisis by exchanging cotton for much-needed gold. Bitterly critical of Northern factors who were buying cotton for 12 or 13 cents and selling it for as much as 19 cents, Washington County planters demanded "the profits of intermediate purchasers." [18]

Despite the national Democratic party's pro-Southern efforts, the nation's economy had developed in such a manner as to compel the South to accept the status of a dependency. Georgia's planters were growing weary of this dependence on the North. Their agitation for direct trade betrayed such a feeling. Mixed with this tension at the top of the social order was the emotional coloration produced among the lower social groups by the suspension fight. These sentiments were superimposed on the psychic violence produced by "Bleeding Kansas." Here, it would seem, were the combustible elements for a great crisis before which the national Democratic party was beginning to betray a fatal incompetence. Fragmentation in the upper echelons was rendering it impotent. On the state level, at least insofar as Georgia was concerned, there was a growing tendency for Democratic leaders to act independently of the national party organization. While Joseph E. Brown was regarded by many of his followers as a second Andrew Jackson, his ideology more nearly resembled that of John C. Calhoun. An unmitigated State rightist, Governor Brown refused to continue the Cobb-Johnson formula of balance-of-power politics. As the leader of Georgia Democracy he insisted

[18] Proceedings quoted in Sandersville *Central Georgian*, November 26, December 3, 1857. Many Georgians agreed with J. N. Bethune of the Columbus *Corner Stone* that direct trade would come only after all tariffs were eliminated. See Elberton *Star of the South*, January 12, 1860, for Bethune's views. In 1857 Bethune organized a second "Columbus Movement" which did considerable propagandizing for free trade. For activities of the second "Columbus Movement" see Augusta *Constitutionalist*, January 7, 1857; Milledgeville *Federal Union*, January 6, May 26, 1857; and Sandersville *Central Georgian*, December 17, 1857.

on more independence than either of his predecessors had cared to exercise.

At the height of the suspension fight Governor Brown appointed John W. Lewis to the superintendency of the State-owned Western and Atlantic Railroad.[19] A vigorous and capable public official, Lewis soon vindicated Brown's belief that no "good reason exists why a State may not manage a great public work of this character with as much honesty, economy, and success as a corporation." [20] By 1860 the Western and Atlantic was earning about one-half million dollars annually.[21] This impressive showing quickly met with popular approval. Much of the earlier opposition to this project in state socialism evaporated as Young Hickory was acclaimed the State's most efficient administrator in many decades.

Governor Brown's treatment of the State road embraced more than merely changing superintendents. Most of the employees were promptly replaced. So sweeping were the changes that the Cassville *Standard* facetiously apostrophized in midsummer of 1858 that the Western and Atlantic had become the "Cherokee Baptist Railroad." [22] It was inevitable that the Governor should collide with John H. Lumpkin, for years the road's leading custodian of patronage. A close friend of Howell Cobb, Lumpkin had long been a key figure in the State Democratic machine. The private correspondence of Howell Cobb warrants the inference that both of Brown's predecessors had simply ratified Lumpkin's nominations for a large portion of State road jobs.[23] When the Brown ax began to fall on the heads of these Lumpkin appointees, the North Georgia Democrat was naturally embittered. He complained to Cobb

[19] Johnston, *Western and Atlantic Railroad,* 51; Coulter, *Georgia,* 262.
[20] Quoted in Fielder, *Life and Times of Joseph E. Brown,* 139.
[21] Johnston, *Western and Atlantic Railroad,* 106–107.
[22] Quoted in Athens *Southern Watchman,* July 29, 1858.
[23] John H. Lumpkin to Howell Cobb, October 14, 25, 1858, in Cobb MSS.

of Brown's dictatorial handling of the railroad. He also informed the Secretary of the Treasury that the Governor had secretly promoted his own chances as a compromise nominee in the party's deadlocked convention of 1857. This was especially disappointing, Lumpkin lamented, because he had counted on Brown to help him in his bitter fight against James Gardner, Jr.[24]

The Brown-Lumpkin feud redounded to the advantage of the Governor. Increasing monthly returns from the State's railroad were beginning to bear out the wisdom of his managerial policy.[25] With a flair for the dramatic, the Governor and his friends were purposefully squeezing some convincing political arguments from the Western and Atlantic financial reports. With one eye fixed on the Democratic national convention of 1860, Secretary Cobb realized the necessity of conciliating this modern Cincinnatus who was the State's Chief Executive. Hence the Secretary of the Treasury intervened as peacemaker. This was not a novel role for the Secretary and, as on other occasions, he was to labor under something of a handicap. He must have known that the price Brown was likely to exact would doubtless improve the Governor's already propitious station in the party. Nevertheless, Cobb and his friends, all anxious that the cabinet member succeed President Buchanan, were willing to pay a high price in return for a friendly delegation at the next Democratic national convention. Consummated on the eve of the gubernatorial contest of 1859, this *rapprochement* between the Cobb-Lumpkin and Brown factions assured Cobb of a friendly delegation at the forthcoming Democratic national con-

[24] *Ibid.* See also Hill, *Joseph E. Brown and the Confederacy,* 6–8, for an account of the preconvention activities of L. N. Trammell, a Brown supporter.

[25] Financial reports of the Western and Atlantic appear in frequent issues of the Milledgeville *Federal Union* during the last months of 1858; *Senate Journal, 1858,* 17.

clave, while, on the other hand, Lumpkin was compelled to forego his perennial quest for the State's highest office. Governor Brown's freedom in the distribution of State road patronage was secured; and of still greater significance was the bargain to award the incumbent a second nomination, which, in reality, amounted to a second term as Chief Executive. Now something of a President-maker, the wily Brown had indeed become the real boss of Georgia's Democracy.[26]

While Governor Brown and Secretary Cobb were settling a major dispute within Georgia's Democratic household, smoldering Kansas burst into flame. The Southern view of the Kansas question was succinctly put by Georgia's H. R. Jackson, former minister to Austria, when he explained that "the slaves were brought into the Territory under the Constitution of the United States, and are now the property of their masters." [27] The proslave Lecompton Constitution, so named from the place in Kansas where it was drafted, therefore called for a referendum late in 1857 on the issue, the constitution with slavery or the constitution without slavery.[28] Should the constitution without slavery be the choice of the voters, then "slavery was to exist 'no longer' in the state 'except that the right of property in slaves now in this Territory shall in no measure be interfered with.' " [29] When the vote was finally taken in late 1857, the official count showed over 6,000 for the constitution with slavery as against approximately 600 for the constitution without slavery. This election was certainly not an

[26] Joseph E. Brown to Howell Cobb, October 25, 1858, February 23, May 4, 1859, in Cobb MSS.; John H. Lumpkin to *id.*, October 25, November 14, December 29, 1858, February 21, 1859, *ibid.*; Robert E. Martin to *id.*, December 28, 1858, *ibid.*; John H. Lumpkin to [?], March 13, 1859, *ibid.*; J. W. Spullock to John H. Lumpkin, November 16, 1859, *ibid.*

[27] Quoted in Milledgeville *Federal Union*, November 30, 1858.

[28] Beveridge, *Abraham Lincoln*, II, 529; Craven, *Coming of the Civil War*, 388; J. G. Randall, *The Civil War and Reconstruction* (New York, 1937), 158.

[29] Quoted in Randall, *The Civil War and Reconstruction*, 158.

exception to the customary corrupt voting that abounded in Kansas during the fifties. Free-soil elements stayed away from the polls. It is conceivable that they did so to preserve the Kansas question. They naturally denounced the election returns as a travesty.[30]

Anxious to dispose of this irritating subject, President Buchanan reasoned that the Lecompton Constitution would at last bring an end to the long reign of terror in Kansas.[31] He therefore urged Congress to accept it. Political expediency was certainly on the side of the President. It has already been observed how administration opponents everywhere were making political capital out of Kansas. They expected to employ it for the *coup de grâce* in the state and Congressional elections of 1858. Buchanan hoped to avert this by promptly admitting Kansas with the Lecompton Constitution and "restoring peace and quiet to the whole country." [32] It might be argued that precedent was also on the side of the administration, for many states had come into the Union without popular referendums on their constitutions.[33] Whether morality was on the President's side was, of course, the crux of the dispute. In fact, this was at the bottom of the whole slavery controversy for the simple reason that both sides had utterly failed to heed the Hebraic injunction to beware of "the fruit of the tree of the knowledge of good and evil." Morality had produced such perversions that the disputants in the slavery struggle were unable to recognize that "good" was just as great a menace to the survival of the Union as "evil." [34]

[30] Craven, *Coming of the Civil War,* 388; Frank H. Hodder, "Some Aspects of the English Bill for the Admission of Kansas," in Vol. I of American Historical Association, *Annual Report,* 1906 (Washington, 1908), 210.

[31] Beveridge, *Abraham Lincoln,* II, 529.

[32] Quoted in Randall, *The Civil War and Reconstruction,* 159.

[33] Beveridge, *Abraham Lincoln,* II, 529.

[34] Craven, *Coming of the Civil War,* 388; Hodder, "Some Aspects of the English Bill," *loc. cit.,* 210; Chisholm, "Reëstablishment of Peacetime Society," *loc. cit.,* 7.

That Stephen A. Douglas believed President Buchanan was about to make a farce of popular sovereignty was, of course, of tremendous political significance, for it constrained the Illinois Senator, long regarded by many as the party's ablest leader and theretofore the strictest partisan, to break with the administration.[35] Because he opposed the Lecompton Constitution he was furiously attacked and finally read out of the party by the Buchanan group. Here was the genesis of the fight which was to wreck the Democratic party and eventually the Union. To break the Congressional deadlock over the Lecompton Constitution Representative William H. English of Indiana offered the celebrated bill named in his honor. The English Bill called for the people of Kansas to vote on the proslave Lecompton document as a whole. If accepted, the Territory was to become a state at once; if rejected, Kansas would be denied statehood until she had enough inhabitants to entitle her to one representative in Congress.[36] Despite the scornful attacks of Senator Douglas, the measure was adopted.[37] When Kansas voted in August, 1858, as prescribed by the English Bill, the Lecompton Constitution was decisively rejected. Thus ended the Kansas controversy. No longer did the original reason for the Republican party exist.[38] As for the Democratic party, the flavor of death had doubtless become nauseous among the higher echelons of its hierarchy.

Amidst the invidious exchanges over the Lecompton muddle, Abraham Lincoln addressed (June 16, 1858) his prophetic "house divided" speech to the Illinois State Republican convention, which nominated him for the United States Senate. The new leader's opponent was Stephen A. Douglas, whose biting attacks on the English Bill during the preceding months had enraged the powerful Buchanan

[35] Beveridge, *Abraham Lincoln*, II, 528, 534.   [36] *Ibid.*, 560.
[37] *Ibid.*, 561.   [38] Craven, *Coming of the Civil War*, 389.

faction of the Democratic party. Lincoln challenged his prominent opponent to a series of joint debates. The speechmaking which followed was of mediocre quality.[39] It was heavily freighted with tedious repetitions, red herrings, set questions, "explanations," and attempts to "explain" "explanations." [40] Lincoln turned his innate shrewdness to greatest advantage at Freeport, where he proposed the most celebrated of his set questions which, it will be recalled, bore an amazingly striking resemblance to the tedious queries that were contrived by certain Georgians during the campaign of 1856.[41] "Can the people of a United States Territory," asked the Republican candidate, "in any lawful way, against the wish of any citizen of the United States exclude slavery from its limits prior to the formation of a State Constitution?" [42] This question was cleverly designed to aggravate Douglas' troubles. By the Kansas-Nebraska Act Congress had empowered the territories to ban slavery only to have the Supreme Court declare three years later in the Dred Scott Case that Congress had no power over slavery in the territories. Lincoln was simply asking Douglas whether he favored the act of Congress or the Court's ruling. The Senator replied by upholding the Court's decision and, at the same time, asserting that slavery could be prevented in the territories by unfriendly legislation.[43] Standing on the jumbled ruins of the national Democratic party, Stephen A. Douglas was proclaimed the victor in a campaign which had transformed Abraham Lincoln into a figure of national prominence.[44]

[39] J. G. Randall, *Lincoln the President* (New York, 1945), I, 127–28; Paul M. Angle (ed.), *The Lincoln Reader* (New Brunswick, 1947), 232, 245.

[40] Randall, *Lincoln*, I, 126–28; Craven, *Coming of the Civil War*, 392.

[41] Montgomery, "A Georgia Precedent for the Freeport Question," *loc. cit.*, 200–207.

[42] Quoted *ibid.*, 200.

[43] Binkley, *American Political Parties*, 201; Craven, *Coming of the Civil War*, 292–93.

[44] Randall, *Lincoln*, I, 126–28; Myrta Lockett Avary (ed.), *Recollections*

"It seems to me . . . nothing can save the Democratic party of the South . . . except the admission of Kansas as a slave state."[45] The opinion was that of Thomas W. Thomas, for many years the stormy petrel of the Democratic party in Georgia. It was addressed to A. H. Stephens, patron of Stephen A. Douglas. The time was January of 1858, just a few weeks after the Lecompton (proslave) Constitution had been approved in a Kansas election. A few weeks later Thomas wrote Stephens another letter. This time he informed his friend that administration spokesmen in Georgia were charging both Stephens and Toombs with exploiting the Walker appointment (to the Kansas governorship) "to cover up Douglas's sins on the Kansas question."[46] Early in February Governor Brown wrote Georgia's Douglas spokesman. If Kansas was denied statehood because of her proslave constitution (Lecompton) then, explained Brown, his duty as Governor was plainly outlined in the fourth resolution of the Georgia Platform. A State convention, he cautioned, would be mandatory if such a contingency eventuated.[47] It may be concluded that during the first few months of 1858 administration Democrats were exerting more than a modicum of pressure on Stephens in the hope that he might influence Senator Douglas to support administration policy in Kansas.[48] That Howell Cobb was directing this project is borne out by his private correspondence.[49] Governor Brown's participa-

of *Alexander H. Stephens* (New York, 1910), 41; E. Ramsey Richardson, *Little Aleck: A Life of Alexander H. Stephens* (Indianapolis, 1932), 180.

[45] Thomas W. Thomas to A. H. Stephens, January 21, 1858, in Phillips (ed.), *Correspondence*, 428.

[46] *Id.* to *id.*, February 7, 1858, *ibid.*, 431.

[47] Joseph E. Brown to *id.*, February 9, 1858, *ibid.*, 431.

[48] Milledgeville *Southern Recorder*, August 24, 1858.

[49] Howell Cobb to Col. [J. B. Lamar], March 10, 1858, in Cobb MSS.; Milledgeville *Federal Union*, January 19, 1858; Augusta *Chronicle and Sentinel*, October 7, 1858; James Jackson to Howell Cobb, July 14, 1858, in Brooks (ed.), "Howell Cobb Papers," *loc. cit.*, 238; Howell Cobb to A. H.

tion was consistent with the bargain he and Cobb were
working out at this time with respect to State patronage,
the Governor's political future, and the complexion of
Georgia's delegation at the next Democratic national convention. Howell Cobb, an old Jacksonian Democrat, and
A. H. Stephens, a nostalgic Whig turned Democrat, were
thus facing each other in battle array. The prize for which
they were contesting was the presidency of the United
States. Always the astute politician, Cobb had the blessing
of President Buchanan, while Douglas, whose cause Stephens stubbornly espoused, possessed an unyielding purpose and an overwhelming determination to succeed.

Georgia's Democratic press was as severely jarred by
Douglas' behavior as that party's leaders. According to the
Chronicle and Sentinel (American) the following journals
were pro-Douglas: Augusta *Constitutionalist,* Macon *Tele-
graph,* Wilkes *Republican,* and Lumpkin *Palladium.* The
same journal reported the following papers as opposed to
Douglas: Milledgeville *Federal Union,* Athens *Southern
Banner,* Cassville *Standard,* Columbus *Times and Sentinel,*
Albany *Patriot,* Cartersville *Express,* and Macon *State Press.*
Not all Democratic papers took sides, however. The follow-
ing were adjudged as neutral with respect to the bitter
fight between the administration and Senator Douglas:
Griffin *Empire State,* Marietta *Advocate,* Rome *Southerner,*
Dalton *Times,* and Atlanta *Intelligencer and Examiner.*[50]

A sanctuary for nostalgic Whigs, Georgia Democracy had
failed to democratize many of these political outlanders.
Despite three or four years apprenticeship, A. H. Stephens,
Robert Toombs, the editor of the *Constitutionalist* (J. A.
Nisbet), and many others simply refused to democratize

Stephens, September 8, 1858, in Phillips (ed.), *Correspondence,* 442–44. See
also Johnson and Browne, *Life of Alexander H. Stephens,* 338.

[50] Augusta *Chronicle and Sentinel,* October 7, 1858.

themselves.[51] Hence there was some basis for the *Federal Union's* complaint that "it is something remarkable that the leniency towards Mr. Douglas for his defection, is cherished by those who formerly belonged to the whig party." [52]

Caught in the cross fire of the Buchanan-Douglas fight, Georgia's Democracy offered a perfect target to American party editors, who, for the most part, were content to aggravate their opponents' difficulties. "Would to God that the South was as true to her principles as Douglas is to his," moralized the *Southern Recorder* during the bitter exchanges in Congress over the English Bill.[53] It has been observed that the English Bill called for the submission of the Lecompton Constitution to the voters of Kansas. In August, 1858, Kansans rejected this notorious instrument. American editors promptly began blasting their opponents with the severest admonitions. "Have they [Democrats] not already done it [excluded slavery from a territory] far more successfully than the Black Republicans could have done?" inquired the distraught *Southern Watchman*.[54] "If there has been any treason to the South," moaned the *Southern Recorder*, "the Southern National Democrats are the traitors, not Mr. Douglas." [55] "SOLD—Yes, sold!", wailed the *Enquirer;* "knocked off to a *low bid,* and still *lower* bidder—an individual known in political circles as 'Bill English.' " [56]

[51] Milledgeville *Federal Union,* September 14, 1858; Athens *Southern Watchman,* September 2, October 14, 1858; Augusta *Chronicle and Sentinel,* October 27, 1858; Milledgeville *Southern Recorder,* October 12, 1858; Cassville *Standard* quoted *ibid.,* October 5, 1858; James Jackson to Howell Cobb, July 14, 1858, in Brooks (ed.), "Howell Cobb Papers," *loc. cit.,* 238.
[52] Milledgeville *Federal Union,* October 5, 1858.
[53] Milledgeville *Southern Recorder,* May 25, 1858.
[54] Athens *Southern Watchman,* September 16, 1858.
[55] Milledgeville *Southern Recorder,* October 12, 1858.
[56] Quoted *ibid.,* October 26, 1858.

When Stephens journeyed to Illinois to counsel with Douglas during the latter's campaign for re-election, the American press taunted this former Whig for going West to "placate the distracted Democracy." [57] Better copy was provided for American editors when Douglas announced at Freeport that while the Supreme Court had ruled slavery could not be kept out of the territories, yet territorial residents were empowered to prevent slavery simply by adopting unfriendly legislation. Pouncing on Douglas' "Freeport heresy" with a chorus of "I told you so," American journalists insisted it was a logical sequence of both the Democratic platform of 1856 and the policy outlined by James Buchanan in his letter of acceptance.[58]

Failure to discipline Douglas was a severe blow to the Democratic party's national leadership. Cobb certainly felt the Douglas rebuff had done irreparable damage and so expressed himself after the Senator's re-election.[59] Despite the Secretary's humiliation, he seems to have had no desire to invoke the Georgia Platform for the purpose of registering a protest against what had happened to Kansas. Brown had, it is true, warned Stephens that in case Kansas was rejected then a State convention would be necessary. However, neither Brown nor Cobb would appear to have been willing at this time to subject their political organization to the kind of test the calling of a State convention would surely engender. Of all men, Cobb, one of the political architects of 1850, appreciated how easy it was for a political organization to be dashed to pieces before the impact of popular indignation. The Secretary of the Treasury was

57 *Ibid.*, August 24, 1858; Athens *Southern Watchman*, October 21, 1858.

58 Milledgeville *Southern Recorder*, September 14, 28, October 26, 1858; Athens *Southern Watchman*, October 7, 14, November 25, 1858; Augusta *Chronicle and Sentinel*, September 29, 1858.

59 Howell Cobb to J. B. Lamar, November 4, 1858, in Cobb MSS.; Johnson and Browne, *Life of Alexander H. Stephens*, 338; Milledgeville *Federal Union*, October 5, 1858.

looking forward to the Democratic national convention of 1860, where he hoped that somehow party problems would be resolved. Governor Brown, now the real master of the State party machine, did not care to take on additional worries on the eve of his campaign for re-election.

XII

VOTE OF CONFIDENCE

DESPITE the Cobb-Brown understanding, Georgia's Democracy approached its biennial conclave in 1859 with a normal complement of potential defections. The understanding between the Secretary of the Treasury and the Governor had been a three-cornered one. Brown was to have a second term and his control over State-road patronage was to continue; Cobb was to have a friendly delegation at the Democratic national convention in 1860; and John H. Lumpkin, who was giving up his gubernatorial ambition, was to replace Alfred Iverson in the United States Senate.[1] It would appear that Senator Iverson was not consulted about these deals. He was simply to be dropped. At least, that was the story published by the Atlanta *Southern Confederacy*, an anti-Brown paper.[2] Naturally this story was played up by the minority press.[3] When the powerful *Federal Union* flayed Senator Iverson two weeks in advance of the Democratic State convention, the *Southern Confederacy*'s story moved a step closer to confirmation.[4] The junior Senator's friends hurried to his defense by giving him a testimonial dinner in Griffin in mid-July.[5] In speaking to his friends Iverson took a very pessimistic view of the future, foretelling with amazing

---

1 John H. Lumpkin to Howell Cobb, February 21, 1859, Joseph E. Brown to *id.*, February 23, 1859, and John H. Lumpkin to [?], March 13, 1859, in Cobb MSS.

2 Milledgeville *Southern Recorder*, April 5, 1859; Atlanta *Southern Confederacy* quoted in Athens *Southern Watchman*, April 14, 1859.

3 Milledgeville *Southern Recorder*, April 5, 1859; Athens *Southern Watchman*, April 14, 1859.

4 Milledgeville *Federal Union*, May 31, 1859.   5 *Ibid.*, July 26, 1859.

accuracy forthcoming events.[6] Senator Iverson's gloomy predictions were not well received by the Democratic press.[7] The incident had the effect of identifying him with the extreme Southern-rights or radical wing of his party. The slightest encouragement to this group was always something of a threat to the national Democratic party, which both the Cobb-Brown-Lumpkin and the Stephens-Gardner-Nisbet factions still believed the best safeguard of the Southern way of life.

A greater threat to Empire State Democracy came from another quarter. Embittered because of his failure to capture the Democratic nomination for Governor in 1857, James Gardner, Jr., publisher of the influential *Constitutionalist,* had never forgiven either Cobb, who had supported Lumpkin then, or Brown, who had unexpectedly received the nomination. Brown's State-road program, as well as his banking policy, was a frequent subject for the sarcastic quips of the hypercritical Gardner.[8] On the national level the Augusta editor was a source of incomparable grief to Cobb. Taking his cue from A. H. Stephens, Gardner turned out frequent editorials in support of Senator Douglas. This naturally infuriated Cobb and provoked him to make a desperate effort to immobilize Douglas' Georgia mouthpiece. In this venture the Secretary of the Treasury sought the assistance of J. M. Smythe, the able founder and editor of the old Augusta *Republic.* At Cobb's request Smythe urged Gardner to repudiate Douglas. When Gardner refused, Smythe proposed to the Secretary of the Treasury that an administration journal be founded in Augusta.[9]

[6] Speech of Alfred Iverson quoted *ibid.*

[7] Augusta *Constitutionalist,* August 6, 1859; Macon *Georgia Telegraph* quoted in Milledgeville *Federal Union,* August 9, 1859.

[8] Augusta *Constitutionalist,* February 2, 1859; Griffin *Empire State,* January 6, 1859; Milledgeville *Federal Union,* January 18, February 1, 8, 1859.

[9] J. M. Smythe to Howell Cobb, May 28, June 3, July 19, 1859, in Cobb MSS.

While at least $2,000 was pledged to this project in journalism, it fell through when the *Constitutionalist* reluctantly endorsed a second term for Brown.[10] Refusal by one of the State's leading Democratic editors to repudiate Senator Douglas was, however, a severe blow to Cobb's presidential aspirations. Unless the State convention was willing to do more for him than Gardner, the Secretary of the Treasury could hardly expect national party leaders to support him in his fight for the presidential nomination.

More powerful than other dissident groups within Georgia's Democracy was the Southern-rights element. Disgusted by the loss of Kansas, this wing of the party was either apathetic or openly hostile to the national administration. That Southern rightists were taking over the county organizations was convincingly demonstrated by the press accounts of local party gatherings. Utterly mortifying to the Democratic high command was the *Enquirer*'s (American) habit of quoting the cold references to President Buchanan which were being voted with increasing frequency in local party meetings.[11] The *Times and Sentinel* (Democratic) was reported to have described Secretary Cobb's political future as hopeless in the face of this frozen apathy.[12] That the Athens Democrat was uneasy is attested by a letter he wrote shortly before the Democratic State convention to J. B. Lamar, his Macon kinsman. Expressing his conviction that unless the convention endorsed the national administration he would stand before his cabinet associates as a repudiated man, he continued by instructing his kinsman that he was caught in the cross fire of mutually antagonistic wings of Georgia's Democracy. These he crisply labeled the "Douglas—slave trading—antiadministration

[10] *Ibid.*; Augusta *Constitutionalist*, June 18, July 30, 1859.

[11] See, for example, Milledgeville *Federal Union*, April 12, May 3, June 14, 1859.

[12] Quoted in Athens *Southern Watchman*, May 17, 1859.

party." [13] The mutual scorn of these two groups was exceeded only by their common contempt for the Buchanan administration, whose Georgia spokesman was Howell Cobb. Here indeed were the combustible elements of a major party crisis. Only Governor Brown seemed capable of preventing the pulling and hauling of dissident groups from wrecking the party.

While Joseph E. Brown had numerous bitter critics, yet they and the manner in which they had been created doubtless constituted his greatest single political asset. The Governor's most violent assailants were those who objected to his handling of the State road and his banking policy. The most corrosive shafts that were hurled at the Governor appeared in the *Constitutionalist* (Democratic) and, according to the *Federal Union*, in the Savannah *Republican* (American). [14] Characterizing Brown as "a creature of accident" and "the spawn of a party quarrel," the *Republican* provoked the *Federal Union* to counter with what had become an endemic defense. [15] "If he [Brown] had sold himself body and soul to the Banks and Railroad corporations," boasted the *Federal Union*, "he would have been a very proper man for the Republican school of politicians." [16] This credo had been hammered out by the Governor and his satellites during the early months of Brown's term. Reports of the proceedings of local Democratic conventions warrant the inference that by 1859 this old Jacksonian creed had swollen into a substantial stream of political thought. [17] Hence Governor Brown could write Cobb six weeks before the convention that he expected to be renominated with ease. [18] It has already been observed that

[13] Howell Cobb to J. B. Lamar, May 23, 1859, in Cobb MSS.
[14] Augusta *Constitutionalist*, February 2, May 21, 1859; Milledgeville *Federal Union*, March 15, 29, 1859; Griffin *Empire State*, January 6, 1859.
[15] Quoted in Milledgeville *Federal Union*, March 15, 1859.
[16] *Ibid.*, March 15, 1859.   [17] *Ibid.*, April 12, 19, 26, 1859.
[18] Joseph E. Brown to Howell Cobb, May 4, 1859, in Cobb MSS.

these local party gatherings were generally not enthusiastic about President Buchanan. Consequently Cobb's reflections on the forthcoming State convention were less sanguine than the Governor's.[19]

Four hundred delegates assembled at Milledgeville on June 15 for the Democratic party's biennial nominating convention. Three resolutions were presented and summarily adopted, two of them by unanimous votes. The first of these resolutions reaffirmed the party's faith in the Cincinnati platform on which President Buchanan had stood in 1856; the second was a tepid endorsement of the Buchanan administration; and the third called for Brown's renomination by acclamation. Despite its moderate tone there was a show of opposition to the second resolution. Its opponents clustered around J. E. Blount of Randolph County. Blount spoke boldly against endorsing the Buchanan administration. H. R. Jackson, a Cobb spokesman, made an eloquent defense of the President, after which the convention acted decisively on the second resolution, adopting it by a vote of 374 to 34.[20] It may therefore be said that the convention endorsed the government at Washington. Cobb appeared satisfied, although he expressed the opinion that endorsement had not been emphatic enough.[21] The American press naturally attempted to make political capital out of the second resolution. The *Republican,* generally more sympathetic toward the national administration than most American journals, thought the second resolution amounted to a repudiation of the nation's Chief Executive, while the *Southern Watchman* and the *Southern Recorder* agreed that Buchanan had been "damned with faint praise." [22]

[19] Howell Cobb to J. B. Lamar, May 23, 1859, in Cobb MSS.

[20] Proceedings quoted in Milledgeville *Federal Union,* June 21, 1859.

[21] Howell Cobb to J. B. Lamar, June 21, 1859, in Cobb MSS.

[22] Savannah *Republican* quoted in Milledgeville *Federal Union,* July 23, 1859; Athens *Southern Watchman,* July 7, 1859; Milledgeville *Southern Recorder,* June 28, 1859.

While Democratic leaders had difficulty in guiding their party through the preparatory stages of the campaign of 1859, their assignment was simple when compared to the problems confronting their opponents. During the early months of 1859 American party editors argued at length over how to wage a campaign against Governor Brown.[23] As the months wore on it became increasingly evident that minority party leaders did not relish the prospect of a contest with the popular Governor.[24] Yet they could hardly escape one. Complaining that the Democrats were forcing them into a contest, American party editors suddenly professed to see great virtue in changing their party's label.[25] "There is now forming a great national party of conservative opposition," declared the *Southern Watchman* early in May. This party was represented as the hope of the South. It alone could save the Union and the constitution, asserted the *Southern Watchman*.[26] The derelict American party was therefore formally banished in June when its central executive committee advised against holding a State convention.[27] In the next breath, however, the committee announced an "Opposition party" convention for July 3. It was to be held in Milledgeville and was addressed specifically to Americans, Whigs, and independent Democrats.[28]

Instead of ending the vacillation of minority editors and inaugurating a program of decisive action, the behavior of the American party's central executive committee added

[23] Athens *Southern Watchman*, March 31, 1859; Columbus *Enquirer* quoted in Milledgeville *Southern Recorder*, April 5, 1859; *ibid.*, May 17, 24, 1859; Macon *Journal and Messenger* quoted in Milledgeville *Federal Union*, March 22, 1859; Columbus *Enquirer* quoted *ibid.*, April 12, 1859.

[24] Milledgeville *Southern Recorder*, May 17, 1859; Athens *Southern Watchman*, March 31, 1859.

[25] Athens *Southern Watchman*, May 5, 1850; Milledgeville *Southern Recorder*, May 17, 1859.

[26] Athens *Southern Watchman*, May 5, 1859.

[27] Address of the central executive committee of the American party quoted in Milledgeville *Federal Union*, June 14, 1859; Joseph E. Brown to A. H. Stephens, June 4, 1859, in Phillips (ed.), *Correspondence*, 444-45.

[28] Milledgeville *Federal Union*, June 14, 1859.

to the general state of the minority's bewilderment. The *Enquirer, Journal and Messenger,* and *Southern Recorder* continued to advise against fighting Governor Brown, while the *Citizen* and the *Republican* were determined that the "inflated Cherokee Baptist" should have an opponent.[29] The position of those who would lose the governorship by default was based on an interesting bit of speculation. If Governor Brown were unopposed, explained the *Southern Recorder,* then many Democrats would not bother to vote.[30] Consequently if the Opposition would turn out in full strength on election day, its slate of candidates for Congress and the legislature would be victorious.[31] The true policy of the Opposition party, declared editor R. M. Orme of the *Southern Recorder,* was not to try to manufacture enthusiasm against Brown, but rather to fight Democracy on national issues, its most vulnerable salient.[32] It was entirely consistent, therefore, to pass up the gubernatorial contest. Sensing the trickery in this plan, the vigilant *Federal Union* chided those of the Opposition who were content to let Brown win by default.[33]

On July 20 a group of Opposition party leaders assembled in Macon. In the confusion which attended the postponement of the convention originally scheduled for Milledgeville on July 3, a smaller group showed up in the capital city. This latter group never reached the Macon conclave.[34] The Macon delegates freely scolded President Buchanan, adopted a resolution asserting that nonintervention did

29 Milledgeville *Southern Recorder,* June 28, 1859; Columbus *Enquirer* quoted *ibid.;* Milledgeville *Federal Union,* June 28, July 5, 1859.

30 Quoted in Milledgeville *Federal Union,* July 19, 1859; Milledgeville *Southern Recorder,* July 12, 1859.

31 Milledgeville *Southern Recorder,* July 12, 1859.

32 *Ibid.,* June 28, July 12, 1859.

33 Quoted *ibid.,* July 5, 1859.

34 Milledgeville *Federal Union,* July 19, 1859; Athens *Southern Watchman,* July 21, 1859; Augusta *Constitutionalist,* July 23, 1859; Milledgeville *Southern Recorder,* July 26, 1859.

not preclude the right of Congress to protect slavery in the territories, unsuccessfully offered the gubernatorial nomination to several of the party's most prominent figures, and adjourned to meet again on August 10 in Atlanta.[35] The Macon *State Press* (Democratic) pronounced the Opposition's first convention a "fizzle," while the *Republican* (Opposition) assured its readers the gathering had gone off well.[36] The *Southern Watchman* (Opposition) thought the delegates had done well by having done nothing, while the *Citizen* (Opposition) was certain an excellent platform had been constructed.[37] The satirical *Federal Union* observed that ". . . the whole Menagerie of opossums, coons, and wild cats, besides many other animals, are to be let loose in Atlanta. . . ."[38]

According to prearrangement the adjourned Macon convention reassembled in Atlanta on August 10 during "a wet gloomy spell of weather that typified the spirits and prospects of the party it represented."[39] This meeting would appear to have been unusually well attended, the *Southern Watchman* reporting a thousand delegates present.[40] After approving the action taken at Macon, the delegates took up the question of a nomination.[41] According to the correspondent of the Savannah *Morning News*, a nomination was made after the Opposition candidate for Congress in the fourth district had unwittingly exposed the plan of party leaders to name an opponent for Governor Brown only if pressure from the floor forced them to do

[35] Report of the proceedings quoted in Milledgeville *Southern Recorder,* July 26, 1859.

[36] Quoted in Augusta *Constitutionalist,* July 27, 1859.

[37] Quoted *ibid.,* July 30, 1859; Athens *Southern Watchman,* July 28, 1859.

[38] Milledgeville *Federal Union,* August 2, 1859.

[39] Avery, *History of Georgia,* 93–96.

[40] Athens *Southern Watchman,* August 18, 1859. See also Milledgeville *Federal Union,* August 23, 1859.

[41] Report of the proceedings quoted in Milledgeville *Southern Recorder,* August 16, 1859.

so.[42] Consequently Warren Akin received the nomination. An obscure lawyer from Cass County, he had served as legal counsel for the State road until dismissed by Governor Brown.[43] He was in poor health and therefore unable to conduct an active campaign.[44] The *Southern Recorder,* ostensibly the Opposition party's leading journal, was manifestly lukewarm to a nomination.[45] His warning just before the Macon convention that the party should not attempt to manufacture enthusiasm against the Governor was doubtless very distressing to editor R. M. Orme when he discovered that he had misspelled Akin's last name at least four times in reporting the convention's proceedings.[46]

Encouraged by the hastily improvised Opposition party, Governor Brown announced immediately after his renomination that, although he would not canvass the State for re-election, he expected to win by 30,000 votes.[47] Opposition leaders accepted the Governor's challenge and set out to detach Democracy's dissident elements. In the main, Opposition strategy was to underline the failures of the national administration, although, when expedient, Brown was freely excoriated. This mode of attack had a tendency to identify the minority with Southern-rights dogma. As a matter of fact, before the canvass was concluded Opposition dialectics had acquired a ring that was not unlike the cries of the old Southern Rights party of 1850–1851. The threatened Iverson purge provided Akin and his col-

[42] Savannah *Morning News* correspondent quoted in Milledgeville *Federal Union,* August 23, 1859.

[43] Report of the proceedings quoted in Milledgeville *Southern Recorder,* August 16, 1859; Milledgeville *Federal Union,* August 30, September 6, 1859.

[44] Warren Akin's letter of acceptance quoted in Athens *Southern Watchman,* August 25, 1859.

[45] Milledgeville *Southern Recorder,* August 16, 1859.

[46] *Ibid.*

[47] Joseph E. Brown to A. H. Stephens, June 4, 1859, in Phillips (ed.), *Correspondence,* 444–45; speech of Joseph E. Brown before Democratic State convention quoted in Milledgeville *Federal Union,* June 28, 1859.

leagues a convenient point of departure. Such journals
as the *Southern Recorder* and the *Southern Watchman*
promptly addressed profuse condolences to a Democrat
who in self-defense had identified himself with the Southern-rights wing of his party.[48]

The minority's most dramatic appeal to the Southern-
rights creed came, strangely enough, from Benjamin Hill,
Brown's opponent in 1857. Generally recognized by historians as a Unionist because of his fight against secession in
1861, Hill's behavior in 1859 betrayed that fatal impatience
which was then fermenting in the culture of Southern frustration. This sense of frustration was activated on the one
hand by the consistent failure of the national Democracy
to protect what were considered the "rights" of the South
in the territories, and on the other by the persistent efforts
of Northern moralists to convict the South of "sin." At this
stage of his long and useful public career, Hill's impatience
would seem to have overwhelmed him. Early in August a
letter which he had written to G. M. Dudley of Americus
appeared in several of the State's leading papers. A forth-
right declaration, the Dudley letter amounted to a com-
pendium of Southern-rights ultraism. Demanding that
Congress pass protective legislation for slavery in the territories, Hill called upon the Governor to repudiate the
national Democratic party. The leaders of this party, bitterly complained Brown's former opponent, had traded
the South out of her rights in Kansas. There now remained
but one course open to the South and that was "war—war
in every sense by which the term is defined, or definable."
This strong language cannot be dismissed as the conventional extravagance of a gubernatorial campaign. That Hill
meant what he had written to Dudley is attested by his
unprecedented pledge to support Brown's second canvass,

---

[48] Milledgeville *Southern Recorder*, April 5, 1859; Atlanta *Southern Confederacy* quoted in Athens *Southern Watchman*, April 14, 1859.

if the latter would simply renounce the national Democratic party and offer to assist those who were determined to compel Congress to protect Southern rights in the territories.[49] Even Akin was alleged to have taken a similar stand.[50]

The Opposition attack spared neither wing of the national Democratic party. Both President Buchanan and Senator Douglas were accused of wanton disregard of Southern rights in Kansas. Despite this sweeping assault on the national leadership of the party, Georgia's rival Union Democratic factions (the followers of Buchanan and the followers of Douglas) were unable to bury the hatchet. This was due to the Opposition tactic of frequently asking Brown whether he would support Senator Douglas in case the latter received the Democratic nomination for President in 1860.[51] Obviously the Governor could not answer in the affirmative and keep his peace with Howell Cobb. Usually Brown spokesmen avoided a direct answer by denying the Illinois Senator had even a remote chance of winning the Democratic nomination in 1860.[52] This oblique counterthrust served to remind Gardner and Stephens, both Douglas enthusiasts, that to the Cobb-Brown faction the suggestion of Douglas' nomination was odious.[53] Veering sharply in the direction of "ultra Southern rights" ways and means, the Opposition astutely maneuvered its attack so that Democratic factions were never permitted to forget their differences.

Like previous Georgia campaigns of the fifties, the one

[49] Augusta *Constitutionalist,* August 6, 1859.

[50] Milledgeville *Federal Union,* September 13, 1859; Macon *Georgia Telegraph* quoted *ibid.,* August 23, 1859.

[51] Ellijay citizens to Joseph E. Brown and Warren Akin quoted in Athens *Southern Watchman,* September 22, 1859; *ibid.,* September 15, 22, 1859.

[52] Milledgeville *Federal Union,* September 27, 1859.

[53] Macon *Journal and Messenger* quoted in Augusta *Constitutionalist,* September 10, 1859; Athens *Southern Watchman,* August 25, September 15, 1859.

of 1859 was heavily weighted with tedious legal questions
and explanations. Occasionally the monotony of involved
queries and answers was broken by the biting wit of a
sarcastic editor. For the edification and amusement of his
readers, the editor of the *Federal Union* characterized the
Opposition party as ". . . a compound of the odds and ends
of all parties that have existed in Georgia for the last six
years—

> 'Eye of newt, and toe of frog,
> Wool of bat, and tongue of dog.' " [54]

When Joshua Hill, the Opposition candidate for Congress
in the seventh district, hurried to the capital city to do some
campaigning among those who had gathered for a circus,
the same editor, reflecting on the candidate's itinerary, observed that a "striped politician is not half so funny as a
clown." [55] Among the most acrimonious of the Georgia
journalists of the fifties was J. H. Christy of the *Southern
Watchman,* the Athens Opposition paper. Christy was particularly bitter in 1859. The most frequent victims of his
canards were Governor Brown and Senator Robert Toombs.
The latter he nicknamed "Bobuel" and described as ". . .
that burly blusterer . . . who disgraces the State of Georgia by the occupancy of a seat in the Senate. . . ." The
Senator was an "arch traitor" and a "McWhig" who was
in an unholy alliance with a Governor who was a "pompous
ignoramus . . . , a ridiculously vain and highly inflated
ignoramus." [56]

While the Opposition built its main offensive around
national issues in the hope of arresting the momentum of
a Democracy which had lately been refreshed by Brown's
vigorous leadership, Democrats, on the other hand, depended on the Governor's record to bring them victory.

[54] Milledgeville *Federal Union,* September 27, 1859.
[55] *Ibid.*
[56] Athens *Southern Watchman,* September 8, 1859.

His handling of the State road, his reduction of taxes, and his program for expanding public education made Brown's re-election obligatory, insisted the *Times and Sentinel*.[57] The Governor expressed the opinion that his reorganization of the State road was his most important achievement. While he promised not to take the stump, yet he made it plain that Georgians would frequently be reminded that the Western and Atlantic was paying from $35,000 to $40,000 per month.[58] The *Federal Union* drew the assignment of dressing State-road balance sheets for popular consumption.[59] The task was well handled. In fact, this eager journal would seem to have overplayed the act of squeezing political capital from prosaic financial reports. Opposition spokesmen soon brandished the "$40,000 argument" to taunt former Governor Johnson and to vindicate Hill's charge of 1857 that the State road had been grossly mismanaged.[60]

Aware of the popular appeal of the Governor's antibank crusade, Brown spokesmen baited the "financial interests" by accusing them of making contributions to the Opposition campaign fund.[61] Thus old passions were rekindled. As before, Brown was accused of using the bank question to stir up class feeling.[62] Apparently unaware of the Governor's success in the role of Young Hickory, Benjamin Hill made the mistake of addressing an open letter to Opposition editors in which he charged Brown with a deliberate war on the banks to create feeling in his behalf.[63] "Woolhat" and "horny-handed" voters were not interested in the "cause" of the Governor's campaign against the banks.

[57] Quoted in Milledgeville *Federal Union*, September 20, 1859.

[58] Speech of Governor Brown quoted *ibid.*, June 28, 1859.

[59] *Ibid.*, for duration of Brown-Akin campaign.

[60] *Ibid.*, August 23, 1859; Athens *Southern Watchman*, September 15, 1859.

[61] Milledgeville *Federal Union*, September 13, 1859.

[62] Various Opposition newspapers quoted in Athens *Southern Watchman*, September 22, 29, 1859.

[63] Benjamin Hill to Opposition editors quoted *ibid.*

They knew their Governor had fought the banks. For this reason he was their friend. Hill had simply underscored the most effective Democratic campaign argument.

Democratic strategy of depending on Governor Brown's record to insulate the party against Opposition thrusts worked out very satisfactorily. There was no denying that he had succeeded in making the State road yield a handsome profit, an accomplishment which might have been over-played a bit in view of the fact that the State road had not always been operated at a loss.[64] Moreover, the Governor had been on the popular side in the war against capital and the banks.[65] These things impressed Georgia voters much more than President Buchanan's affray with Senator Douglas over Kansas or Opposition tirades against both these national Democratic leaders. Consequently, Brown amassed the unprecedented total of 63,644 votes as against 42,103 for Akin.[66] The Opposition vote was approximately the same as that polled by Fillmore in 1856. The Governor was some 6,000 votes stronger than in 1857; Akin was weaker than Hill by approximately 4,000 votes.[67] While Brown's decisive re-election was something of a personal victory, yet an equally, if not more, significant aspect of the campaign and its result was the appearance of the social gospel of Jacksonian Democracy blithely astride the credo of John C. Calhoun. The poor man had become identified with Southern rights. Young Hickory was soon to measure him for the Confederate gray.

[64] Savannah *Republican* quoted in Milledgeville *Federal Union*, October 18, 1859. For an up-to-date account of the operation of the State road under Governors Johnson and Brown, see Hill, *Joseph E. Brown and the Confederacy*, 26–30.

[65] Savannah *Republican* quoted in Milledgeville *Federal Union*, October 18, 1859.

[66] Returns quoted *ibid.*, October 25, 1859.

[67] *Ibid.*

XIII

MAGNIFICENT
SOVEREIGNTY

WHILE Georgia was re-electing Governor Joseph E. Brown, another Brown was engaged in a mysterious plan for seizing the Government arsenal at Harpers Ferry and liberating the slaves in the surrounding region. To appraise the effects among Georgians of John Brown's debacle at Harpers Ferry is not easy. The Columbus *Times and Sentinel,* generally more Southern rightist than other Democratic journals, urged the people to unite against those whose deadly propaganda was the cause of this physical invasion.¹ Both the *Republican* and the *Southern Watchman* ridiculed this exhortation as another Democratic effort to promote party interests, the latter journal objurgating that Senator Douglas was "ten thousand times more dangerous" than John Brown.² Although the John Brown incident provoked more than passing comment, especially among Democratic editors, yet many Georgians would seem to have been more alarmed by Senator Douglas, who at this time was airing his views in a series of articles published in *Harper's Weekly.* When a Wisconsin editor's reflection that "Judge Douglas has only one step more to find himself a Republican" reached Georgia, Opposition journals made the most of it.³ The attack on the Illinois Senator extended beyond the domain of journalism. W. H. Stiles rose on the floor of the State legislature to warn that Douglas was more dan-

---

¹ Quoted in Athens *Southern Watchman,* November 3, 1859.
² *Ibid.,* October 27, 1859.   ³ *Ibid.,* October 20, 1859.

gerous than the Republicans because he was operating in the guise of Democracy, supposedly friendly to the South.[4]

During the months following Governor Brown's re-election, when the stage was being set for the presidential contest of 1860, Georgia editors and politicians were acting as they had always acted on the eve of a presidential campaign. Sundry factions, especially within the Democratic party, were maneuvering for advantage.[5] Alarmed by the Democratic central committee's announcement that the State convention to select delegates for the party's national convention would not meet until March, 1860, Howell Cobb's supporters in the legislature summoned a convention for December 8, 1859.[6] This somewhat irregular Cobb gathering resolved to send delegates to Charleston and to instruct them to support the nominee of the Charleston convention, if that body agreed to protect state equality, Southern rights, and the Dred Scott decision.[7] This convention next resolved to present the name of Howell Cobb to the Charleston conclave as one worthy for the presidency. After appointing the State's quota of delegates and endorsing the Buchanan administration, the convention adjourned. Because of the unpopularity of the action taken by this December convention, the Democratic party's executive committee ordered another convention for March 14, 1860. Delegates were elected after heated local contests between Cobb and anti-Cobb factions. When these delegates gathered they carried their bitter fight to the convention's floor. The anti-Cobb faction withdrew temporarily.

[4] Quoted *ibid.*, November 24, 1859; the Augusta *Constitutionalist*, the leading Douglas paper in Georgia, featured the Harpers Ferry raid.

[5] Milledgeville *Southern Recorder*, October 25, 1859.

[6] J. W. Spullock to John H. Lumpkin, November 16, 1859, and John H. Lumpkin to Howell Cobb, November 18, 1859, in Cobb MSS.; Phillips, *Life of Toombs*, 188.

[7] Athens *Southern Watchman*, December 14, 1859; Milledgeville *Federal Union*, December 20, 1859; William G. Delony to Howell Cobb, December 8, 1859, in Cobb MSS.; Phillips, *Life of Toombs*, 188–89.

It named a slate of delegates and then returned to the convention. Thereupon an agreement was reached to combine the anti-Cobb and Cobb tickets into a single delegation of twice the usual size, whereupon it was instructed to vote as a unit at Charleston.[8] Never a union of unalloyed bliss, the Cobb-Brown accord vanished in Howell Cobb's hour of adversity. Governor Brown had chosen to act with A. H. Stephens to block the Secretary of the Treasury's road to Charleston.[9]

Georgia Democracy's convention troubles were a fitting prelude to what was shortly to happen in national party councils. In April and June of 1860 delegates of the national Democratic party held a total of five conventions.[10] At Charleston a group of Southern delegates demanded that the convention resolve that Congress establish and protect slavery in the territories. When Douglas' followers rejected this proposal, William L. Yancey of Alabama headed a movement of bolters. Taking their cue from H. L. Benning, Empire State Yanceyite, twenty-six of Georgia's thirty-six delegates joined the bolters.[11] After fifty-seven ballots, Douglas, the leading contender for the presidential nomination, was still short of the necessary two-thirds majority. As a result of this deadlock the convention adjourned to meet in Baltimore on June 18. The second of the five conventions was held in Charleston by the Yanceyites. While predominately Southern, this group included numerous Northern men who despised Douglas. They were out to vindicate President Buchanan.[12] Like the Douglas delegates, they too decided to hold a convention in June. This convention was to meet in Richmond.

8 Phillips, *Life of Toombs*, 188–89.
9 John H. Lumpkin to Howell Cobb, November 18, 1859, in Cobb MSS.; Phillips, *Life of Toombs*, 189.   10 Randall, *Lincoln*, I, 139.
11 Milledgeville *Federal Union*, May 1, 1859.
12 Randall, *Lincoln*, I, 140.

Between the two Charleston conventions and the Baltimore gathering, the views of Georgia's leading Democrats were published in many of the State's newspapers. A. H. Stephens and former Governor Johnson expressed regret for the behavior of the bolters. Governor Brown doubted the wisdom of what the Yanceyites had done, while Howell Cobb, whose carefully laid plans had gone amiss, let go with an anti-Douglas canard, vowing he would not support the Illinois Senator under any condition.[13]

As prearranged, the third convention was held in Baltimore on June 18. This was the body which nominated Stephen A. Douglas for President and Benjamin Fitzpatrick of Alabama for Vice-President. When the latter declined, H. V. Johnson, former Governor of Georgia, was chosen by the Democratic national committee to serve as Douglas' running mate.[14] Some of the Yanceyites and the "Buchanan Ultras," in Baltimore to participate in the main Democratic convention, now held in that city an irregular convention of their own. This was the fourth of the five Democratic conclaves. After adopting the platform of their leaders, earlier rejected by the original Charleston convention, the Yanceyites and the Buchanan Ultras nominated John C. Breckinridge of Kentucky for President and Joseph Lane of Oregon for Vice-President. The final gathering of Democratic delegates took place in Richmond, where the bolters had been scheduled to meet on June 11. Waiting, however, until the Baltimore convention had adjourned, they discovered that the presumptuous Yanceyites and Buchanan Ultras who had gone to Baltimore had done there what was to have been done in Richmond. Acquiescing in the decision of these splinter parties, the Richmond conven-

[13] Milledgeville *Federal Union,* May 22, 1860; Phillips, *Georgia and State Rights,* 189–90.

[14] "From the Autobiography of Herschel V. Johnson, 1856–1867," in *American Historical Review,* XXX (1925), 317.

tion simply ratified the platform and the nominations of
Breckinridge and Lane.[15] The national Democratic party
no longer existed. Like the North with its Republican
party, the South now seemed to possess what was at least
a potential sectional party.[16]

Amid the pulling and hauling of Democratic factions
on both State and national levels, Georgia's Opposition
party began preparations for the campaign of 1860.[17] Early
in the spring the party's executive committee issued the
call for a State convention. Accordingly, Opposition delegates assembled on May 2, adopted the creed of the "Constitution and the Union," and appointed delegates to attend
a national convention of Constitutional Unionites scheduled for Baltimore in early May.[18] Representing an important segment of the nation's conservatives, this Constitutional Union gathering bolted the party to the Constitution,
the Union, "and the enforcement of the laws." [19] On the
second ballot John Bell of Tennessee became the nominee
for President. Edward Everett of Massachusetts was chosen
as his running mate.

Another party, this one without a Georgia following,
placed a ticket in the field.[20] Meeting in Chicago on May
16 for a three-day session, Republican delegates nominated

15 Randall, *Lincoln*, I, 142.
16 Craven, *Coming of the Civil War*, 416.
17 Dwight L. Dumond (ed.), *Southern Editorials on Secession* (New York, 1931), 34.
18 Milledgeville *Federal Union*, May 8, 1860.
19 Randall, *Lincoln*, I, 144.
20 There was actually a fifth ticket in the presidential race in 1860. The Abolitionists nominated Gerrit Smith for President and Samuel McFarland for Vice-President. While Smith did not seem to take his candidacy very seriously, he voted for himself. See Ralph Volney Harlow, *Gerrit Smith, Philanthropist and Reformer* (New York, 1939), 427. One Georgia editor wrote on November 3 that "should Gerrit Smith be able to draw some fifty or sixty thousand votes in New York, the *fusion* ticket will carry that state. . . ." Quoted in Dumond (ed.), *Southern Editorials*, 208.

Abraham Lincoln of Illinois for President and Hannibal Hamlin of Maine for Vice-President. Aimed at pleasing a vast concourse of conflicting social and political factions, the Republican platform emerged as a well-orchestrated document of considerable proportions. In the main it was a far more restrained and adroit exposition than the party's first platform (in 1856).[21] There was no positive declaration to prohibit the extension of slavery into the territories; rather, all references to this subject were of an oblique character and appropriately so, for, as Professor Avery Craven explains, "No one really expected slavery to expand farther into the territories." [22] There were numerous other planks. One committed the party to what was understood as the protective tariff principle. Another advocated a free-homestead policy. Still others pledged economy in government and the admission of Kansas with her free-state constitution.[23]

A triangular race between the Breckinridge, Bell, and Douglas factions, the presidential campaign of 1860 in Georgia resolved itself into a repetition of the old arguments, the tedious queries, the trite explanations, and the conventional expressions of sanguine hopes and gloomy forebodings. The Breckinridge group was the most formidable of the Georgia factions. It included most of the traditional Southern-rights Democrats as well as the followings of both Governor Brown and Howell Cobb. Brown and Cobb were unquestionably the two most powerful figures in State politics at this time. Robert Toombs, E. A. Nisbet, and H. L. Benning were also laboring in the Breckinridge

[21] Randall, *Lincoln*, I, 172.

[22] Craven, *Coming of the Civil War*, 419. See also J. G. Randall, *Lincoln the Liberal Statesman* (New York, 1947), 24-25; Dumond (ed.), *Southern Editorials*, 382; Ollinger Crenshaw, *The Slave States in the Presidential Election of 1860* (Baltimore, 1945), 58.

[23] Randall, *Lincoln*, I, 172-73.

vineyard. With the exception of Governor Brown, all of these men advocated protective legislation for slavery in the territories.[24] Commonly known as the Southern-rights Democracy, the Breckinridge party was ably defended by such journals as the *Federal Union,* the *Times and Sentinel,* the *Morning News,* the *Telegraph,* and the *Intelligencer.* Weakest of the three factions were the Douglas men. They naturally looked to H. V. Johnson, vice-presidential candidate on the Douglas ticket, and A. H. Stephens for guidance. The *Constitutionalist* provided their strongest editorial support.[25] Except for their loyalty to the Union, Douglas men offered little more than an abiding faith in their ticket. They believed that somehow Stephen A. Douglas would resolve the nation's ills.[26] Stronger then the Douglas Democrats but weaker than the Breckinridge brand of Democracy was the Bell faction. Among the Bell papers were such prominent organs as the *Southern Watchman,* the *Republican,* and the *Chronicle and Sentinel.* Most prominent among Constitutional Union orators were Benjamin Hill and Warren Akin.[27] Like the Douglas men, Constitutional Unionites put their trust in their candidate.[28]

There was a strong undercurrent of conservatism in Georgia throughout the campaign of 1860. This was no less evident among Southern rightists than among Constitutional Unionites and Douglasites.[29] Encouraged by the spirit of the times, Benjamin Hill attempted to capture

24 Milledgeville *Federal Union,* July 10, 1860; Hill, *Joseph E. Brown and the Confederacy,* 34.

25 Milledgeville *Federal Union,* July 10, 1869.

26 Dumond (ed.), *Southern Editorials,* 176, 209; "From the Autobiography of Herschel V. Johnson," *loc. cit.,* 318.

27 Milledgeville *Federal Union,* July 17, 1860.

28 *Ibid.;* Dumond (ed.), *Southern Editorials,* 176.

29 Dumond (ed.), *Southern Editorials,* 176, 207 ff.; Craven, *Coming of the Civil War,* 425–26; Crenshaw, *The Slave States in the Presidential Election of 1860,* 236–38, 241.

the conservative potential by projecting a fusion of Georgia factions.[30] The scars of recent party battles were too deep, however, and Hill's scheme failed.[31] The Breckinridge faction was especially bitter towards Douglas, while Governor Brown, also of the Breckinridge faction, was suspicious of Hill. Without the co-operation of Breckinridge leaders, fusion was doomed. The inertia of partisan strife nourished division, confusion, and uncertainty. In such an atmosphere co-operation was impossible.[32] Consequently, Georgians divided their votes as follows: Breckinridge, 51,893; Bell, 42,886; and Douglas, 11,580.[33] Though Breckinridge led the field, he failed to poll a majority. Conservatism had won in spite of itself. But there was no one to capture and organize the victory. Breckinridge radicals, on the other hand, immediately began a purposeful drive by which they were to move from their defeat of November to a secession victory in January. Since none of the candidates had polled a popular majority, the choice of the State's electors fell to the legislature. Indignant at Lincoln's election, Governor Brown advised the legislature to ignore its duty. The lawmakers nevertheless selected Breckinridge electors, thus giving the radicals their first taste of victory.[34] They were not to be stopped until they had taken Georgia out of the Union.

Having convened early in November, the Georgia legislature was in session when the news of Lincoln's election reached the State. However, before the outcome of the election was known, Governor Brown had delivered a

[30] Dumond (ed.), *Southern Editorials*, 176, 207 ff.; Craven, *Coming of the Civil War*, 425–26; Crenshaw, *The Slave States in the Presidential Election of 1860*, 236–38, 241; Hill, *Joseph E. Brown and the Confederacy*, 34; Milledgeville *Federal Union*, July 10, 1860.

[31] Craven, *Coming of the Civil War*, 427; Hill, *Joseph E. Brown and the Confederacy*, 34; Milledgeville *Federal Union*, July 3, October 23, 1860.

[32] Milledgeville *Federal Union*, July 3, September 11, October 23, 1860.

[33] *Ibid.*, November 27, 1860.

[34] Coulter, *Georgia*, 316.

special message to the legislators recommending, in case of a Republican victory, a convention to withdraw the State from the Union and an appropriation of one million dollars for military purposes.[35] The Governor's message and the news of Lincoln's election reached many Georgians at about the same time. These two incidents seriously threatened the conservative temper which had prevailed during the late campaign. When the legislature reassembled after the Governor's message, many Breckinridge Democrats were on hand "rampant for immediate secession." Their behavior was "impatient, overbearing, dictatorial and intolerant." [36] T. R. R. Cobb, younger brother of Howell, delivered on the night of November 12 a strong appeal for immediate and permanent secession. The next night Senator Toombs shouted an identical plea.[37] On the night of the fourteenth, A. H. Stephens punctured the wall of secession oratory with a sober remonstrance, urging, instead of immediate secession, a State convention to consider Georgia's grievances and co-operation with other Southern states as the most effective means of redressing those grievances.[38] Two days later former Governor Johnson reiterated Stephens' argument.[39] Within less than a week after Johnson's effort the legislature had appropriated one million dollars for military purposes and Governor Brown had signed a bill providing for the election on January 2 of delegates who were to convene a fortnight later in a State

[35] Allen D. Candler (ed.), *The Confederate Records of the State of Georgia* (Atlanta, 1909), I, 199 ff. See also Randall, *The Civil War and Reconstruction*, 187.

[36] "From the Autobiography of Herschel V. Johnson," *loc. cit.*, 323.

[37] Phillips, *Life of Toombs*, 199.

[38] *Ibid.*; Milledgeville *Southern Recorder*, December 25, 1860; "From the Autobiography of Herschel V. Johnson," *loc. cit.*, 323-24.

[39] Milledgeville *Southern Recorder*, December 25, 1860; "From the Autobiography of Herschel V. Johnson," *loc. cit.*, 323-24; Benjamin Hill was acting with Stephens and Johnson.

convention to consider how Georgia should meet the crisis then understood to be facing her.[40]

Amid the campaign for the election of delegates to the State convention Howell Cobb resigned from President Buchanan's cabinet. Three days after Lincoln's election Cobb strongly objected to an elaborate paper the President read to his cabinet. The Secretary of the Treasury suspected certain cabinet members of trying to persuade the President to commit the administration to coercion.[41] Approximately a month later, on December 6, Cobb addressed an open letter to the people of Georgia, advising that after March 4, 1861, there could be no "equality and justice" in the Union.[42] Two days later he left the cabinet.[43] On December 24 Senator Toombs addressed the people of his State through the columns of the *True Democrat*, declaring that "secession by the fourth of March next should be thundered from the ballot-box by the unanimous voice of Georgia on the second day of January next. Such a voice will be your best guaranty for liberty, security, tranquility, and glory." [44] Meanwhile South Carolina seceded and in taking her leave "sent a wave of enthusiasm throughout the lower South. . . ." [45]

Despite these rather favorable circumstances, the secessionists were alarmed. "We are having trouble here [Chero-

[40] Candler (ed.), *Confederate Records,* I, 206–208; "From the Autobiography of Herschel V. Johnson," *loc. cit.,* 324.

[41] Philip Gerald Auchampaugh, *James Buchanan and his Cabinet on the Eve of Secession* (Lancaster, Pa., 1926), 133. For a brief account of Cobb's quarrel with Attorney General (later Secretary of State) Jeremiah Black, see William Norwood Brigance, *Jeremiah Sullivan Black: A Defender of the Constitution and the Ten Commandments* (Philadelphia, 1934), 90.

[42] "Howell Cobb to the People of Georgia," in Phillips (ed.), *Correspondence,* 505 ff.

[43] *Ibid.,* 517–18.   [44] *Ibid.,* 525.

[45] Dwight L. Dumond, *The Secession Movement, 1860–1861* (New York, 1931), 194. See also Arthur Hood to Howell Cobb, December 19, 1860, in Phillips (ed.), *Correspondence,* 524.

kee], and *no one* but *yourself* can quell it," wrote T. R. R.
Cobb to brother Howell on December 15. Continuing,
he strongly urged the former Secretary of the Treasury
to hurry home and make some speeches.[46] "Where are our
speakers?" was the frantic query of a southwest Georgia
extremist on December 19. "The cry of cooperation is
injuring us," persisted this troubled secessionist.[47] As in
1850, Georgia was again in a position to exert a steadying
influence on the nation's affairs. A co-operationist victory
"would have been a death blow to immediate secession
in the West." [48] Former Governor Johnson insisted that
Georgia must co-operate with the other Southern states
rather than secede as a separate State.[49] Benjamin Hill
agreed with Johnson, advising the former Governor of
having received numerous letters urging that the slavery
question be settled short of secession.[50] Despite the efforts
of Johnson, Hill, and other opponents of immediate secession, the co-operationists lost to the immediate secessionists
on January 2 by a vote of 50,243 to 37,123.[51]

The immediate secessionists entered the campaign to
elect convention delegates with several advantages. The
contest was to be short. Throughout the campaign the immediate secessionists argued that withdrawal from the
Union would be peaceful.[52] And, it would be only temporary.[53] The South, continued the secessionists, would re-

[46] T. R. R. Cobb to *id.*, December 15, 1860, in Phillips (ed.), *Correspondence*, 522.

[47] Arthur Hood to *id.*, *ibid.*, 524.

[48] Dumond (ed.), *Secession Movement*, 194.

[49] Flippin, *Herschel V. Johnson*, 161.

[50] T. Conn Bryan, "The Secession of Georgia," in *Georgia Historical
Quarterly*, XXXI (1947), 94.

[51] Milledgeville *Federal Union*, April 10, 1861.

[52] "From the Autobiography of Herschel V. Johnson," *loc. cit.*, 324–25.

[53] Phillips, *Georgia and State Rights*, 204; Bryan, "Secession of Georgia,"
loc. cit., 95; A. H. Stephens, *A Constitutional View of the Late War Between
the States* (New York, 1872), II, 321.

turn to the Union just as soon as her grievances were redressed and certain guarantees were secured.[54] If war did come, it would be short and a Southern victory was assured because the Yankees were cowards. "The people were honest, patriotic and confiding," wrote Johnson; "hence they yielded to the storm cry of secession, trusting that the convention would act wisely and for the best." [55] Antisecession leaders were confused and divided; they hesitated while secessionists purposefully ground out a multitude of resolutions and memorials in their local mass meetings.[56] These were carefully reported in the press.[57] Another weakness of the co-operationists was their lack of a zealous press. Even the *Constitutionalist,* fearful of the disloyalty charge, joined the secessionists.[58]

Approximately 300 delegates gathered in Milledgeville on January 16 to attend what was doubtless Georgia's most important convention since the adoption of the Federal Constitution.[59] Like the conclave of ten years before, this one numbered among its members the State's ablest men. Former Governor George W. Crawford was elected permanent chairman.[60] Other prominent delegates were Senator Toombs, former Governor H. V. Johnson, T. R. R. Cobb, E. A. Nisbet, and the Stephens brothers. Governor Brown, Howell Cobb, and several judges from both the State and Federal courts were given seats.[61] Also present were Robert B. Rhett from South Carolina and W. L. Yancey from Alabama, as well as other commissioners from states which had

[54] Stephens, *Constitutional View of the Late War Between the States,* II, 321.

[55] "From the Autobiography of Herschel V. Johnson," *loc. cit.,* 324–25.

[56] Craven, *Coming of the Civil War,* 431.

[57] Phillips, *Life of Toombs,* 211–14.

[58] Dumond (ed.), *Southern Editorials,* 361, 380–86.

[59] Candler (ed.), *Confederate Records,* II, 212 ff.

[60] *Journal . . . of the Convention . . . of Georgia* (Milledgeville, 1861), 7–8. Hereafter cited as *Secession Journal.*

[61] *Ibid.;* Candler (ed.), *Confederate Records,* I, 213–17.

already left the Union.[62] These visitors naturally exerted strong pressure to get Georgia to join those states which had already seceded.[63] Defeated at the polls on January 2, the antisecessionists seemed powerless to organize and direct a conservative counterthrust. Unlike the convention of 1850, this one was from its inception in the control of the extremists.[64]

On January 18, E. A. Nisbet presented two resolutions to the convention, one declaring the right of secession and the other calling for the appointment of a committee to draft a secession ordinance.[65] Supported by Dr. Alexander Means, Hiram Warner, Benjamin Hill, and the Stephens brothers, former Governor Johnson countered with a series of substitute resolutions calling for a Southern convention and declaring that Georgia would leave the Union unless the conditions demanded were secured by amendments to the Federal Constitution.[66] A lengthy discussion of the rival resolutions followed. T. R. R. Cobb cleverly captured the immediate secessionist argument when he said, "We can make better terms out of the Union than in it!" [67] The co-operationist rebuttal was weak. According to Johnson, A. H. Stephens' speech in behalf of the substitute resolutions was loaded with an overdose of defeatism.[68] When a demand for the previous question forced a vote on the Nisbet resolution, it carried by a vote of 166–130. A committee, wth Nisbet serving as its chairman, was promptly appointed to draft a secession ordinance.[69]

62 By January 16, 1861, South Carolina, Alabama, Florida, and Mississippi had left the Union.

63 *Secession Journal*, 305–306.

64 Bryan, "Secession of Georgia," *loc. cit.*, 97.

65 *Secession Journal*, 305–306.

66 "From the Autobiography of Herschel V. Johnson," *loc. cit.*, 325; *Secession Journal*, 305–306; Candler (ed.), *Confederate Records*, I, 229–30; Dumond, *Secession Movement*, 206–207.

67 Quoted in Bryan, "Secession of Georgia," *loc. cit.*, 99.

68 "From the Autobiography of Herschel V. Johnson," *loc. cit.*, 325.

69 *Secession Journal*, 15–20, 104.

The next day (January 19), after Nisbet reported an ordinance withdrawing Georgia from the Union, Benjamin Hill promptly moved the adoption of Johnson's substitute resolutions. Hill's motion lost by a vote of 164–133. The secessionists had won a narrow victory; a change of sixteen votes would have brought them defeat. A vote was then taken on the secession ordinance. It was adopted by a vote of 208–89, whereupon President Crawford announced it his "privilege and pleasure to declare that the State of Georgia was free, sovereign and independent." [70]

Numerous explanations have been offered for Georgia's behavior in January of 1861. A. H. Stephens reflected that "two-thirds at least of those who voted for the Ordinance of Secession did so . . . with a view to a more certain Reformation of the Union. . . . In other words they acted under the impression and belief that the whole object . . . could better be accomplished by the State's being out of the Union than in it." [71] Importance has been attached to the efforts of Governor Brown, the Cobb brothers, and Senator Toombs.[72] It is conceivable that these men could have prevented their State from seceding had they united with former Governor Johnson, Benjamin Hill, and the Stephens brothers to help organize and direct a conservatism which, on the basis of the presidential election returns, was in the ascendancy as late as early November of 1860. The explanation of the refusal of Brown, the Cobbs, and Toombs to act with the antisecessionists must be sought in the latitudes of economics and psychology, where over-facile generalizations become tempting. The voting in the State convention, however, does offer some clues with respect to the force of economics. On this basis it is demonstrable that secession sentiment was strongest in the coastal

[70] *Ibid.*, 32, 35, 39.

[71] Stephens, *Constitutional View of the Late War Between the States,* II, 321.

[72] Phillips, *Georgia and State Rights,* 207–208.

area, in the newer cotton lands, and in the urban centers, while, on the other hand, delegates from North Georgia, the pine barrens, and the "old cotton lands" manifested a disposition to cling to the Union.[73] Here were the stimuli for a "wave of the future" complex. The radicals must take Georgia out of the Union.

Far more subtle than economics was what has been characterized as the "irreconcilable incompatibility of temper . . . and feeling" between the North and South.[74] For two decades Abolitionists had been fastening the yoke of sin around the neck of the South. Republican talk and action during the months which followed Lincoln's election confirmed the suspicion that the new administration would invoke the power of the national government to sustain this crusade against sin.[75] In such a culture, conservatism rapidly vanished, while radicalism fermented with ease.[76] For example, the normally conservative *Chronicle and Sentinel* declared in December, 1860, that "Georgia, today, would not give a penny-whistle for the Fugitive Slave law of 1850, or all the fugitive slave laws Congress could pass." Continuing, the editor betrayed the "irreconcilable incompatibility of temper" by explaining that "our opposition is to the *animus* of the North, as exhibited in the passage of the Liberty Bills, and finally in the election of an irrepressible conflict representative as the Chief Executive of the States."[77] Expressing a feeling of relief which many must have experienced after the passage of the secession ordinance, the *Federal Union* majestically proclaimed Georgia "a free and independent Republic."[78] "And so

---

[73] Coulter, *Georgia*, 319–20; Bryan, "Secession of Georgia," *loc. cit.*, 101.

[74] Quoted in Craven, *Coming of the Civil War*, 433.

[75] *Ibid.*, 432; David M. Potter, *Lincoln and his Party in the Secession Crisis* (New Haven, 1942), 57, 155, 157, 160.

[76] Craven, *Coming of the Civil War*, 432.

[77] Quoted *ibid.*, 433.

[78] Milledgeville *Federal Union*, January 22, 1861.

the Rubicon was crossed," wrote H. V. Johnson, "and . . . Georgia was launched upon a dark, uncertain and dangerous sea. The secessionists were jubilant. I never felt so sad before. The clustering glories of the past thronged my memory, but they were darkened by the gathering gloom of the lowering future." [79] Immobilized in the strait jacket of glittering sovereignty, Georgia Unionism was awaiting still a more deadly fate, the benumbing force of the Confederate gray.

[79] "From the Autobiography of Herschel V. Johnson," *loc. cit.,* 327.

BIBLIOGRAPHY

Guides

Brooks, R. P. *A Preliminary Bibliography of Georgia History*, in *Bulletin of the University of Georgia*, X, 10A (June, 1910).

Catalogue of the Wimberley Jones De Renne Georgia Library, II. 3 vols. Wormsloe, Ga. (Privately Printed), 1931.

Thornton, Ella May (ed.). *Finding-List of Books and Pamphlets Relating to Georgia and Georgians*. Atlanta, 1928.

Unpublished Source Materials

Executive Letter Book from 1856 to 1861. Georgia State Department of Archives and History, Atlanta.

Governor's Letter Book, 1847–1861. Georgia State Department of Archives and History, Atlanta.

Letter Book: Executive Department, 1852–1859. Georgia State Department of Archives and History, Atlanta.

Minutes of the Executive Department, 1849–1855. Georgia State Department of Archives and History, Atlanta.

Howell Cobb Manuscripts. In private possession. Some of the letters in this collection were available to Ulrich B. Phillips and appear in Phillips (ed.), *The Correspondence of Robert Toombs, Alexander Stephens, and Howell Cobb*. A number were also edited by Robert P. Brooks as "Howell Cobb Papers" in the *Georgia Historical Quarterly*. See "Published Source Materials."

Telamon Cuyler Collection. A few letters dealing with the Nashville convention relate to this study. This collection is in the University of Georgia Library.

Published Source Materials

A. Collected Works

Brooks, Robert P. (ed.). "Howell Cobb Papers," in *Georgia Historical Quarterly*, V–VI. Savannah, 1921–1922.

Candler, Allen D. (ed.). *The Confederate Records of the State of Georgia*, I–II. 4 vols. Atlanta, 1909.

Dumond, Dwight L. (ed.). *Southern Editorials on Secession.* New York, 1931.

Greeley, Horace, and Cleveland, John F. *A Political Text-Book for 1860 Comprising a Brief View of Presidential Nominations and Elections.* New York, 1860.

Moore, J. B. (ed.). *The Works of James Buchanan*, IV–VI. 10 vols. Philadelphia, 1908–1911.

Perkins, Howard Cecil (ed.). *Northern Editorials on Secession.* New York, 1942.

Phillips, Ulrich B. (ed.). *The Correspondence of Robert Toombs, Alexander Stephens, and Howell Cobb,* Vol. II of American Historical Association, *Annual Report*, 1911. Washington, 1913.

Richardson, James D. *A Compilation of the Messages and Papers of the Presidents,* V. 10 vols. Washington, 1908.

Shryock, Richard H. (ed.). *Letters of Richard D. Arnold, M. D., 1808–1876.* Durham, 1929.

B. Official Documents

Acts of the General Assembly . . . of the State of Georgia. 1850–1860. Published separately for each session.

Address of a Portion of the Executive Committee to the Union Democracy and Union Whigs, friends of Pierce and King. Milledgeville, 1852. In the University of Georgia Library.

Address of the Executive Committee to the Constitutional Union Party of Georgia. Milledgeville, 1852. In the University of Georgia Library.

Debates and Proceedings of the Georgia Convention, assembled in Milledgeville, at the Capitol. December 10, 1850. Milledgeville, 1850.

Howell Cobb and Others. *To Our Constituents.* Washington, 1849. In the University of Georgia Library.

Journal of the House of Representatives . . . of Georgia, 1849–1860. Published separately for each session.

Journal of the Public and Secret Proceedings of the Convention of the People of Georgia, Held in Milledgeville and Savannah in 1861. Milledgeville, 1861.

Journal of the Senate . . . of Georgia, 1849–1860. Published separately for each session.

Journal of the State Convention, Held in Milledgeville in December, 1850. Milledgeville, 1850.

The Congressional Globe: Containing the Debates and Proceedings of . . . Congress. Washington, 1845–1860. Published separately for each session.

To the Voters of Newton County. 1850. A leaflet in possession of Dr. E. Merton Coulter.

Newspapers

Macon. *American Republic,* December 10, 1859.

Sandersville. *Central Georgian,* 1852–1855, 1857–1859.

Augusta. *Chronicle and Sentinel,* 1847–1855, 1858.

Augusta. *Constitutionalist,* 1856–1859.

Atlanta. *Daily Examiner,* 1857.

Atlanta. *Daily Intelligencer and Examiner,* September 29, 1857–March 9, 1858.

Savannah. *Daily Journal and Courier,* 1855.

Savannah. *Daily Morning News,* 1857, 1859.

Pittsburgh. *Daily Post,* July 9, 1879.

Savannah. *Daily Republican,* 1851, 1852, 1855.

Calhoun. *Democratic Platform,* September 8, 1859.

Griffin. *Empire State,* 1856, 1857, 1859.

Savannah. *Evening Journal,* 1852, 1853.

Milledgeville. *Federal Union,* 1846–1861.

Griffin. *Georgia Jeffersonian,* 1853, 1854.

Macon. *Journal and Messenger,* 1856.

Savannah. *Daily Georgian,* 1851–1854.

Savannah. *Daily Journal,* December, 1855.

Rome. *Southerner and Commercial Advertiser,* November 4, 1858.

Athens. *Southern Banner,* 1847–1849, 1851–1857.

Augusta. *Southern Field and Fireside.* A few issues of 1859 were used.

Athens. *Southern Herald,* 1850.

Milledgeville. *Southern Recorder,* 1851–1859.

Athens. *Southern Watchman,* 1855–1859.

Athens. *Southern Whig,* 1846–1850.

Elberton. *Star of the South,* 1859, 1860.

Macon. *Telegraph,* 1848.

Rome. *Southerner,* November, 1850.

General Works and Monographs

Adams, James Truslow. *America's Tragedy.* New York, 1834.

Avery, I. W. *The History of the State of Georgia from 1850 to 1881.* New York, 1881.

Barnes, Gilbert. *The Anti-slavery Impulse.* New York, 1933.

Beard, Charles A. and Mary R. *The Rise of American Civilization.* 2 vols. New York, 1927.

Binkley, Wilfred E. *American Political Parties: Their Natural History.* New York, 1944.

———. *The Powers of the President.* Garden City (N.Y.), 1937.

Brooks, Robert P. *History of Georgia.* New York, 1913.

Burgess, John W. *The Civil War and the Constitution, 1859–1865,* I. 2 vols. New York, 1901.

Carpenter, Jesse T. *The South as a Conscious Minority, 1789–1861.* New York, 1930.

Clark, Victor Selden. *History of Manufactures in the United States.* 2 vols. Washington, 1916.

Cole, Arthur C. *The Irrepressible Conflict.* New York, 1934.

———. *The Whig Party in the South.* Washington, 1913.

Cooper, Walter G. *The Story of Georgia,* I. 4 vols. New York, 1938.

Coulter, E. Merton. *Georgia: A Short History.* Chapel Hill, 1947.

———. *College Life in the Old South.* New York, 1928.

Craven, Avery O. *The Coming of the Civil War.* New York, 1942.

———. *The Repressible Conflict.* Baton Rouge, 1939.

Crenshaw, Ollinger. *The Slave States in the Presidential Election of 1860.* Baltimore, 1945.

Curtis, Francis. *The Republican Party, 1854–1904.* 2 vols. New York, 1904.

De Voto, Bernard. *The Year of Decision: 1846.* Boston, 1943.

Dewey, D. R. *Financial History of the United States.* New York, 1924.

Dumond, Dwight L. *The Secession Movement, 1860–1861.* New York, 1931.

Dunning, W. A. *Studies in Southern History and Politics.* New York, 1914.

Faulkner, Harold Underwood. *American Economic History.* New York, 1943.

Fish, Carl Russell. *The Rise of the Common Man.* New York, 1927.

Fite, Emerson D. *History of the Presidential Election of 1860.* New York, 1910.

Hamer, Philip May. *The Secession Movement in South Carolina, 1847–1852.* Allentown, Pa., 1918.

Hockett, Homer C. *The Constitutional History of the United States, 1826–1876,* II. 2 vols. New York, 1939.

Hodder, Frank H. "Some Aspects of the English Bill for the Admission of Kansas," in Vol. I of American Historical Association, *Annual Report,* 1906. Washington, 1908.

Howe, Daniel Wait. *A Political History of Secession to the Beginning of the American Civil War.* New York, 1914.

Howell, Clark. *History of Georgia,* I. 4 vols. Chicago, 1926.

Johnson, Amanda. *Georgia as Colony and State.* Atlanta, 1938.

Johnston, James Houstoun. *Western and Atlantic Railroad of the State of Georgia.* Atlanta, 1932.

Kent, Frank A. *A History of the Democratic Party.* New York, 1928.

Knight, Lucian Lamar. *A Standard History of Georgia and Georgians,* I–II. 6 vols. Chicago, 1917.

Meyer, Balthasar H. (ed.). *History of Transportation in the United States before 1860.* Washington, 1917.

Myers, William Starr. *The Republican Party, A History.* New York, 1928.

Nichols, Roy Franklin. *The Democratic Machine, 1850–1854.* New York, 1923.

Phillips, Ulrich B. *A History of Transportation in the Eastern Cotton Belt to 1860.* New York, 1908.

————. "The Southern Whigs," in *Essays in American History.* New York, 1910.

————. *The Course of the South to Secession.* New York, 1939.

————. *Georgia and State Rights.* Washington, 1902.

————. *Life and Labor in the Old South.* Boston, 1929.

Potter, David M. *Lincoln and his Party in the Secession Crisis.* New Haven, 1942.

Randall, J. G. *The Civil War and Reconstruction.* New York, 1937.

Schlesinger, Arthur M., Jr. *The Age of Jackson.* Boston, 1945.

Schmeckebier, L. F. *History of the Know Nothing Party in Maryland.* Baltimore, 1899.

Sherwood, Adiel. *A Gazeteer of Georgia.* Atlanta, 1860.

Shryock, Richard H. *Georgia and the Union in 1850.* Durham, 1926.

Simms, Henry H. *A Decade of Sectional Controversy.* Chapel Hill, 1942.

Smith, Theodore Clarke. *Parties and Slavery, 1850–1859.* New York, 1906.

Stanwood, Edward. *A History of the Presidency from 1788 to 1897.* New York, 1898.

The South in the Building of the Nation, IV. 12 vols. Richmond, 1909.

Wittke, Carl F. *We Who Built America; the Saga of the Immigrant.* New York, 1939.

Biographies, Autobiographies and Reminiscences

Angle, Paul M. (ed.). *The Lincoln Reader.* New Brunswick, 1947.

Auchampaugh, Philip Gerald. *James Buchanan and his Cabinet on the Eve of Secession.* Lancaster, Pa., 1926.

Avary, Myrta Lockett (ed.). *Recollections of Alexander H. Stephens.* New York, 1910.

Beveridge, A. J. *Abraham Lincoln, 1809–1858,* II. 2 vols. New York, 1928.

Black, Chauncey (ed.). *Essays and Speeches of Jeremiah S. Black. With a Biographical Sketch.* New York, 1885.

Blaine, James G. *Twenty Years in Congress.* 2 vols. Norwich, Conn., 1886.

Boykin, Samuel. *A Memorial Volume of the Honorable Howell Cobb.* Philadelphia, 1870.

Brigance, William Norwood. *Jeremiah Sullivan Black: A Defender of the Constitution and the Ten Commandments.* Philadelphia, 1934.

Buchanan, James. *Mr. Buchanan's Administration on the Eve of the Rebellion.* New York, 1866.

Cleveland, Henry. *Alexander H. Stephens, in Public and Private. With Letters and Speeches, Before, During and Since the War.* Atlanta, 1866.

Coulter, E. Merton, *Thomas Spalding of Sapelo.* University, La., 1940.

Craven, Avery O. *Edmund Ruffin, Southerner.* New York, 1932.

Curtis, G. T. *Life of James Buchanan, Fifteenth President of the United States,* II. 2 vols. New York, 1883.

Dyer, Brainerd. *Zachary Taylor.* Baton Rouge, 1946.

Fielder, Herbert. *Life and Times of Joseph E. Brown.* Springfield, Mass., 1883.

Flippin, Percy S. *Herschel V. Johnson of Georgia, State Rights Unionist.* Richmond, 1931.

Foote, Henry S. *War of the Rebellion: or, Scylla and Charybdis. Consisting of Observations upon the Causes, Course, and Consequences of the Late Civil War in the United States.* New York, 1866.

Forney, John W. *Anecdotes of Public Men.* New York, 1873.

———. *Anecdotes of Public Men.* 2 vols. New York, 1873–1881.

"From the Autobiography of Herschel V. Johnson, 1856–67," in *American Historical Review,* XXX, 1 (January, 1925).

Griffis, William Elliot. *Millard Fillmore, President of the United States.* Ithaca, N.Y., 1915.

Harlow, Ralph V. *Gerrit Smith, Philanthropist and Reformer.* New York, 1939.

Hendrick, Burton J. *Statesmen of the Lost Cause: Jefferson Davis and His Cabinet.* Boston, 1939.

Hill, Benjamin H., Jr. *Senator Benjamin H. Hill of Georgia. His Life, Writings and Speeches.* Atlanta, 1893.

Hill, Louise Biles. *Joseph E. Brown and the Confederacy.* Chapel Hill, 1939.

Johnson, R. M., and Browne, W. H. *Life of Alexander H. Stephens.* Philadelphia, 1884.

Johnson, Zachary T. *The Political Policies of Howell Cobb.* Nashville, 1929.

Knight, Lucian Lamar. *Reminiscences of Famous Georgians.* Atlanta, 1907.

McCulloch, Hugh. *Men and Measures of Half a Century.* New York, 1888.

Mallory, Daniel (ed.). *The Life and Speeches of Honorable Henry Clay.* Hartford, 1855.

Memoirs of Georgia. 2 vols. Atlanta, 1855.

Miller, Stephen F. *The Bench and Bar in Georgia.* Philadelphia, 1858.

Milton, George Fort. *The Eve of Conflict: Stephen A. Douglas and the Needless War.* New York, 1934.

Nevins, Allan. *Frémont, The West's Greatest Adventurer,* II. 2 vols. New York, 1928.

Nichols, Roy Franklin. *Franklin Pierce, Young Hickory of the Granite Hills.* Philadelphia, 1931.

Northen, William J. (ed.). *Men of Mark in Georgia.* 6 vols. Atlanta, 1910.

Pearce, H. J., Jr. *Benjamin H. Hill.* Chicago, 1928.

Pendleton, Louis. *Alexander H. Stephens.* Philadelphia, 1908.

Phillips, Ulrich B. *Life of Robert Toombs.* New York, 1913.

Richardson, E. Ramsey. *Little Aleck: A Life of Alexander H. Stephens.* Indianapolis, 1932.

Randall, James G. *Abraham Lincoln: From Springfield to Gettysburg,* I. 2 vols. New York, 1945.

Randall, James G. *Lincoln the Liberal Statesman*. New York, 1947.

Rowland, Eron A. *Varina Howell, Wife of Jefferson Davis*. 2 vols. New York, 1931.

Sargent, Nathan. *Public Men and Events from the Commencement of Mr. Monroe's Administration, in 1817, to the close of Mr. Fillmore's Administration, in 1853*, II. 2 vols. Philadelphia, 1875.

Schurz, Carl. *Life of Henry Clay*, II. 2 vols. New York, 1888.

Smith, William E. *The Francis Preston Blair Family in Politics*, II. 2 vols. New York, 1933.

Stephens, A. H. *A Constitutional View of the Late War Between the States*. 2 vols. New York, 1872.

Stovall, P. A. *Robert Toombs, Statesman, Speaker, Soldier, Sage*. New York, 1892.

Swisher, Carl Brent. *Roger B. Taney*. New York, 1936.

Von Abele, Rudolph. *Alexander H. Stephens*. New York, 1946.

Waddell, James D. *Biographical Sketch of Linton Stephens, containing a selection of his Letters, Speeches, State Papers, Etc.* Atlanta, 1877.

Wade, John Donald. *Augustus Baldwin Longstreet*. New York, 1924.

Articles in Periodicals

Brooks, Robert P. "Howell Cobb and the Crisis of 1850," in *Mississippi Valley Historical Review*, IV (December, 1917), 279–98.

Bryan, T. C. "The Secession of Georgia," in *Georgia Historical Quarterly*, XXXI (June, 1947), 89–111.

Chisholm, G. B. "The Reëstablishment of Peacetime Society," in *Psychiatry*, IX (February, 1946), 3–11.

Cole, Arthur C. "The South and the Right of Secession in the Early Fifties," in *Mississippi Valley Historical Review*, I (December, 1914), 376–99.

Coulter, E. Merton. "A Georgia Educational Movement During the Eighteen Hundred Fifties," in *Georgia Historical Quarterly*, IX (March, 1925), 1–33.

Craven, Avery O. "Georgia and the South," in *Georgia Historical Quarterly*, XXIII (September, 1939), 220–35.

Greene, Helene Ione. "Politics in Georgia, 1853–54: The Ordeal of Howell Cobb," in *Georgia Historical Quarterly*, XXX (September, 1946), 185–211.

Harrington, Fred Harvey. "Frémont and the North Americans," in *American Historical Review*, XLIV (July, 1939), 842–48.

Johnson, Z. T. "Geographic Factors in Georgia Politics in 1850," in *Georgia Historical Quarterly*, XVII (March, 1933), 26–36.

Montgomery, Horace. "The Solid South Movement of 1855," in *Georgia Historical Quarterly*, XXVI (June, 1942), 101–12.

————. "A Georgia Precedent for the Freeport Question," in *Journal of Southern History*, X (May, 1944), 200–207.

Owsley, Frank L. "The Fundamental Cause of the Civil War: Egocentric Sectionalism," in *Journal of Southern History*, VII (February, 1941), 3–18.

Perkins, Howard C. "A Neglected Phase of the Movement for Southern Unity, 1847–1852," in *Journal of Southern History*, XII (May, 1946), 153–203.

Phillips, Ulrich B. "An American State-Owned Railroad," in *Yale Review*, XV (November, 1906), 259–82.

Schlesinger, Arthur M. "Tides of American Politics," *Yale Review*, XXIX (December, 1939), 217–30.

Tankersley, Allen P. "Basil Hallam Overby, Champion of Prohibition in Ante-Bellum Georgia," in *Georgia Historical Quarterly*, XXXI (March, 1947), 1–18.

INDEX

tem in, 1; on Wilmot Proviso, 17; during crisis of 1850, p. 19; indifference to Nashville convention in, 21-22; prosperity of, 28-29; method of elections in, 28 n.; rights of, in territories, 30; on Compromise of 1850, p. 34, 132; saves Union, 34, 43; party structure in, 37, 43, 54-55, 84-85, 98, 117, 186; on Scott, 65, 75; Whigs of, 86; vote of, in 1852, p. 90; Union Democrats rebuked by, 93; opponents of Pierce in, 94; owns railroad, 105; supports Pierce, 115-16, 166; conservatism of, 123, 134, 242-43; Know-Nothing party in, 127, 135, 139; editors endorse Kansas-Nebraska Bill, 131, 133; Senate of, 132; Democracy of, 133, 163, 182, 183, 203, 205, 213, 219, 224, 232, 239; politics in, 137, 185, 232, 241; second drive for Southern unity in, 144, 147; accepts Republican challenge, 156; Congressional delegation of, 160; Americans of, 161-62, 172, 177, 189, 191; journalists of, 186, 233, 237; opponents of Buchanan in, 190, 217-18; on Walker, 191; public figures of, 197; direct trade of, 209; planters of, 210; voters of, 235; behavior at Charleston, 238; grievances of, 244; crisis in, 244-45; extremists of, 246, 248; urged to secede, 248; withdraws from Union, 243, 249-51

Georgia Platform, 33-34, 38-39, 41, 46, 62-64, 91, 93, 103, 131, 156, 217, 220; approved by Johnson committee, 45; endorsed, 100, 141, 142, 147, 159; author of, 104

Georgians, 90, 116, 123, 133, 145, 146, 149, 156, 157, 160, 175, 185, 216, 234; urged to support Pierce, 109, 124; partisan politics among, 126; urged to end partisan strife, 142-43; active at Cincinnati convention, 167; aroused by Brown, 206-207; reaction of, to Harpers Ferry raid, 236

Germans, 153; liberals among, 126; Jews among, 127
Greeley, Horace, 161, 184
Griffin, 222; Whigs of, 138
Griffin *Empire State*, 170, 181, 218
Griffin *Jeffersonian*, 98, 107
"Gubernatorial Convention of Republican Citizens," 102; see also Robert Toombs

Hale, John P., 85 n.
Hall County, 115
Hamlin, Hannibal, 241
Haralson, Hugh, elected to Congress in 1848, p. 14
Harpers Ferry, 236
Harper's Weekly, 236
Harris, Thomas D., advises Cobb, 61, 93, 117
Heirs of Jackson, 175-76
Henry County, Democratic harmony meeting in, 80; Whigs of, 138
Hill, Benjamin H., 234; in election of 1852, p. 86; in election of 1855, p. 158; nomination of, for Governor in 1857, p. 194; in election of 1857, pp. 195-202, 207, 235; defeat of, 202, 203; on Union, 204, 231; on Southern rights, 231; in election of 1860, pp. 242-43; urges co-operation, 246, 248; loses to secessionists, 249
Hill, Edward Y., 17 n.
Hill, Joshua, 233
Hillyer, Junius, 100; delegate-elect to Nashville convention, 23; speaks for Cobb, 54; in election of 1856, pp. 173-74
Hilton, R. B., editor, 96
Holsey, Hopkins, 91; editor, 1; Jacksonian, 1, 50, 62, 88, 97; urges liberal party, 3, 60; on Johnson, 46, 81; on politics, 64, 85, 88-89; denounces Regulars, 67, 73; views of, on Tugalo ticket, 83; tribute to, 89 n.; on Pierce cabinet, 93-94; opposes Cobb, 97, 117, 118; resigns post, 98, 99; favors Buchanan, 177 n.
Homesteads, 131, 241
House of Representatives, 122, 169,

Kentucky, 167, 179, 183
Keystone State, *see* Pennsylvania
King, William Rufus, candidate for vice-presidency in 1852, p. 76
Kingston, anti-Compromise demonstration in, 31; political rally in, 109, 112, 115
Know-Nothing party, 123, 124, 129, 133, 135, 138, 142, 145, 147, 149, 155, 179, 186; genesis of, in Georgia, 126, 185; secrecy of, 127-28; raids of, on Whig membership, 128; a Whig trick, 137; national council meets, 141; State meetings of, 140-41, 146; strategy of, 143; ritual of, 149
Kossuth, Louis, 70, 87

Laboring class, defense of, 206
La Grange, Ga., 195
Lamar, Henry G., 192
Lamar, John B., 85; predicts disunion in 1850, pp. 18-19; Cobb complains to, 224-25
Lamar, L. Q. C., 119
Lane, Joseph, 239, 240
Lecompton Constitution, 213-15, 219
Lewis, John W., superintendent of State road, 211
Liberalism, nineteenth-century type of, 156, 166
Liberty Bills, 250
Lincoln, Abraham, 147, 173; nomination of, for Senate in 1858, p. 215; debates with Douglas, 216; nomination of, for presidency in 1860, p. 241; elected to presidency in 1860, pp. 243, 250
Lincoln-Douglas debates, *see* Abraham Lincoln and Stephen A. Douglas
Liquor-license system, 135
"Little Aleck," *see* Alexander H. Stephens
Liverpool, 209
Locofocoism, 3, 87
Lomax, Tenant, editor, 139, 144
Longstreet, Augustus B., 149
Louisiana, 91, 167, 183
Louisville, Ky., 149
Louisville (Ky.) *Times*, 149

Lumpkin, John H., 79, 190, 191, 192, 193, 223; Democratic party leader, 2, 211; advises Cobb, 61, 107, 117, 119, 121, 212; elected to Congress, 153; relations of, with Brown, 212-13, 222
Lumpkin *Palladium*, 218

McDonald, Charles J., 6-7, 42, 52, 79, 91, 104, 109, 112, 116, 185; Democratic leader, 2, 117-18; nomination of, for Governor in 1851, pp. 39, 44; campaigns for Senate, 118-21, 202
Macon, 26, 42, 75, 77, 84, 127, 140, 146, 153, 169, 183, 224, 228, 229, 230
Macon *Georgia Citizen*, 187; supports Scott, 65, 113; urges Berrien for Governor, 113-14; on Know-Nothing party, 128-29; on Opposition party, 229
Macon *Georgia Telegraph*, 2, 136-37, 153; supports Southern Rights party, 29; opposes Georgia Platform, 39; advises Southern-rights Democrats, 116-17; on Douglas, 218; supports Breckinridge, 242
Macon *Journal and Messenger*, 2, 32-33, 36, 53, 104, 127, 172, 192, 228; supports Cobb, 50; on Scott, 65; rebukes Cobb, 73; on Iverson, 121; supports Stephens, 138; supports Fillmore, 178, 180, 183
Macon Regency, 50, 53
Macon *State Press*, 218, 229
Maine, 179, 180, 241
Manufacturing, advocated, 4
Marietta *Advocate*, 218
Marietta *Union*, 99; charges plot, 83-84, 87; criticizes Cobb, 97
Maryland, 183
Massachusetts, 32, 160, 240
Means, Dr. Alexander, 248
Mexican War, 7, 20
Michigan, 165
Milledge, John, advises Cobb, 117-18
Milledgeville, 2, 27, 33, 45, 57, 63, 69, 77, 120, 153, 158, 163, 168, 192, 194, 226, 227, 228, 247

INDEX